An Introduction
to Hmong Culture

D0864372

An Introduction to Hmong Culture

YA PO CHA

McFarland & Company, Inc., Publishers

Jefferson, North Carolina, and London

LIBRARY OF CONGRESS CATALOGUING-IN-PUBLICATION DATA

Cha, Ya Po, 1968–
    An introduction to Hmong culture / Ya Po Cha.
        p.   cm.
    Includes bibliographical references and index.

    ISBN 978-0-7864-4951-4
    softcover : 50# alkaline paper ∞

        1. Hmong (Asian people) — Social life and customs.
    2. Hmong Americans — Social life and customs.   3. Hmong
    language — Terms and phrases.   4. Proverbs, Hmong.   I. Title.
    DS509.5.H66C48   2010
    305.895'972 — dc22   2010030886

British Library cataloguing data are available

©2010 Ya Po Cha. All rights reserved

*No part of this book may be reproduced or transmitted in any form
or by any means, electronic or mechanical, including photocopying
or recording, or by any information storage and retrieval system,
without permission in writing from the publisher.*

On the cover: *(clockwise from top)* Hmong people living at the edge of
the world; traditional Hmong embroidery; Hmong people farming
the hillsides of Ban Romklao, Thailand; Anna Vang (left) and Chia
Vang wear traditional White Hmong costumes

Manufactured in the United States of America

*McFarland & Company, Inc., Publishers
    Box 611, Jefferson, North Carolina 28640
    www.mcfarlandpub.com*

ACKNOWLEDGMENTS

I would like to thank Kathy Vue, Neil Hollander, Rebecca Doolittle and Xee Yang for helping with editing. For spending the time to clarify certain aspects of Hmong culture to me, I would also like to thank my cousin Chong Leng Cha and uncle Kou Chai Vue.

A special thanks goes to Kahm Xiong and Cindy Moua for their fabulous artwork and my wife and children for their contributions and patience. I am forever in debt to my gracious friends Linda Contreras and Sue M. Mote for their encouragement and editing.

Lastly, my father is my inspiration and my mentor; he paved the way for me in the Hmong world. No words can express my gratitude to him for the role he plays in my life and in writing this book. Thanks a million, Dad.

TABLE OF CONTENTS

INTRODUCTION

On a hot August afternoon in 2008, Sacramento, California, sheriff deputies were summoned to a house on 37th Street in the south part of the city. When deputies arrived, they found 16-year-old Phong Vang lying on the front lawn with several bullet wounds in both legs. Inside the house, they found the boy's father, 54-year-old Ka Thao Vang, dead from a self-inflicted gunshot wound to the head. According to relatives and friends, Ka Thao was a gentle person. He was just enraged about the way his son had been behaving. Ka Thao saw his son as a failure and a disgrace to the family. The son, on the other hand, was simply being an urbanized American teenager — hanging out with friends and acting irresponsibly.

The conflict between Ka Thao and his son is extreme, but it is not an isolated case. It is just an example of what is happening to Hmong families across the United States and the conflicts stemming from the lack of understanding between the generations.

There is a generational language gap and cultural shift for Hmong in the United States.* This shift is inevitable as Hmong went from leading an agrarian life to the modern world in the blink of an eye. The first-generation immigrants still think they are living in the primitive, war-scarred past whereas the second and third-generation Hmong are living in present-day America. This disconnect causes a lot of turmoil in Hmong families of all socioeconomic levels. Educating Hmong children about their cultural heritage is a way to bridge the generations and bring harmony to Hmong families.

Today, in the native homelands of Hmong people in southwestern

*Andrea C. Withers. "Hmong Language and Cultural Maintenance in Merced, California," Bilingual Research Journal, 28 (2004): 299-318.

China and Southeast Asia, Hmong try to escape the primitive lifestyle in the rural mountainous regions and descend to the cities in the lowland to become economically, academically, and technologically more competitive. These are usually young people who become assimilated to the dominant culture and abandon their own heritage. This is a worldwide phenomenon. Many do become successful but at a heavy price: the loss of their identity.

The Hmong culture is losing its authenticity as well as its practicability as members of the older generation pass on. Each successive generation becomes less and less capable of retaining the culture. The practice of shamanism is a perfect example of our vanishing cultural traditions. My father and his five brothers were all shamans. Together, there are 24 male first-generation cousins in my immediate Cha family, and only four among us have acquired the practice. None of them is able to perform the task satisfactorily if his life depended on it, and shamanism is what our spiritual health depends on. My family is not alone in this dilemma. Shamanism might very well become a thing of the past if the trend continues, and shamanism is only one component of Hmong culture. Other aspects of the culture are also in need of preservation.

Studies have shown that by acknowledging immigrant students' cultural values and identity, their self-confidence and self-esteem are elevated. Thus, they perform better in school.* Hmong students have historically under-achieved in school. In the many years I have been teaching Hmong as a heritage language, I have seen major changes in my Hmong students. When they have acquired Hmong literacy, learned about our history, and have come to understand the values of Hmong culture, Hmong students become proud students. Many of my students do their senior projects on a topic related to Hmong culture. They wear Hmong clothes, with all those jingly coins, to school for cultural events. I truly believe that when Hmong students know who they really are, they behave better, and they are more eager to learn. This is one more reason why we need to preserve the Hmong culture.

In the bilingual, multicultural world of the Hmong people, we need to take a proactive approach to preserving the authentic culture. Where there are no Sunday schools to attend, no private schools to send the kids

---

*Sonia Nieto. "Critical Multicultural Education," in Critical Multiculturalism, ed. Stephen May (Philadelphia: Falmer Press, 1999): 209–235.

to, and no lessons on Hmong culture in mainstream society, it is imperative that we take responsibility for preserving our heritage. Documenting our culture in writing is one way to preserve it. In the subsequent chapters, the foundation to Hmong culture is discussed. Regional variations, certain differences in dialect and practices occur and will be noted by Hmong readers, but for the most part the basics of the Hmong culture are universal and are illustrated in this book.

There has been a lot of writing about Hmong people and culture. Most works were written by non–Hmong who have spent time with Hmong people. Lately, Hmong scholars have begun to contribute to the chronicling of our lives. We are starting to paint a clearer picture of our own culture and history through primary resources.

I am not a scholar or an anthropologist with research experience on Hmong. I am just an ordinary Hmong. I was born in a small Hmong village in the highlands of Laos. I lead a Hmong life and teach Hmong literacy, culture and history in a high school in Sacramento, California. Over 95 percent of my students are Hmong. I am the oldest son, a husband, a father and an outspoken member of a large clan. What I have to offer in this book is insight into the Hmong people's way of life — a way of life that needs to be perpetuated.

My personal and professional experiences have taken me beyond what the average Hmong man would normally do, and have allowed me to see different sides of the current dilemma for Hmong. I grew up in the old world of subsistence farming as Hmong people have practiced it for thousands of years. The experience has allowed me to understand what it really means to be Hmong. I wasted my early adolescent years feeling hopeless in a refugee camp in Thailand, an experience that made me appreciate the life I am living now. Having a degree in chemistry and teaching high school science for more than ten years have made me a data-driven person able to remain objective. I have traveled to some of the most remote Hmong villages of Yunnan and Quizhou Provinces in China. Recently, I spent a summer in Hmong villages of northern Thailand. I visited Hmong students in villages, boarding schools and colleges in Thailand and southern China. In those parts of the world, young people have to make a hard choice between total assimilation into the dominant society, hoping to succeed, and keeping the Hmong identity, hoping for a miracle. I am forever grateful to not have to choose.

I am a practitioner of Hmong religion, traditions and cultural rituals.

I have performed in various capacities at funeral services and wedding ceremonies. My father is a shaman, and I was drawn to the practice at an early age. With all these experiences, I have come to understand and appreciate Hmong culture from the inside and out.

In college, my English professor gave me the book *Ishi in Two Worlds: A Biography of the Last Wild Indian in North America* by Theodora Kroeber and suggested that I read it. I didn't understand why she would tell me, and only me, to read that book. Nearly a quarter century later, I finally get it. Our struggle to survive as a culturally distinct people may soon be over as it was for Ishi's tribe. In China, Hmong struggle to stay afloat economically. In the countryside of Thailand and in the jungles of Laos, thousands of Hmong peasants are still trying to steer clear of political persecution. In the Western world, education and assimilation overshadow Hmong language and cultural heritage. Our traditions, culture and commitment to being Hmong are diminishing. For the estimated 8 to 12 million Hmong throughout the world, the way of life our ancestors have fought hard for and treasured for thousands of years may be vanishing before our eyes. I feel like I am dangling on barbwire as I write these chapters.

There is no bible to dictate Hmong traditions, culture and life. The language and lifestyle differ slightly between regions and subgroups. The traditions and practices described here may be different from those practiced in other parts of the world. I have tried to be objective. I have also tried to cover a broad spectrum of the Hmong experience worldwide and still make the information comprehensible and practical. There are no exaggerations. I have tried to show Hmong people and the conflicts we face today — the basics of Hmong culture.

In practice, Hmong cultural rituals stretch far beyond the basics. Certain subgroups or sectors of the Hmong population may place greater emphasis on certain aspects of the Hmong culture. Some cultural rituals may be more practical in certain parts of the world than in others due to political or societal norms. The detailed examples of rituals and traditions used in this book should reflect those of White Hmong in California, where I come from.

Regional differences aside, all aspects of Hmong culture are interconnected. From birth to death, from art to religion, and from Heaven to earth, everything is woven together. To lose one aspect of Hmong culture is like losing one leg on a table. There is a proverb that says, "One leg cannot stand erect, one hand clapping cannot make a sound" (*ib ceg sawv tsis ntseg, ib teg npuaj tsis nrov*). Only keeping certain pieces of Hmong culture cannot sustain a cultural heritage.

Like all cultures, language is the bond that holds Hmong culture together. Our language is ancient and literacy is barely emerging. As residents in societies where we must master the dominant language to survive, Hmong language languishes. If we do not maintain our language, it will not be possible to retain our culture. In the face of this, there is literature and writing dedicated to educating young people in the Hmong language. There are also institutions that increasingly place emphasis on Hmong culture and history. This book is part of that movement.

Until recently, Hmong people have lived in isolation as the rest of the world advanced economically, educationally and technologically. Hmong have only entered the academic and technological world in the last four decades, and yet we have made giant strides in the Western world. In China and Southeast Asia, progress is slow due to the lack of educational opportunities, but there is hope for future generations. Hmong people worldwide may still be isolated physically, but no longer intellectually. This is a great opportunity for us to establish a global community.

As Hmong people become more educated, we become more aware of our history and culture. In the world where education is revered, we learn about other cultures and how other people value their own cultural history. We are starting to think about our own culture as other people show interest in us. Now we are in the process of connecting with our past — some for the first time. There are research studies and news articles about Hmong being published. However, we are barely starting to realize the work that still needs to be done, with credibility, on the cultural traditions of the Hmong people.

Throughout history, Hmong people have adapted to different environments and social changes. Our ancestors learned to survive under extreme social and political climates. Today, the adaptation continues. The more fortunate who have entered the Western world still find it difficult to adjust and adapt to the demands of industrialized and highly literate society. We have taken the characters of a foreign language and phonetically fine-tuned them to transcribe our oral language in an attempt to develop our literacy. Where opportunities are granted, we let go of the crude farming implements in exchange for pen and paper — tools vital to making a living. Where opportunities are hard to come by, young people change their names and physical appearance to be in congruence with the norm to improve their chances of survival. We have learned to camouflage ourselves with the elements of our current environment and thrive. This book provides suggestions on things we can do to survive and yet still retain our cultural identity.

As a people, Hmong are in a transitional period. Some, especially the elders, continue to dwell in the past, dreading life in the demanding modern world. Younger individuals become oblivious to our past and eagerly join the dominant culture. Then there are those of who want to maintain our identity, our culture and our way of life, but also want to embrace the benefits of the modern world. These are the ones faced with the challenge of retaining and maintaining our cultural traditions, and blazing a middle trail for those eager for a new way of life.

In recent years, Hmong youth have shown a renewed interest in their cultural heritage. I have conducted several workshops on Hmong culture. I have also attended similar workshops conducted by others. In every case, rooms were packed and the audiences always had more questions than the presenters could answer. Young people want to know who they are. They want to understand the cultural rituals being performed in the community. They want to know what to do when their turns have come. There are days where I spend whole periods answering questions on topics such as weddings, shamanism, dream interpretation, funeral rituals, history, social issues, etc. It is to these people that I most gratefully address this book.

This book presents a holistic perspective of the Hmong way of life. It touches on a broad spectrum of the Hmong culture, but can't cover everything. I have attempted to phonetically spell Hmong words in English and translate them throughout the text. It is my hope that this book will both inform and instill pride in Hmong youth. Most importantly, I hope this book empowers people to maintain and retain our rich and beautiful culture.

1 HMONG HISTORY

> Nine generations of paternal ancestors are not to be destroyed; three generations of maternal relatives are not to be disrespected. (*Cuaj tiam txwv zeej tsis txhob rhuav; peb tiam neej tsa tsis txhob thuam.*)
>
> — a Hmong proverb

To fully appreciate the Hmong culture, one has to know how hard our ancestors have fought to retain it. This chapter summarizes thousands of years of Hmong history and the struggles our ancestors endured. More detailed discussion is emphasized during the Cold War era because that marked an important point in the history of the Hmong people when we emerged out of isolation and into civilization.

Every ancient civilization has left evidence of its existence behind. The Egyptians left geometrically perfect pyramids. The Romans left their towering structural columns and gigantic stadiums. Hmong left nothing—not even grave sites. Hmong may not be known to the world as an ancient civilization, but our ancestors survived for several thousand years.

From folktales, religious rites, oral history and (Chinese government) documentaries, historians have been able to piece together a sketchy timeline of Hmong ancient history. More accurate and detailed accounts of the history in the last several centuries have been made possible because of the research and literary works of emerging Hmong scholars in China and the United States. The great leaders and war heroes of the past have not been commemorated in books or mirrored in statues for us to marvel at. They dwell in the legends and songs of Hmong peasants from generation to generation.

Ancient Hmong leaders were not exactly pharaohs, but they were heroic and brave. They were proud people who fought hard to institute freedom for the Hmong people of past and present. If it were not for them, Hmong would have vanished from the earth like many other ethnic groups that once existed in an ancient world ruled by ruthless emperors and dictators of ancient China. It was these great leaders that made it possible for Hmong to continue to survive until this day.

For nearly 5,000 years, Hmong have lived in the shadows of imperial China. Hmong have always detested Chinese oppressions. Hmong cringe at the sight of callous Chinese warlords. On the other hand, Hmong have learned to adore the beauty of Chinese youth. We have always envied the knowledge and wisdom of Chinese scholars. We have a strong desire for the power of their Heavenly emperors. Hmong have expressed these thoughts and feelings in songs, folktales and rituals. At the same time, Hmong continually feud with the Chinese from generation to generation in a never-ending battle.

Since the beginning, Hmong have always been known to lead an independent agrarian lifestyle. For as far back as historians can trace, Hmong were perfectly content with what they could grow, hunt, raise, make or trade for. Hmong have always lived a hard life, but have lived it with pride and dignity. Hmong would not hesitate to drop the handle of a hoe and pick up that of a sword or whatever weapon was available to fight to the death for our freedom. The truth is we just wanted to be free — free from other people's rules and oppression. This philosophy has not changed to this day.

With reference to Chinese mythology, Hmong history can be traced back to about 4,600 years ago in central China along the Yangtze River basin. Hmong were a subgroup of the larger collection of ethnic groups referred to by the Han Chinese as Miao. Hmong were direct descendants of the Miao king, Chi You (*Txiv Yawg*). He was a mythical ruler. He ruled over 81 different clans in a kingdom called Jiuli (*Kuj Cuab Cuaj Lig*). Chi You was the first to forge tools and weapons out of metal. Agriculture and laws were first established in his kingdom. Huang Di, the Chinese Yellow Emperor, waged a lengthy war with Chi You and his people. After many years of war, Huang Di combined forces with his nemesis Yan Di. Together, they finally defeated Chi You at the Battle of Zhuolu. When Chi You was killed in battle, the Jiuli Kingdom was captured by Huang Di and his people, who were the predecessors of the Han Chinese. Survivors of the Jiuli tribe scattered southward.

The descendants of Chi You went on to live in desolated areas, without significant developments until 1,000 years later at which time they established the San Miao Kingdom (*Kuj Cuab Peb Hmoob*). That kingdom is believed to have been located in southern China in the vicinity of Zi Shui River (*Dej Ntshav*) in Hunan Province. San Miao was a great agricultural center ruled by Hmong for about 1,000 years. Two of the great rulers of the time were Taotie (*Thaub Them*) and Huan Tuo (*Huam Thuav*). Hmong religious beliefs were much like what we have these days, with ancestral spirits being the primary spiritual deities of worship. The spirits of the land and the Heavens were of great significance. Hmong established laws that were fair and equitable for everybody.

San Miao was eventually conquered by the Han Chinese about 3,200 years ago. A lot of people were killed in the many years of battle. During the fall of San Miao, Hmong were slaughtered to near extinction. Some managed to escape and scattered into the rugged mountainous highlands of the south and west. Those who were not able to escape were either executed or turned into slaves. Men were killed. Women and children were sold into slavery. The escapees continued to live in seclusion, but were free from oppression. From there on, Hmong were never able to re-establish a kingdom of their own.

For about 1,000 years, following the fall of San Miao and up to the birth of Jesus, Hmong did not leave a lot of evidence of their presence. Chinese historical records do not make any reference to Hmong people during this period of time. That may be because the Hmong population dwindled to such a small number that they did not pose a threat to the Chinese. For whatever reason, there is a huge gap in the history of the Hmong people.

When the Han Dynasty came into power about 2,200 years ago, Hmong were living in harmony with nature. They were, by and large, on their own in small, isolated, self-sustaining communities. Hmong were spared the large-scale battles of other ethnic groups. They were able to live off the land and govern themselves. They hunted and gathered natural resources to be traded with the Chinese for material goods. That was a period of many centuries of peace that the Hmong people enjoyed.

During the Tang Dynasty, around A.D. 600, Hmong lived in a feudal society where the feudal lords were wealthy people who were hard workers themselves. These feudal lords owned extensive properties that they leased to less fortunate families who became their tenants. These local lords had the might to protect themselves and their subordinates. The feudal lords were able to fend off foreign aggression and settle civil disputes. The tenants, in return, paid the feudal lords for land use and protection by giving them a certain percentage of their harvest. Then Tang emperors started collecting tax from the feudal lords. Subsequent Tang emperors increased the taxation and demanded greater physical labor from the Hmong people. In early A.D. 800, Hmong started rebelling against the Chinese. These rebellions prevented the Chinese government from overly taxing the people. During this period, Hmong and the Han respected each other to the point where conflicts were settled without trying to annihilate one another. Hmong lived this way continuously for many centuries during and after the Tang Dynasty.

The Yuan Dynasty came into power in the 13th century. The Yuan emperors were Mongols. The Mongols were ruthless rulers. As a result, Hmong combined forces with the Han Chinese to overthrow the Yuan Dynasty. Wu Tian Bao (*Vwj Theeb Pov*) led Hmong warriors to fight against the Mongols. With the Chinese and Hmong fighting for the same cause, the Yuan Dynasty did not rule for long. After the fall of the Yuan Dynasty, Wu Tian Bao had complete authority over an extensive region covering what today are Hunan, Hubei, Guizhou and Guangxi provinces. His reign lasted for many decades. Under his rule, Hmong were able to have peace and harmony. It is times like these that Hmong yearned for and sang about for centuries and still do.

The Ming Dynasty did not gain power until Wu Tian Bao had long passed on and Hmong had once again come under Chinese rule. Even so, the emperor started out with a great relationship with all ethnic groups throughout southern China, including the Hmong. The emperor collected a small tax from Hmong regional rulers and left the rest of the people alone. However, as successive emperors came into power, they became more demanding and greedy. When the demand from the Chinese officials became increasingly unbearable, Hmong began to see it as oppression.

In the 1400s Hmong started rebelling again. Ordinary people rose to leadership. Men, young and old, dropped their farming equipment and grabbed swords and spears to go to war. War heroes such as Meng Neng (*Moob Neeb*), Li Tian Bao (*Lis Theeb Pov*), and Li Zai Wan (*Lis Txawj Vam*) became legends when they marched into battle with thousands of their fellow Hmong countrymen. Many battles were won and lost. Hmong became a sore point for the emperor, so he deployed over 57,000 Chinese soldiers to come down on Li Zai Wan and his 2,000 rebels and their families. Hmong were outnumbered so they had to retreat, leaving the locals to defend themselves. The Chinese also promised Hmong regional leaders wealth and independence if they would switch sides. The losing battles and trickery of the Chinese officials persuaded many Hmong regional leaders to betray Li Zai Wan and surrender to the Chinese. As they did so, the Chinese were able to subdue the rebellion and they killed Li Zai Wan along with all his followers. So much for the promises; local leaders were killed and Chinese officials moved in.

As a result of this failed rebellion, the Ming emperor of the time came down on the Hmong people harder and more ruthlessly. The regional Hmong rulers who were promised sovereignty for defecting to the Chinese were murdered. Hmong people were forced to speak only Chinese, worship Chinese gods and wear only Chinese clothes. These Hmong were referred to as "cooked Hmong" (*Hmoob siav*) by the Chinese, because they had been fully assimilated by force. Every locale was placed under the watchful eyes of resident Chinese authorities and soldiers. Hmong were forced to house and feed these Chinese officials.

In the remote areas the Chinese were not able to conquer, Hmong were able to live free from Chinese domination, but they were in constant fear of being attacked. These Hmong were referred to as "raw Hmong" (*Hmoob nyoos*). Small-scale fighting continued, but total domination by the Chinese was never achieved.

There were two reasons why the Chinese were not able to conquer the Hmong completely. One of the reasons was the fact that the raw Hmong re-established themselves in treacherous mountaintops which the Chinese soldiers were not able to reach. The other reason was that the cooked Hmong would inform the raw Hmong of any plan the Chinese concocted. In this way, they were able to evade Chinese military crackdowns.

For a long time, there was a sense of resentment between the cooked Hmong and the raw Hmong. The cooked Hmong were accused of being traitors and the raw Hmong created a hostile environment for the cooked Hmong. The truth is that Hmong were able to remain pure and retain their cultural identity for many centuries due in part to the help of the ones who were forced to assimilate.

In 1622, the Chinese started erecting a southern wall to the west of Hu-Nan. Chinese authorities built this wall to isolate Hmong from Chinese towns and cities. The wall was about 60 miles long and 15 feet high. It has been torn down since, but it served as a reminder as to how much of a threat Hmong posed to the Chinese. Hmong were forced to live under these conditions until the end of the Ming Dynasty in 1644.

The Qing Dynasty brought a sigh of relief at its beginning. The Manchurians (rulers of the Qing Dynasty) exhausted their manpower to overthrow the Ming Dynasty. As a result, the first Qing emperor could not afford to assert great restraint on the people. Besides, like most of his predecessors, the first Qing emperor was sympathetic to his citizens in general. As a result, for the first century under the Manchurians, Hmong actually faired better than they had under the Mings.

At the beginning of the Qing Dynasty, Hmong were able to live independent, self-sustaining lives and worship the spirits of their ancestors and the land. Hmong, like other ethnic groups, were allowed to rule themselves regionally with fairly low taxation going to the emperor. Each government post was occupied by one Manchu and one Han Chinese official. China was a large country controlled by insufficient numbers of Manchurian officials. Over time, the central government started to lose control. Regional officials started to assert their own influence. Toward the latter part of the Qing Dynasty, the emperor had very little influence over regional warlords. This proved disastrous for the Hmong. During the Qing Dynasty, Hmong suffered far worse and more Hmong perished than during all the previous dynasties combined.

Problems started with heavy taxation. Then the Chinese started claiming rights to the land. Hmong leaders were lured into death traps by Chinese officials. Ultimately, Chinese authorities were sent to take control of villages and towns. Rich Chinese merchants resettled in Hmong villages and towns and claimed the fertile lands. Citizens had to pay the Chinese rent for the land that was once their own. Loans were imposed with a five percent monthly interest. If Hmong were not able to pay, a percentage of the yield of the next harvest would be taken as payment. Chinese authorities also divided Hmong families into small groups of around a dozen. If one person from a group violated a law, the whole group got punished. If a Han Chinese was killed by a Hmong, all members of his group would be executed in retaliation unless the perpetrator was turned in to Chinese authorities by the group itself.

Isolated areas where no Chinese had ever set foot before were explored and conquered by Chinese soldiers. The plan was to lure, conquer and eliminate those who opposed Chinese authorities. There was a genocide of ethnic minorities throughout southern China, and Hmong were just one of these ethnic minorities. During this period, many ethnic groups were wiped from the surface of the earth. By 1737, tens of thousands of Hmong had been massacred, villages burned and land seized and given to the Chinese soldiers.

During the Qing Dynasty, Hmong mounted many rebellions against Chinese rule. Many Hmong kings were proclaimed and perished. Many war heroes became legends. Wu Ba Yue (*Vwj Paj Yias*) was one such hero. Wu was a self-proclaimed Hmong king during the Qing Dynasty, and was a powerful leader with a lot of loyal followers. Legend has it that he was educated, well-trained in martial arts, intelligent and passionate. His nearly 100-pound (45.5 kg) dagger could not be stopped in battle. Unfortunately, he was betrayed by a clansman. As a result, in 1795 he was captured and executed by the Chinese. He left a chilling legacy of power, betrayal and destruction.

Ultimately, the ruthless repression by Chinese authorities and devastating defeats led many Hmong to migrate farther south into Laos and Vietnam for the first time.

Bao Da Du (*Pob Tuam Twm*) was born not too long after the death of Wu Ba Yue. Bao was an extraordinary leader with a superior physique and martial arts skills. He gained high status in the mid–1800s as an ingenious military leader. He was admired by his followers and feared by enemies. In 1869, he was in command of Hmong soldiers in a battle known as Huang Piao (*Faj Plob*) Battle, defending Hmong territories against Chinese suppression forces. Bao and his men lured, trapped and killed nearly 20,000 Chinese soldiers in a single battle.

Zhang Xiu Mei (*Tsab Xyooj Mem* or *Tsab Xyawm Mej*) was a revered leader who led Hmong rebellions along with Bao Da Du. There were other ethnic groups such as Dong Zu (*Toom*), Bu Yi Zu (*Puab Yib*), Yi Zu (*Yiv*), and Chinese that he took under his wing. Under his leadership, a large portion of southern China was reclaimed and ruled by Hmong for a couple of decades. During this period of time, with the protection of Zhang's forces, Hmong were able to continue to live the way they had done for thousands of years.

To combat Zhang's forces, Chinese authorities resorted to military consultants from the Western world to crack down on Hmong. Because of the advantage of the handgun and modern rifle, the Chinese prevailed.

Bao and his forces retreated to a mountaintop in Hmong country called Lei Gong Shan (*Roob Lej Koob Sab*). Bao was killed in battle. In 1871, Zhang was eventually captured and taken to the emperor. On that last, fateful journey to Beijing, he left Hmong with the following song:

> There is work to be done, do
> There is clothe to be sewn, sew
> This year I have parted
> I will return in the next life
> To reclaim land for us to farm
> To reclaim land for us to govern
> Kill the enemy to extinction
> For revenge
>
> *Muaj num kav tsij ua*
> *Muaj paj ntaub kav tsij nrhia*
> *Xyoo no kuv ncaim lawm tiag,*
> *Lwm tiam kuv li rov los,*
> *Txeeb liaj teb rau peb cog,*
> *Tua teb tua chaw rau peb kav,*
> *Tua Suav rog kom tu tsav,*
> *Los pauj peb*

As the war raged on Hmong suffered greatly, but they were strong-willed and enduring. The Chinese, on the other hand, brought in cannons and rifles from the West. They also tried to demoralize the Hmong by digging up the graves of the deceased — disturbing the spirits of the ancestors. This action struck at the core of Hmong belief, which is ancestor worship. For Hmong, this is like cutting off the roots to a tree. Another strategy the Chinese used was to destroy everything in their path — homes and crops in the path of war were burned and destroyed. This turmoil drove Hmong to desperation. Some became traitors in order to stay alive, which proved fatal to Hmong people. In the end, hundreds of thousands of Hmong surrendered. Hundreds of thousands more were killed or died from starvation. This was the bloodiest era in Hmong history. It is said that the blood of Hmong in the final battles flowed like a river.

In the years following the Qing Dynasty, China went through a lot of military and political turmoil. The focus of the nationalist movement shifted away from ethnic genocide. The communist revolution that followed also put greater focus on foreign aggressions rather than internal turmoil. That eased the tension between Hmong and Chinese. Along the way, many Hmong joined the forces of these movements and some rose to become high-ranking military leaders during and after the Communist revolution.

In the 19th century, Hmong continued to migrate into Southeast Asia. Wave after wave of Hmong families migrated into Laos and Vietnam. The flow of Hmong refugees continued well into the early 1900s. In Southeast Asia, Hmong settled in the highlands, which the Vietnamese and Laotian natives did not inhabit. For nearly a hundred years, Hmong led peaceful lives. With new, fertile virgin forests, Hmong adapted to slash and burn techniques as opposed to tilling with oxen and water buffalos as they were used to doing in China. Hmong continued their self-subsistence farming way of life and worshipped their ancestors as well as spirits of the land and Heaven.

Living off the land was not easy, but the prospects were much better than ever before. With a vast open range, Hmong raised cattle, goats and pigs to supplement their diet. They cultivated rice and corn as main staples. By this time, the opium trade in China was running rampant and the cooler climate of the highlands was perfect for opium cultivation. Thus, opium became the main cash crop for Hmong people. Trading came by way of Chinese merchants drawn by horses and mules coming into the Hmong villages from China. Hmong were reluctant to go to the lowlands and interact with the natives. Those who did usually became sick and died. Only when the French asserted their colonial power to collect tax and demand corvee labor from all Laotian citizens were Hmong forced to go down to the lowlands.

In the early 1900s, Hmong were being taxed unfairly. A contributing factor to the overtaxation was the corrupt Laotian tax collectors. Tax collectors ordered Hmong to pay for every stump of the sizeable trees that were cut down to clear the way for farming. Furthermore, personal tax was so high that poor families had to sell their children to pay the tax collectors. So when Hmong people could not pay their taxes some rebelled. The rebellion was a combined effort among Hmong in China, Laos and Vietnam.

In Laos, rebels were led by the messianic Pa Chay Vue (*Paj Cai Vwj*). Vue led a strong resistance of blatant refusal to pay the tax collectors. When the tax collectors went back without money, the French sent soldiers. The French soldiers were greeted by angry Hmong men armed with homemade muskets at the base of the mountains. This rebellion was called the Crazy War.

In Vietnam, Vuong Chinh Duc (*Zoov Leej Vaj*) organized Hmong men to rebel against the French colonial oppression. At the height of the war, Hmong rebels took control of a large portion of northern Laos and Vietnam.

Unfortunately, not all Hmong supported the rebellious effort. The majority of Hmong just stood by and watched as Vue was assassinated and his followers were beheaded. Vuong, on the other hand, was captured and incarcerated. Many Hmong lost their lives.

As a result of the rebellion, the French dealt directly with Hmong, establishing local Hmong clan leaders called Kaitong (*Kiab Toom*) who answered directly to the French.

During World War II, many Hmong men were involved in the fighting, but the Hmong villages were spared. Hmong people, for the most part, stood by and watched the fighting, because the bulk of the fighting was between the French and the Japanese in the low lying areas to determine who would have control over Laos. Hmong people called it the Japanese War. Prior to the war, many Hmong children were sent to school for the first time. Among the first wave of Hmong students was Vang Pao (*Vaj Pov*). He joined the Lao Royal Army and quickly climbed up the ranks. Vang Pao went to battle for the French. During this time, French missionary Yves Bertrais was developing the Roman Popularized Alphabet (RPA) writing system for the Hmong people. By 1953, Hmong people were learning how to read and write in their own language.

During the Vietnam War, Vang Pao and a handful of Hmong elders agreed to secretly help the United States Central Intelligence Agency (CIA) combat the spread of communism in what was known as the Cold War. Young Hmong men were recruited, trained and armed by the CIA. Hmong soldiers were given the responsibilities of rescuing downed U.S. pilots and cutting off the Ho Chi Minh trail that cut through Laos. This went on for more than two decades where nearly every able Hmong man was given a gun to protect his village and thousands of young men were sent to the front line. At the same time, Hmong continued to slash and burn away ancient jungles and live off the highlands of Laos.

Ironically, Hmong were fighting against their own kind during the Cold War. All the Hmong people in Vietnam lived in Northern Vietnam, and so they were under total Communist rule. They didn't have a choice but to become Communists. A faction of the Hmong people in Laos joined the Communist movement under the leadership of Fai Da Lao (*Faiv Ntaj*

Lauj). For the most part, Hmong were on opposing sides of the conflict, and they were fighting against each other. Communist influence swept from east to west across northern Laos. The majority of Hmong people strongly disliked Communist ideologies, so they stayed just ahead of the Communist infiltration. As such, Hmong migrated westward toward the Mekong River. To stay ahead of the war and to find new virgin forests to sustain their way of life, Hmong made their way across the Mekong River and were well into Thai territory by the late 1950s.

As the Cold War intensified and the Communist movement gained strength, Communists infiltrated Hmong villages. As early as 1960, Hmong were abandoning their highland villages and fleeing into the lowland by the thousands. Hmong were taking refuge in cities and towns that had once been inhabited exclusively by native Lao ethnics. Hmong became refugees of war in Laos long before the country fell to the hands of communists.

When the U.S. forces pulled out of Southeast Asia in May of 1975, communists gained complete control of Laos. General Vang Pao's followers and sympathizers became targets of retaliation. Fearing for their lives, hundreds of thousands of Hmong, Mien, Kher and Laotians fled to Thailand. Many of these refugees perished in the Mekong River by drowning or being shot to death by communists on boat patrol.

Once in Thailand, Hmong received refugee status and refugee camps were established inside Thailand to accommodate the hundreds of thousands of refugees. From the refugee camps, Hmong were dispersed into the Western world — mainly to France and the United States of America. Today, the vast majority of Hmong living outside of Asia came from Laos.

The current estimate of the Hmong population worldwide is between 8 million and 12 million. It is impossible to get an accurate count for various reasons. The bulk of the population resides in southwestern China. Laos, Vietnam and Thailand are home to a few hundred thousand Hmong each. There are also several thousand Hmong living in countries such as France, Canada, Australia and Argentina. In the United States, the Hmong population is about 300,000 with the majority living in California, Minnesota and Wisconsin.

According to Yuepheng Xiong, a pioneering Hmong historian, Hmong-Chinese are divided into five subgroups: Black (*Hmong Dub*), Red (*Hmong Liab*), White (*Hmong Dawb*), Green (*Hmoob Ntsuab*) and Flower

Top: A segregated Hmong village called Nampendin in Thailand. This is a typical village that is situated above the clouds but below the peak of the mountain. Cities and towns lie in the valley in the background. *Above:* Hmong people farming the hillsides of Ban Romklao, Thailand, carrying 100-pound bags of ginger on their backs the same way their ancestors have done for generations.

Top: The agrarian life seems dirty and primitive, but it comes with a low level of stress as it revolves around the natural cycle of life. *Above:* Hmong have always enjoyed the leisure life on top of the mountain as the world passes by below.

It is not uncommon to find Hmong people living at the edge of the world.

Hmongs (*Hmong Paj*).* The subgroups are named for the general appearance of their clothes. The dialects spoken by the subgroups vary from minor to unintelligible differences. In the United States, for example, there are only two subgroups of Hmong: White and Green. These two subgroups are practically the same except for minor differences in the detail of their cultural and religious practices. Their clothing designs are different in that the Green Hmong men's trousers are loose and baggy, whereas White Hmong men's trousers are fitted more snugly. White Hmong originally wore clothes made of undyed hemp fibers, so their clothes evolved into white skirts for the women. Green Hmong traditionally dyed their clothes with delicate designs, so the women's skirts are multi-colored. As for the language, there are slight dialectic variations with few uniquely different words. The two dialects are quite intelligible to one another. These subgroups can be categorized further due to regional differences in their costumes. White Hmong, for example, can be subdivided into Black (*Dub*), Striped (*Txaij*) and Flowery-Headwear (*Phuam Paj*) Hmong. There are no cultural or language differences among these groups of people. Though subdivided, all Hmong came from one humble root, and we are practically the same throughout the world.

Yuepeng Xiong. "INK," Hmong Magazine, Vol. 1, Spring 1997.

There have been tremendous developments for Hmong within the last 30 years since we migrated into the Western world. Hmong Americans now have the means to reach out to our fellow Hmong in other parts of the world — even the ones living in the most remote corners of China. We are reconnecting slowly.

Throughout history, there have been unique and consistent traits of Hmong. We have always wanted freedom. We have maintained an agrarian lifestyle. Our commitment has remained the same. Survival has always been a constant struggle. However, things are looking up for Hmong. Today, many Hmong have embarked on a new quest — the quest for a formal education. As a result, Hmong will never be the same again.

2 PARENTS AND THEIR CHILDREN

Animals that are not loyal to their masters will die, people who are not loyal to their parents will be poor. (*Tsiaj tsis hwm tswv yuav tuag, tub ki tsis hwm niam hwm txiv yuav pluag.*)
— Kou Shue Cha

Hmong people have strong ties with extended family members, aunts, uncles, grandparents, nieces, nephews, etc. Members of the family depend on and support each other. Without a family, there is no life. That is why Hmong families seem so large. We tend to cluster in large numbers under the same roof, with three or four generations living together. The core of the family, however, centers around parents and child. The bond between the generations keeps the clan alive, but an elderly woman will tell you that the key to making a marriage work is the children.

There is a Hmong proverb that says, "We raise crops to await hunger, we raise children to await old age" (*ua qoob ua loo los npaj tshaib, tu tub tu kiv los npaj laus*). Hmong people have children because they want to have somebody there to care for them when they can no longer take care of themselves. In the Hmong world, there have never been government pensions or subsidies for seniors. Retirement homes are jailhouses. When people get old and can no longer fend for themselves, they rely on their children to care for them. Those without children foresee that suffering in the later years. This is still the popular belief among Hmong parents. Sadly, the younger generation does not seem to share the same philosophy. In early 2007, 78-year-old Choua Sue Lee (*Tshuas Xwm Lis*) from Sacramento, California, was sent to a nursing home because he had no immediate family members who could take care of him. His wife and only son had both passed away the year before. At the nursing home, Mr. Lee became depressed, and he refused to eat. He died a few months later. Mr. Lee was a well-respected and highly influential person in the Hmong community. He was well versed in Hmong cultural rituals with many disciples. It is hard to imagine that such a great man would succumb so easily. Thus is the nature of first-generation Hmong immigrants.

Hmong parents always want at least one son. This is not because a son will love them more, but because a daughter will marry into another clan and become an outsider. A son has the inherent right to the family name and to be the family heir. When there is no heir to the family name and the father dies, the family name perishes. No matter how prosperous a daughter becomes, her children will bear the family name of another clan.

A son is obligated to take care of his parents when they become old. If there is more than one son, the responsibility for the parents lies in the youngest. That, however, does not mean that the older sons are off the hook. All children owe their parents the love and care they were provided when they were young. When the parents become less capable, the roles are reversed. As any elder would say, "Old old become a little child" (*laus laus ua mi nyuam yaus*). It means when a person becomes old, he or she becomes like a child who needs attention, care and nurturing. The obligation parents and children have for each other is the bond which is the basis of Hmong family values.

It is arguable that a daughter can just as well take care of her parents. Physically, it is possible that a daughter can care for and shelter her parents to the end. However, when she is married to her husband, she is incorporated spiritually into her husband's family. Because of this she cannot remain part of her parents' family spiritually — not even if she divorces her husband. What this means is that the daughter cannot tend to her parents spiritually. In fact, the parents cannot even die inside her house, because that will violate her husband's guardian spirits. When my family was still living in the refugee camp in Thailand, I knew an old lady we called Auntie Chia Thong (*niam tais Txiaj Thoob*). She had no sons so she lived with her daughter's family. When she became very sick and about to die, her daughter took her out to the side of the house. The old lady died there. For her funeral, they made a makeshift hut with just a few thatches of grass, barely enough to provide shade for her body during the funeral rituals. The funeral was just overnight, with the bare minimum required for the soul to depart into the spiritual land of oblivion. That is the extent to which a daughter can take care of her parents. Chia Thong did not have an heir or any close family members from her husband's side, so she did not have a house to die in. As if that is not bad enough, a daughter cannot worship the spirits of her parents after they die. So, in the Hmong world, a daughter can take care of her parents physically when they are alive, but never spiritually.

The clannish nature of Hmong society favors a son. A family that does not have a son is viewed as a burden to the clan and community, because such a family will not contribute much to the community. A family without a male heir will need everybody else to see the parents to the end. From the clan perspective, Hmong people value their sons more than their daughters. Even when a son is a looser, the elders say, "He will come around." This is the belief that a looser son will mature and wise up. Then, he will do the right thing and become a productive member of society. A daughter, on the other hand, has to conduct herself properly and it is not in her best interest to be out helping the clan in ceremonial or religious rituals. If she is mischievous and becomes old, she will not likely marry into a decent family, and she will be a disgrace to her parents. A son can always redeem himself, but not a daughter. This is justifiable culturally, but it is unfair to the daughter from a contemporary perspective. Daughters are not allowed to be contributing members of the clan or community or to explore life. Boys, on the other hand, are given more freedom to explore and develop the habits that are needed to become contributing clan members. Because of this, some girls will get married at a young age just to get away from their parents, while the sons take advantage of their freedom and get into trouble. Such is the nature of a clannish society.

In the Hmong world, it is just as crucial for a family to have a son as it is to have a father in a family. There is an interdependency between father and son that makes life unsettling if one or the other is missing. It is this connection that makes Hmong people treat fatherless children and childrenless parents differently from everybody else. This practice is referenced in the proverb, "Respect the father, give the son meat and respect the son, give the father wine" (*saib txiv pub tub nqaij, saib tub pub txiv cawv*). When a man is young, people respect him because of his father and when he is old people respect him because of his son. For a young boy, when people feast they give him meat out of respect for his father. When the man becomes old, people only respect him if he has a respectable son who other people can rely on. So when people drink they will invite the old man to drink with them out of respect for his son. This is evident in the Hmong world in which orphans get treated as second class citizens in the community. Likewise, elders who do not have a son do not get invited to gatherings and celebrations outside of their immediate families. So the interdependency between father and son is more than just a personal thing.

Just because Hmong parents have greater hopes for and expect more from their sons does not mean that they love their sons more than their daughters. Normally, parents love their children equally. Some parents actually love their daughters more. My grandfather always said that he loved his two daughters more than his six sons because he knew the girls were only going to live with him for just a short time — then they would be gone forever. And, indeed, my father and uncles were with my grandparents until the end, and my aunts parted when they got married. They only saw each other once every few years thereafter. During the last three decades of my grandmother's life, she lost contact with her daughters. Only my father and uncles were there for her until the end. When she passed away in 1988, none of her daughters made it to her funeral. Hmong parents do love both boys and girls equally. They just have different expectations for members of each gender.

Although the preference leans toward a son, a daughter is also important to the family. A daughter is said to keep the house warm. As a child, a daughter keeps the mother company. As she grows up, suitors will keep ghosts and thieves away as they come around to court her. She also does all the light household chores, such as cooking and cleaning. A daughter's burden can only be lightened by a sister-in-law brought in by a son. It is said that the daughter is the guest and the daughter-in-law is the caretaker (*nkauj nyab nkauj tab, nkauj muam nkauj qhua*). A daughter provides parents with affection. She is the one who reminds the parents that they are loved. When the son goes astray, she keeps him in line. A daughter bears the right to be critical of how the son takes care of the parents. Hmong parents who do not have a daughter will always be sad and feel unloved. A daughter has a place in the parents' heart which nobody else can replace.

A daughter holds a special, highly regarded, position in Hmong religion. When a "faulty religious practice" develops, the daughter becomes the savior (*muam phauj tsawm*). The daughter has the final say in how rituals can be performed. At the funeral of any elder, the daughters and sisters take their positions at the helm in the ceremonial services. They are there to show love and to make sure the deceased is being treated fairly. So, a couple that does not have a daughter or a man who does not have a sister would be very depressed. Each gender plays a unique role in a Hmong family and the double standard is a part of Hmong culture.

In modern day Hmong society, it is difficult to balance gender equity and still keep customs intact. The Hmong culture and customs no doubt seem antiquated. Many still refuse to change and change can be different. These days, daughters are still being married off. Sons are still expected to bring wives into the family to help support the family. Rituals are still performed and decisions still made almost exclusively by men. The boys are pushed harder in school. Boys also are allowed to be more adventurous than girls. There is gender inequity in the Hmong world. Some people, especially girls, see this inequity and jump ship. I think the most favorable thing to do is to understand the culture and the circumstances surrounding it and work toward change.

As a matter of fact, there are changes on the horizon already. We are seeing daughters at their parents' home more often even long after they are married off. My sister Mai Lee and her husband, Chue Soua Vang, visit my parents more often than my wife and I do. More girls are allowed to go away for college, and they are not being pressured to get married at a young age. The boys are encouraged to do household chores. As this trend continues, the double standard in the Hmong world will soon be a thing of the past. So goes the culture and customs, but cultures are always changing anyway. It is important that the sons will have to continue to carry the family name and perform the religious rituals, but everything else can be compromised.

Communication between parents and children is challenging in every culture. Hmong people are no exception. Hmong parents and their children speak different languages literally, if they talk at all. This is inherent — customarily, Hmong children are discouraged from talking back to their parents. They are also taught to not question their parents' authority and actions. My father has always said, "When I tell you to do something, don't question me. What you need to know is that it will never kill you." I am sure other Hmong parents are similar. Obedient children are supposed to act like robots and follow orders. In fact, children are not to even look at their elders when being talked to. Looking at an elder when he is talking is a sign of disrespect. By the time children become young adults, they have grown accustomed to the idea that questioning their parents' authority is not culturally acceptable. Communication is a learned behavior which can be easily changed with awareness and education.

Normally, parents and children of the same gender feel more comfortable communicating (e.g., father and son or mother and daughter) than those of opposite genders. That is because in the Hmong community it is taboo for a mother to have a close relationship with her son and for a father to have a close relationship with his daughter. I have seen mothers who try to talk to their sons, and it appears as though they were talking to dummies. A father and a grown-up daughter's display of affection is deemed inappropriate.

Communication between parents and their teenage children is especially difficult when children grow up in a bilingual/multicultural world. I have, on many occasions, been a mediator between Hmong parents and their children. A good example is my cousin Jimmy Cha, who was born and raised in the United States. His parents speak very little English and are very traditional. He, on the other hand, is more fluent in English than Hmong. Jimmy lives a dual-life of Hmong at home and American pop culture at school. One evening a few years ago, I got an urgent call from Jimmy's mother. When I got there, I saw that Jimmy had a knife in his hand and was ready to kill himself. I convinced him to lay down the knife and start talking. The reason he wanted to end his life was because he wanted to get married. It was all a misunderstanding. The issue was easily settled by allowing him to get married even though he was only 18 and a high school dropout. Hmong people used to call this kind of dilemma "chopping down the bed posts" (*ntov ncej txag*). Then again, miscommunication can be attributed to the lack of cultural capital in Hmong children.

Teenage girls have traditionally not received much affection and open communication from their fathers. Hmong fathers have to learn to communicate directly with their daughters as opposed to through their wives. It used to be that the father would not tell a daughter what to do. It is "the mother's job," as my father-in-law would say. When the girls do something inappropriate, the father would just blame the mother for it. This is evident at Hmong New Year celebrations where mothers dress their daughters up very nicely and follow their every move the whole time they are out. Meanwhile, the fathers are usually out with their friends doing their own thing. In the Western world, Hmong fathers are starting to open up the communication channel between them and their daughters, but there are still too many who are just as archaic as their forefathers have been for generations.

Hmong parents have high expectations of their children. The sons are expected to become responsible and to take care of the family when they grow up. Daughters are expected to be loyal and subservient. Oftentimes, sons grow up with the notion that it is manly not to do household chores. Chores are the girls' responsibility. Often times, the sons grow up having authority over their sisters. This is a practice we often see at family gatherings. Hmong have not bought into the idea of catering, so we still do our own cooking at every ceremony and celebration. On such occasions, I see young men helping with some of the laborious tasks of putting a feast together. However, the bulk of the work lies with the women (young and old). Be it the cooking, washing dishes, setting up the table or cleaning up, it is the women and their daughters who do all the work. I believe that this is a practice all Hmong people need to evaluate; they need to face the fact that men and women need to both help carry their share of the responsibility. Better yet, parents need to model and instill in their children that it is just as acceptable for men to cook and clean as for women to mow the lawn and change the engine oil in the family car if it is a way of sharing the workload.

Regardless of the gender, all parents expect their children to be loving, caring, obedient, hard-working, and of course, stay in school. At a young age, children do as their parents say. As children grow up, some continue to do whatever their parents ask of them in order to get them to participate in Hmong cultural traditions. Some children grow up hating being told what to do and eventually give up trying to understand and take part in rituals at functions. Yeng Vang, for example, was obedient and well disciplined. He learned how to play the bamboo reed pipe or kheng (*qeej*) at the age of 10. By the time he became a teenager he had mastered it, but he stopped practicing for two reasons. First, he got involved with the wrong crowd and fell behind academically. Second, he was not asked to perform at funerals because he was just a child. He lost interest in it as a result. These days, he does not remember a thing about kheng. Yeng is not alone. There are many more who have been pushed hard both at school and home. Without the proper guidance and support some become burnt out and give up on both.

What is a more realistic expectation of Hmong sons and daughters these days is for them to know their manners (*paub kev cai*). To know Hmong manners is to have a general understanding about every aspect of our culture. Such knowledge may be quite profound, but it is also essential to keeping the culture alive. Having proper personal conduct around elders is necessary. Religious ceremonies, weddings, and funeral rituals are occasions where good manners and traditions are expected to be exhibited. Most important is knowing who you are. These are examples of traditional manners.

Developing authentic manners is the first step in the upbringing of a child. A person with proper manners may not have acquired a body of knowledge well enough to perform at cultural ceremonies, but he knows enough not to embarrass himself on such occasions. As tradition has it, there are only a few who are motivated and gifted enough to learn to take the lead and be in charge of ceremonies and celebrations. An occasion where young people these days are clueless is a funeral. A person who knows his manners would conduct himself properly so others would not look down on him. For example, when he donates money to the family of the deceased, which is a common practice, he knows the proper channels to go through and when the family gives thanks, he knows how to respond. There are those who see such practices every day, but are reluctant to learn. Some don't take the time to learn or do not have the proper guidance. In any case, knowledge is not inheritable or innate. It has to be learned. Parents lead the way and their children will follow suit as Tou Ger Xiong talked about in his popular comedy shows where his father took him to a funeral. Tou Ger's father started wailing upon arrival, so Tou Ger just wailed and blew his nose, mimicking his father.

Traditionally, Hmong people who have mastered a certain body of knowledge are reluctant to show or teach children of others who are not likely to be benefactors. Keeping knowledge as a family secret has made it difficult for Hmong people to pass their cultural traditions and practices from one generation to the next. The culture could be easily retained by subsequent generations if every teachable moment were not wasted and knowledge and skills were not kept from inquiring minds. We see it in old Chinese martial arts movies all the time. When a kung fu master teaches his disciples, he keeps one lethal move a secret and only teaches it to one student he trusts the most. Such is the case with Hmong masters as well. In the Hmong world, when a body of knowledge is not entirely passed on to others and the keeper of the knowledge does not have an inheritance, the knowledge is gone when the master dies. Knowledge has to be passed on from one generation to the next or it is lost.

Often, Hmong parents have dreams that go unfulfilled. These parents sometimes push their children hard so their children can accomplish what they themselves could not accomplish. In such cases, parents weigh in on their children's future. This is a common mistake that happens a lot in the Hmong world. Children are steered toward a certain traditional skill, career path or profession of their parents' choosing. I know of many young people whose parents want them to become doctors, lawyers and teachers. When these young people have their career choices chosen for them, the result is often quite disappointing. Parents should allow their children to explore their own interests and talents and chose their own path.

This day and age, children are very vulnerable to external influences. These external forces include video games, the internet, peer pressure, drugs, street gangs, and more. If not carefully monitored and guided, children can get tangled up in very dangerous predicaments. These are issues that uninformed parents cannot comprehend. Uneducated Hmong parents are not aware of the complexity of these problems. As such, many families are torn apart by children who get involved in drugs and gang activities. In some cases, parents and grandparents are taken advantage of, if not abused, by their children and grandchildren. This is an issue that is emotionally charged, and there are no easy solutions. Factor in the unbreakable bond between parents, children and grandchildren, and it spells disaster. My cousin Tong Cher (*Tooj Tsaub*) is a perfect example. He is a 28-year-old man who lost his job, wife and three children in a nasty divorce. Now he gets Social Security benefits and is living with my uncle and aunt who are in their mid–70s and ill. Among other drugs, he is addicted to methamphetamine. All his money goes toward his drug addiction, and he freeloads off his parents. They will not kick him out of the house because they love him. He is constantly in a state of semi-consciousness thanks to methamphetamine. Anybody with logical sense would just throw the son out, but my uncle and aunt would not do that. Tong's problem goes way back to his pre-adolescent years when he was left alone at home to do whatever he wanted and go wherever he chose to as my uncle and aunt were busy tending to their farm every day from dawn until dusk. Where Hmong parents used to have complete control over their children, now under the watchful eyes of modern civic codes, many Hmong parents watch helplessly as their children are dragged into the world of gangs, drugs and losers.

Hmong parents and their children will continue to struggle. There are no parenting classes and obedience schools for Hmong people, so individuals are going to have to deal with these issues individually with the help and support of families, friends, and community leaders. Ultimately, it comes down to the inseparable bond between Hmong parents and their children that has made life worthwhile for everybody. It is the relationship between Hmong parents and their children that defines family, and ultimately dictates our culture.

3 CUSTOMS AND VALUES

On the inside we are family, on the outside we are relatives.
Opened doors make us family, closed doors make us a village.
(*Qas ntawg yog neej, qas nraug yog tsav. Qheb rooj yog yig, qos rooj yog ib zog.*)
— an affirmation of how all Hmong are related

People throughout the world have unique cultural values. Hmong are no different. Although the basic values and customs remain the same, Hmong people live very differently from one region to another. We have learned to adapt to the dominant culture under which we live. Because of this, there are differences in the way we see and value things in different parts of the world. Western influence has also altered our views and philosophy and thus has shifted our cultural values and customs. Overall, Hmong are still Hmong no matter where we live.

Hmong people have always lived in a patriarchal world. From the family unit to society at large, men make all the decisions. In addition, elders are to be respected by young people regardless of stature. Generational order is also a very important concept. Being a patriarchal society, women always take a backseat. A large sector of the Hmong population still lives this way, especially in China and Southeast Asia. In the West, Hmong men have learned to share the responsibilities and the decision-making process with Hmong women.

Humbleness and modesty are defining characteristics of being Hmong, particularly in the older generation. Hmong people not only live off the earth, but we are down-to-earth as well. A man with a body of knowledge will not show it off until there is a need to. A girl with a rep-

32

utation of being beautiful and graceful will not brag about her beauty. If you compliment a Hmong elder for a job well done, his response would probably not be "thank you." Instead, you might hear something like, "Oh, it is just mediocrity," or, "It's nothing." Hmong are not only restrained at responding to compliments, we don't give compliments liberally. This is starting to change among people who are westernized, especially when they have some education.

Hmong people have an awkward way of complimenting others. If you see a beautiful baby, you should not tell the parents that the baby is beautiful. The proper way to compliment an adorable baby is to say the baby smells of poop (*tsw quav*). The rationale behind this is that beauty is attractive to both human beings and spirits. If a child is regarded as being beautiful, evil spirits might snatch the child's soul. When the baby is regarded to be unattractive, both human and spirits would shy away and the baby will not get sick. So next time you extend a good gesture toward a Hmong and you don't get the expected response, don't take it personally. It is a cultural thing.

Traditionally, Hmong people are quite thankful, but we don't say it at every turn. Young Hmong people these days say "thank you" all the time. Until recently, however, Hmong used to take the expression "thank you" by itself offensively. That is because there is a proper way to say thank you. The proper way to express one's appreciation is to say the words "thank you" very subtly, follow with a phrase explaining the circumstances and a humble acceptance of the deed that warrants it. When a person visits relatives that live far away, and they have prepared a meal in his honor, he needs to thank them. Once everybody has settled at the table and are getting ready to eat, he should thank the family. As the guest, he stands up with plate and spoon in hand, call out the head of household and thanks him. He thanks the family to the effect that they didn't have to go out of their way to prepare a meal for him, which is such an inconvenience for them. (*Ua tsaug os mog, nej tsis cia li tseem npaj zaub npaj mov rau kuv noj thiab es luab luab lim nej xwb os.*) In return, the head of the family will respond by saying that it is a humble meal and they can't afford better, so there is no need to say thanks. (*Tsis txhob ua tsaug os, koj tuaj deb deb tuaj los cav npaj tsis tau ib pluag zoo mov pub koj noj es tsis txhob ua tsaug.*) The words of choice may differ individually, but the basic idea of saying thank you and responding to a thank you is the same. Each situation warrants a different phrase of thanks. At a wedding, for example, the words and hand gesture of thanks vary drastically from those used at a funeral service.

In the Hmong world, gender inequity is alive and well. Woman need to respect not only their men, but men in general. They should not demean men (*hla txiv neej tob hau*). A wife should not defy her husband's actions or his decisions. This would disgrace him in public (*rhuav ntsej muag*). A woman should not physically walk past a man's immediate forefront nor extend any part of her body over any part of a man's body. A woman should not reach over a man's head to grab something above him. The same goes for children. They are held to the same standards as women. Another man can, however, walk past another man's personal space with courtesy. If a man needs to walk past another man's immediate front to get to another part of the room, he must politely pardon himself and proceed in a submissive, crouching position. This is basically the same polite manner Westerners would show, except for the lowering of one's posture.

Hmong children are usually taught to not argue with people who are older than they are. They should not look elders in the eyes when talked to. Children are not to question the will of their parents or elders. This is a sign of obedience and respect, but it is often contradicted by Western behavior. Hmong children who listen to their parents (*mloog lus*) are revered by Hmong elders as being respectful; however, those who are educated in the Western world are taught the opposite.

In the Western culture, showing respect toward an elder is to address a man as Mister and a woman as Miss or Mrs. It is not the same in the Hmong world. There are no such simple titles. My students are so used to calling me Mr. Cha in school that when they see me in the community that is what they call me. Hmong parents and elders would look at their children and me with confusion, for there is a Hmong way to show respect by properly addressing someone. That is simply to call each other by kinship plus first name. For example, you should address your neighbor as Uncle Tom instead of Mr. Thompson. Hmong people recognize both blood and marital kinships. So to properly address someone, the first name has to be preceded by the term of the relationship. A stranger is just a relative that has not been acquainted. Once two people meet, they can always find out how they are related. If two people have the same last name and there is no established relationship, they can always be brothers. Hmong believe that people with the same last name are all blood relatives many generations back. Two men with the same last name must either be brothers, father and son, or grandfather and grandson. For example, when I talk to my father's older brother, I would call him "tzee hlaw Tong Ger"(*txiv hlob Tooj Ntxawg*). The direct English translation for that is older father Tong Ger. So instead of addressing people with a surname, Hmong people address each other with kinship. Hmong people have no established official or academic titles such as president or doctor. If any such terms are used, they are borrowed from other languages.

Hmong refer to ourselves as relatives (*tub Hmoob neej tsa*). It means that all Hmong of different last names are related by marriage. Two people of different last names must be related by marriage somehow. Two perfect strangers can determine their relationship to each other by figuring out if there are existing marriages between their two clans. If no mutual relatives are found, as long as there is a relative with the same last name, an arbitrary relationship can be established and they can address one another accordingly. So it is not unusual when two strangers meet and the first thing they talk about is how they are related and then they start treating each other like old friends.

Before a kinship can be established between two strangers, they can arbitrarily address each other with a presumptuous kinship. For example, if you meet someone with the same last name as you but he looks slightly older than you, you can start by calling him older brother (*tij laug*). For someone who seems much older than you but younger than your father, you can call him younger father (*txiv ntawm*). Even if that person has a different last name, it is still safe to treat him in that manner. This is how Hmong people have treated each other for generations.

The terms used to define relationships between people in the Hmong world are quite extensive. Unlike Westerners, Hmong treat relatives of their own clans differently than the way they treat those who are related by marriage. For example, my father's younger brother is tzee tzer (*txiv ntxawm*), meaning younger father. His older brother is my tzee hlaw. My mother's brother, on the other hand, is da lao (*dab laug*) meaning old spirit. In Western culture they are all uncles without differentiation. The same goes for aunts, cousins and so on and so forth.

Kinships are inter- and intragenerational. In other words, kinship between people reflects both birth order and generational order. My father and his two dozen or so first cousins share the same grandparents. Therefore, they all belong to the same generational order even though their ages might vary significantly. They refer to each other as brothers. I am not in their generational order. I am in the next order along with my second cousins, and we all consider each other brothers. That automatically places my father and his cousins in the greater paternal hierarchy in the Hmong world — even though some of my brothers may be older than my father's brothers, we are still the lesser order. The generational order not only has great implications in establishing kinship among people but also in marriage practices and religious rituals as well.

It can be confusing sometimes when there is more than one relationship between two people due to multiple marriages between members of two families. In such a case, both parties agree on a relationship and name each other accordingly. Figure 3.1 shows how a girl will address relatives from both paternal and maternal families. Paternal grandparents are paw (*pog*) for grandmother and yer (*yawg*) for grandfather. Her father's brothers are tzee hlaw (*txiv hlob*) and tzee tzer (*txiv ntxawm*). Her male cousins with the same last name are considered brothers (*nus*) and those of a different last name are cousin-brothers or nuber (*nus npaws*). Female cousins are all sisters. Relatives from the mother's side of the family are named differently. Grandmother and grandfather are nia tai (*niam tais*) and yer tzee (*yawm txiv*) respectively. A maternal uncle is da lao (*dab laug*) and his wife is nia da lao (*niam dab laug*).

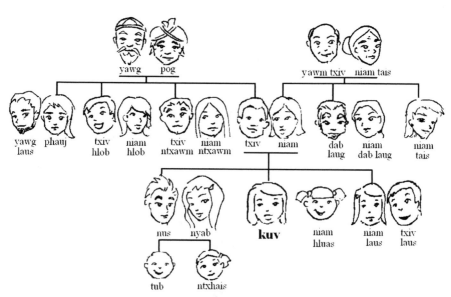

Figure 3.1: Kinship from a girl's perspective

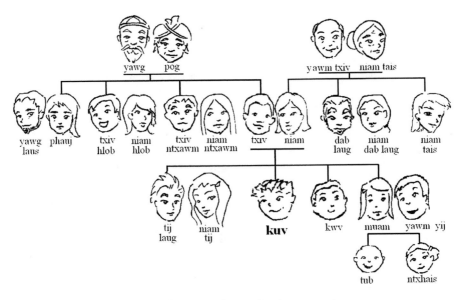

Figure 3.2: Kinship from a boy's perspective

The mother's sister is nia tai (*niam tais*) just like the maternal grand-mother. Nia lao (*niam laus*) is used for an older sister, and nia hlua (*niam hluas*) for younger sisters. She calls her brother nu (*nus*) and sister-in-law nyah (*nyab*). Her older sister is nia lao (*niam laus*) and her husband is tzee lao (*txiv laus*). As for a younger sister, it's nia hlua (*niam hluas*) and tzee hlua (*txiv hluas*) for her husband. All the nieces and nephews are considered children with tou (*tub*) for the boys and xai (*ntxhais*) for the girls.

For a man, relatives from the father's side of the family are basically the same except for gender differences among siblings (see figure 3.2). Tzee hlaw and tzee tzer's children are treated as brothers and sisters where an older brother is tee lao (*tij laug*) and a younger brother is ker (*kwv*). An older brother's wife is niathi (*niam* tij). The younger brother's wife is nia tzer (*niam ntxawm*). A sister is simply moua (*muam*). The children of the pao (*phauj*) are ber (*npawg*) for the male cousins and moua ber (*muam npaws*) for female cousins. These kin names are from the White Hmong dialect. Other dialects are mostly the same except for minor differences. Hmong do not use the term cousins as Westerners would. All cousins of the same generational order are regarded as brothers and sisters no matter how distant the relationships are. Those of the higher order are regarded as mothers and fathers and the ones next down the line are all children.

Once a person is married and has children, kinship becomes a totally different ball game. Hmong people no longer address their relatives the same way. Married people usually address their relatives the way their children would ordinarily address them to get the children accustomed to the kinship. For example, normally a man would address his sister as moua (*muam*). However, his children would address her as pao (*phauj*), so when he has children he should start calling her pao to get his kids used to calling her that. For a married couple, they address all relatives from both sides of the family exactly the same way. After all, they are just one entity.

Hmong people take the generational order very seriously. It is also important for religious purposes. So, knowing one's position in the generational order of the clan and in relations to relatives outside of the clan is an essential part of being Hmong. As a courtesy, people will address each other accordingly. My mother's distant cousin, for example, will call me son — Ya Po (*tub Yaj Pov*) — because I am like a son to him or her. It might seem difficult to get the relationships straight but with practice, it can be done with ease. Hmong people have great respect for kinships — it is part of knowing one's manners (*paub kev cai*).

Knowing how to address people with the proper name is just as important as knowing how to greet them. Over the generations, Hmong have adopted many ways of greeting people from their host societies. Here are some of the things a person can do to show respect to visiting guests in the Hmong world. The expression nyaw jong (*nyob zoo*) is a fairly new expression adopted from the Laotian expression *sabaidee*, which means good health. The handshake was also fairly recently adopted from Western cultures. Naturally, Hmong people will say "nyaw jong" to each other and extend the right hand to shake each other's hand to greet. The traditional greeting, however, is to call out a person's name and acknowledge his presence with a short phrase depending on the situation of the encounter. If you are at home and you have a visiting guest, the greeting is in the form of a question: "You have come" (*Koj tuaj los*)? The guest will respond, "Yes, I have come" (*Kuv tuaj os*). If you are somewhere other than at your own home, the greeting should be "You come, too" (*Koj tuaj thiab los*)? For men, a handshake furthers the cause (again adopting Western culture). The responder would say, "I come, too" (*Kuv tuaj thiab os*). For women a handshake is not necessary — on the contrary, it is a taboo for women to shake hands or for a man to shake the hand of a woman. In the Western world, where Hmong have become less traditional, handshakes between the genders are becoming more acceptable.

There are ways to properly treat visitors to make them feel welcome. Ignorance is never nice in any culture, including the Hmong world. When visitors arrive at a person's doorstep, they should be received with a warm welcome. For example, if your mother's sister comes over to visit your family, the moment you see her you should call out to her, "Nia thai, kaw thoua law" (*Niam tais koj tuaj los*)? It is as if you were asking, "Aunt you have come?" You have to invite her into your home and offer her a seat, telling her to sit down (*Zaum os*). You either get the person she came to visit to come talk to her or you simply sit with her and start a conversation. It is not proper to ask why she came, if she's hungry, or, more importantly, when she will be leaving. Those are taboo questions. What you should do is offer her a cup of water or a drink. If she is from out of town, cook her a meal whether she is hungry or not. Throughout her stay you need to keep talking to her and keep her occupied. When she leaves, you insist on her staying longer. If she must go, and she has not indicated the purpose of her visit, you may ask the purpose of her visit as she is about to leave. When she leaves, bid farewell to her by saying, "Nia thai, mooh haw toua aw" (*Niam tais mus ho tuaj os*), which means "Please come back to visit again."

Even when there is a more responsible person in the house with you when there are visitors, you still need to welcome your guests warmly. You should call out to them by the specific kinship and name. You are not to go anywhere. You can help by bringing the guests water or cooking for them. Do not ask them what you can help them with. You are expected to know how to make them comfortable and welcome.

Married women walk a very fine line between being proper and being flirtatious when it comes to receiving guests. When the husband or other adult males are home, women usually direct male visitors to the men. The men usually direct female visitors straight to the women. Usually, closely related guests and hosts will strike up a casual conversation. It is rather uncomfortable and might cause speculation for a host to talk casually or whole-heartedly with a guest of the opposite sex who is a stranger. It is culturally sensitive when a woman is home alone and she has male visitors or vice versa. When a woman receives male visitors, she has to be very careful, especially when the guests are not her immediate family members. If she is too friendly and warm, male visitors might interpret it as if she is flirting with them. If she is reserved, they might interpret that as poor manner. So it is difficult being a woman in such a situation and that is why when male visitors show up at a person's home and there is no man in the house, respectable visitors don't even come inside the house. Women should be polite. They should ask and answer questions succinctly and directly when it comes to guests of the opposite sex. It is difficult for Hmong married women to be polite, and others will always judge one way or another.

To be proper is to be modest and humble. Hmong people will judge those who are conceited (*muaj plhus*) negatively. People who don't understand how Hmong people function perceive Hmong proper behavior as being shy or obedient. When someone compliments you on certain task or characteristics, you are not to thank them but to tell them it is not worth the compliment. For example, when somebody says your shirt looks pretty, you are supposed to reply by saying that it is not pretty or that it is ugly. That may sound awkward to people of other cultures, but it is proper for Hmong people. Westernized and educated Hmong may act differently sometimes, but modesty is still the norm.

As in other cultures, interrupting others while they are in the middle of something is rude. One needs to pardon or excuse himself or herself before interrupting somebody or violating their personal space. When interrupting somebody who is talking, for example, you should say, "Excuse me, I am going to interrupt you..." (*thov txim kuv yuav txiav koj lus*), and then proceed to say what you need to say. Whereas in the Western world you ask and get acknowledged before you can proceed, Hmong people, sometimes, do not ask and wait for an answer before interrupting.

Another area where Hmong traditions could easily be misinterpreted is table manner. Traditionally, Hmong did not have a lot of china and utensils. As a result, we resorted to sharing spoons and eating out of community dishes. Food was served in large bowls placed on the table, and people ate from the bowls, sharing several spoons. In modern times and in more modern health-conscious societies, the sharing of spoons has become a thing of the past. Sharing food from large, conveniently-located community bowls is still practiced. This is usually done without serving spoons, except for rice. Individual forks and spoons are used to serve food directly out of the community dishes. This is an enduring practice that seems weird to outsiders, but Hmong people have never done it any other way.

Good table manners are very important as well. When there are guests in the house or at large gatherings, table manner is not so much how you conduct yourself during dining. Instead, a greater emphasis is placed on when to dine. At large gatherings, it is hard to accommodate everybody at the same time, so the men eat first. This tradition is still practiced in the larger segment of the Hmong population. At gatherings, there are usually some rituals or formalities done before people start eating. Women and children usually don't participate in these formalities at the table. For people who do not understand these formalities well, it is best to just go with the flow — if the people in charge of the gathering choose to invite certain individuals to sit first, then watch to see who is being invited. Usually, the elderly men are asked to sit first. Then, the more mature men are asked to sit to fill up the seats at the table. In such cases, young men or women should wait, even if they were invited to sit. A young person should avoid being seated first and feeling awkward about not knowing what to do during the proceeding. A safe thing to do is to follow people of one's own age group. I have seen young men who do not know the protocol sit at the table with a bunch of elderly men and everybody looks at them strangely — sometimes even stare them down.

When the men are done eating, the women and children may eat. Sometimes, the women and children are left with less than their fair share, but it is improper to complain. Sometimes, someone purposely saves some food for the women and children so that they get to eat. Hmong families often prepare large quantities of food so that there is plenty for all. A practical way to avoid treating women and children as second class citizens is to set up two tables or dining areas. One table is set for all the men, and in a different room there is another table for the women and children. After the formalities, everybody eats. Sometimes the women and children start eating before the men are done with their lengthy rituals.

Let us examine a shaman ritual to illustrate proper table norms. When the feast is prepared and the table is set, the elders are usually invited to sit at the table first. The head of the table is usually the middle seat against the back wall of the home, and it is here the shaman normally sits during the feasting. This is easily recognizable because the shaman, or *suka*, altar is placed on the back wall. Hmong people refer to it as the upside (*sab pem toj*). The shaman and the elders will be honored. The younger men are to show respect by kneeling twice to each honoree following a phrase of carefully chosen words of acknowledgment. It may go something like this, "(Relationship and name of honoree) thank you, we rely on you to come perform a religious task for the family, but we don't have a nice meal or a nice cup of drink to place in front of you, we just ask for your help without substance." ([*Hais txiv neeb lub npe*] *ua tsaug os mog, tias vam vam koj tuaj ua neeb kho ntsuj kho hlauv los twb tsis muaj zoo kab phaj tus ntxuag pib deg khob caw rau koj lub xub ntiag es tsuas thov koj lub zog qhuav qhuav xwb no mog.*) After a round of kneeling for everyone, the shaman will say thank-you and the eating begins.

Normally, during the meal every dish is supposed to be within everyone's reach. There should be no asking for anybody to pass this or that. It is rude to have your neighbors do things for you while eating. It is the responsibility of the server to make sure the different dishes are evenly distributed throughout the table. While eating, one should not get up and stoop over others or the food to reach for a dish that is out of arm's reach. If the host sees that a guest cannot access a certain dish, he will reposition the dish or ask for another serving to be placed where it can be reached. Hmong people usually do not garnish their food or decorate the dining table.

The host of a gathering has many responsibilities. The host has to make sure all the important guests get to eat at the table. He or she needs to make sure all the guests, young and old, have eaten before they leave. He or she should encourage the cooks to make more than enough food for everyone. Leftovers can be offered to guests to take home. Another responsibility of the host or hostess is to make sure the dishes have the proper taste. For example, a host should make sure meat dishes are salted to taste so guests do not have to ask for salt. Most importantly, the host needs to lead the feast and outlast everyone else eating at the table. A host should be courteous.

A person becomes an important guest when he ventures outside of his or her own community. We say, "Go become a guest" (*mus ua qhua*). When visiting relatives of a different clan who live in a different town, they often slaughter a chicken or pig to honor their guest. A cow or a water buffalo is rarely used. In such occasion, the guest needs to properly thank them. This is a two-fold ritual. If it is a chicken, then usually they would just slaughter it without informing the guest. If it is a pig or a larger animal, the host usually informs the guest first. In doing that, the host would sit the guest down and give him two shots of liquor or wine. He then asks the guest not to go anywhere that day because an animal is being slaughtered in his honor. The guest is asked to join the family for a feast. At that moment, the guest (as the modest person he should be) needs to refuse with all his effort, albeit calmly and politely. Eventually, the host family will prevail and the pig is slaughtered.

When the meal is prepared, the table is set and everybody is seated, the guest needs to thank the host and his family before eating. How to thank them may vary regionally and may depend upon how knowledgeable the guest is in Hmong traditions. A simple way is to stand up, call out the host by name, hands cupped together, and say, "Thank you [add kinship], you didn't need to but still you slaughtered an animal for me to feast on." (*Ua tsaug os, nej tsis cia li haj tseem tua tsiaj tua txhuv rau kuv noj thiab.*) In return, the host will simultaneously respond that it is nothing at all and if he was well off, he would have done more and for the guest not to be sad (*Txhob ua tsaug os, koj tuaj deb deb tuaj xyuas peb ib zaug los txom txom nyem es twb pam tsis tau ib pluag zaub pluag mov raws li lub siab xav rau koj noj es txhob tu siab*). The elders would probably have an extensive saying to make the appreciation seem more genuine. Often times, they shed some tears and share their thoughts on such a joyous occasion. As for a person less knowledgeable in Hmong traditions, a brief thank you is sufficient, and is much better than not saying anything at all.

For just any feast, a host or members of the host family are expected to sit at the table and eat until all the guests have excused themselves from the table. The host should insist that the guests continue to eat until full (*noj tiag kom tsau*). If a member of the host family eats his or her fill and just leaves the table, that will make the guests uneasy, and they will pretend to be full even when they are still hungry — and will stop eating.

When someone is a guest, there is also protocol for manners. When asked to join the host for a meal, the guest is supposed to say no. Only when the host insists should the guest eat. Once the guest is full, he lays down his spoon and tells the host for him or her to continue eating (*koj mam noj*). The host will insist that you eat some more, but just tell them you are very full (*tsau lawm os*). As a courtesy, the guest should continue to sit at the table and wait for the host to finish eating. Normally, the host will instruct the guest to get up and walk around (*sawv ncig*). Only then should the guest politely excuse himself from the table. To do this the guest can say, "I am getting up without waiting for you" (*sawv tsis tos nej*), and then get up and walk away from the table.

Hmong are unpretentious people. They often hide their needs and wants. When a person is being offered a drink, he or she should say no at first. Only if the person making the offer insists should the offer be accepted. That is proper manner for Hmong people. A polite person just doesn't go around casually asking or demanding things. Such a person is said to not have proper manners.

In essence, proper manners bring respect and honor. Inappropriate manners will bring shame to the family and the clan (*poob ntsej muag*). Hmong people usually don't ridicule others or confront them face to face. However, people will talk and spread rumors when it comes to improper personal conduct. That is when reputations and family honor can be ruined.

These are customs that have been carried on from generation to generation. In the Western world, we have adopted new norms and customs. Sometimes these norms are not consistent with traditional ones, but usually the newly-incorporated norms are more practical. As cultures change, it is reasonable to let go of what seems outdated — for example, waiting for the men to eat first while the women and children watch. These days, some families allow men, women and children to eat together at the same table.

A well-mannered person needs to be mindful of what he or she wears. Hmong people usually do not wear revealing clothes. Revealing clothes make people uncomfortable (*laj laj ntsia*). A well-mannered person should know what not to wear when out in public. When living with multiple generations in the same household, it is inappropriate to wear just anything — not to mention wearing nothing at all. People are usually quite judgmental about what young women wear. Whether you are the daughter or daughter-in-law, the clothes you wear have to cover the whole body loosely. Avoid shorts and tube-tops or spaghetti straps, especially when adult male family members are around.

At the same time, however, Hmong do not see women's breasts as sexual objects. Do not be surprised if you see older Hmong women walk around with bare breasts or breastfeeding babies in front of other people. Breastfeeding is a natural part of childbearing, and that is just the way Hmong people see it. Of course, in the Western world exposing the breasts is inappropriate, and we are mindful of that.

Hmong women should avoid certain types of conversations and actions. There are things a woman should not say or do in order to avoid being judged negatively by her in-laws. This can vary from family to family and from region to region. In the United States, for example, a woman should never joke around with her father-in-law. This is improper. For most Hmong people, a daughter-in-law is not allowed to go into her father-in-law's bedroom. Likewise, he is not allowed to go into the son and daughter-in-law's room either. For some people, this is against their religion. Men have limitations as well. For example, a man who shows affection for his sister-in-law or daughter-in-law is asking for harsh judgment. Of course, these things are just taboos, but not taking them seriously can lead to serious consequences.

To have proper manners is to act and talk properly. Hmong people have high regard for young people who are knowledgeable in Hmong mores, values and customs. A young man who is well-versed will bring honor and praise to himself, his family, and his clan. A young woman who is proper gives her family hope that she will find a decent husband or marry into a reputable family. In general, young people who are well-mannered simply bring a positive light to the world around them.

Ironically, young people these days learn in school that questioning authority is not only acceptable, but is the right thing to do. They learn that men and women are equal. That nobody should take a backseat to another person's cause. They learn that parents should not punish their children physically or psychologically. It is against the law. Some of these things are contradictory to what has been discussed in this chapter. This is part of the problem Hmong parents have faced for decades in the Western world.

Some Hmong parents find themselves at odds with their children because they expect the children to carry themselves properly among Hmong elders when the parents themselves do not know how. It is important for Hmong people to retain and maintain our culture and pass it on to our children. At the same time, we need to be aware of the societal norms of the dominant society so that we can avoid conflicts with the law.

From experience and observations of teenagers over the years, I believe that it is difficult for children to please their parents and still maintain self confidence in a civilized society. It is also difficult for Hmong parents to teach their children Hmong values and customs and still be supportive of their endeavors. Living in this dual-society is a constant challenge, but Hmong parents have to provide leadership and guidance for their children. Some parents may not be educated, but they can still be involved in their children's education. Parents cannot just preach Hmong values and culture, they have to practice these values and culture as well. Hmong parents need to support their children in education and model good manners at home.

It is quite a challenge, but it is fulfilling, for it is a gift of life to truly be a part of two cultures.

I think it is more challenging for women than for men to be successful in mainstream society and still respect Hmong cultural values. The ways women contribute to the family and community are changing, but men still expect women to fill the traditional roles in Hmong society. As we become more conscientious of women's rights, Hmong people are starting to become more aware of gender inequality. The men are starting to heed the advice of their wives. In fact, in some families, the wives or mothers make the important decisions when it comes to family affairs and the men make the decisions when it comes to cultural, religious and community affairs. There is a lot more that the Hmong community needs to understand about modern Western culture, but much progress has been made in the two decades.

It is exciting to see the customs and culture of a people transform from a patriarchal society toward one with equal rights for everyone. At the same time, it is also disheartening to see a culture that has survived for thousands of years disappear in just a matter of decades. We have to take these changes in stride, for I have stared into the eyes of the older generation who seem to have lost everything they value and what they stand for. I have also stared into the eyes of young children who will become the leaders of tomorrow. They have one thing in common and that is hopelessness (due to the fact that they are losing their cultural identity, and there is not much they can do about it as individuals). One thing is for sure though, and that is the fact that we need to remember who the Hmong people are and preserve our cultural values and customs for future generations.

4 CULTURAL TRADITIONS

With wedding traditions you can follow others, but with religion you cannot. (*Tshoob kos mas yoog tau luag, kev cai dab qhuas mas yoog tsis tau.*)

— Hmong words of wisdom

Traditions include the rituals, customs, beliefs, practices and intuitions of a people. Hmong people have a wide array of traditions. Nobody knows for sure which traditions are genuine and which ones were adopted from other cultures. That is because Hmong are heavily influenced by the dominant societies that they live under. When these adopted traditions become second nature, it becomes part of us after many generations.

The tying of yarn around the wrist, for example, has become very popular. However, it is not a traditional Hmong practice. It is a Lao custom. I remember when my father took me to his Laotian friends to initiate me as their godchild. They would tie these cotton threads around my wrist and chanted weird words that I did not understand. These days, we do it to newborns, special guests, newlyweds or just about whenever and to whomever feels right. It has become a Hmong custom.

Another practice that is not native to Hmong is the handshake. This is a way of greeting that we have adopted from the West. Then there is dancing, singing and so on.

It is unknown whether some traditions are Hmong originals or have been adopted. Suka (*xwm kab*) (see chapter 7 for more detail) is such a tradition. Suka is a religious ritual to honor the guardian spirit of prosperity (as well as the name of a spiritual deity that Hmong people worship). There are many folktales to explain how suka came about. Some say it is the worship of the deceased mother to help protect the health and wealth of the family. Others say that this is a practice that Hmong adopted from the Chinese a long time ago. It is supposedly the Chinese equivalent of the God of wealth, Tsai Shen Yeh. Whatever the case, its origin is uncertain. Every Hmong family seems to practice suka or something similar to it.

There are long-standing traditions that are genuinely Hmong. A good example is the popular Hmong New Year. Right behind Hmong New Year is the new crop celebration, which is more like harvest festival in the Western world. Another good example is the resting day during the full moon of each month, which resembles the weekend in the Western calendar. Other traditional practices include chanting, singing, playing the reed pipe or kheng (qeej) and many more.

Hmong New Year

Hmong New Year has been around for as long as Hmong have been around. Hmong call New Year chia pe chao (*tsiab peb caug*). To celebrate New Year is "to eat" chia pe chao. Eat refers to the wining and dining that take place during the celebration. Chia is a word that does not have a literal meaning, but it is well understood to mean New Year. Thirty is the 30th day of the 12th month on the Hmong lunar calendar or new moon of the next lunar cycle (Hmong are convinced that a lunar month is normally 30 days). To Hmong people, the New Year marks the conclusion of the annual crop cycle. Rather than celebrating the arrival of the first day of the New Year, Hmong celebrate the departure of the current year. The reason is to get rid of all that is old and to cast away the misfortunes along with the passing of the current year. It is a time to renew everything in preparation for the arrival of the New Year, so when the new day dawns everything is anew.

New Year marks the beginning of the new crop cycle. The new crop cycle starts in what Hmong call the first month. This usually falls in late November or early December on the Western calendar for Hmong people in Southeast Asia. In China, where the climate is milder and the crop cycle starts later in the year, Hmong New Year is usually celebrated in February. This coincides with the Chinese New Year. Every few years, when the lunar calendar falls behind the Western calendar and the actual orbit of the Earth around the sun, Hmong people change the New Year to a month later.

Traditionally, New Year is made up of three parts. The first part is the festivity of each family or nawchia (*noj tsiab*). The real wining and dining occur at this time. This is the part that has been largely neglected in non-agrarian Hmong communities. Next is the religious ceremony. Lastly, we have the community social gathering.

New Year celebration occurs at a time in which all the field work is done and members of the community have the leisure to prepare for the New Year celebration. The festivities begin with the renewal of the shaman spirits and New Years feast. For families that have a shaman, both are lumped into one. In either case, a sizeable pig is butchered. Each Hmong family usually raises a barrow hog, a neutered male pig, to a fairly large size for the occasion. Such an animal is called bouachia (*npua tsiab*). In a good year, an ordinary family should have raised a plump, fat barrow that might weigh up to 500 pounds. Right before New Year, the pig is butchered. Relatives and friends are invited to come join the family for a feast. A lot of eating and drinking is expected during this New Year feast.

At such a feast, one can expect to find a wide array of traditional dishes being prepared. Usually, some of the most authentic dishes are served. In large extended families, a good portion of the fresh meat is consumed, but certain parts of the bouachia are meant to be saved. Usually the ribs with skin intact are preserved and saved for later. Whole ribs are cut out with the meat and skin intact (*nqaij sawb*). They are smothered with salt and hung to dry. The leftover fatty parts are fried to extract the lard.

The size of the bouachia is indicative of the success of the family during the passing year. A big pig means the family has done well. A family with a small or no pig at all probably had a tough year. A bigger pig being butchered also means that there will be more meat left over after the New Year feast. For short term, the remaining pork is to be served to families and friends who will visit during the New Year resting period. For long term, the meat is much needed during the slashing of a new forest or clearing of an old field for farming (*luaj teb*). In the world of slash and burn farming, this is the most physically challenging work in the farming cycle. It is also done during the driest season. A family that butchers a large bouachia will have meat left over to supplement its diet during this period of strenuous work. Less fortunate families will have a tougher time. The fat from the pork will also provide oil for cooking and fuel for lighting at night. For some, the meat and lard will last well into the rainy season, which is about five months long.

The religious ceremony phase of the New Year celebration begins at the individual households in the late afternoon on the 30th day of the 12th lunar month. The oldest male of each household takes a bundle of bamboo leaves and waves them with a sweeping motion throughout the whole house, uttering words to force out all evil spirits and bad luck. The words he utters may be as follows:

> The old year has passed and the New Year is arriving. What I am sweeping is not the souls of the children, the mother, the father or the crops and wealth. What I am sweeping are the sickness, evil spirits and bad luck to vanish along with the old year. I sweep them into the edge of the world so my family's eyes will not see and our ears will not hear them again.
>
> *Xyoo laus tas xyoo tshiab tuaj. Kuv cheb no kuv tsis cheb plig tub plig ki, plig niam plig txi, plig qoob plig loo, plig tsiaj plig txhuv, plig nyiaj plig kub. Kuv cheb no kuv cheb mob cheb ntsaj, vij sub vij sw dab ntub npau suav kom nrog xyoo laus mus. Yam twg yam tsis zoo, kuv cheb lawm ntuj hnub coog hli kawg kom xyoo tshiab tuaj kuv ib tse nees nkaum leej ntsej tsis hnov muag tsis pom.*

Usually he starts in the bedrooms and then goes through the kitchen, living room and out the main door. The bundle of bamboo leaves is then taken to the religious leader's house. The ceremony at the religious leader's house is called luchia (*lwm sub* or *lwm tsiab*), which means ridding of negative spiritual forces.

All members of each clan should attend their respective luchia ceremony. If a person is tied up somewhere and cannot participate, his or her shirt can be brought in as a substitute. Tools and weapons such as knives, axes, hoes and guns should be brought there too. Weapons and tools will be spiritually cleansed at this time, so that mishaps with them will not occur during the next year. The bundles of bamboo leaves are tied with red fabric strings, and they are inserted into a large rope woven out of grass. A small tree, called paocha (*pos ncag* or *pos lwm qaib*), is cut, leaving some leaves at the top. When these trees are not available any tree with green leaves can be substituted. One end of the long rope is tied to the paocha just beneath the leaves. The other end is tied to the bottom of the tree. The rope is pulled out and held up to form a loop. When all members of the clan have arrived, the head of the clan or the religious leader, which is usually the oldest male, will conduct the ceremony. The religious leader holds the paocha in one hand and a live rooster in the other. All clan members walk through the loop, circling the vertical section of the rope. The religious leader waves the rooster over their heads. At the same time, he utters words to ward off all evil spirits and misfortunes to pass with the concluding year. He then bestows upon his clan members a prosperous, healthful and joyful incoming year. This marks the ending of the passing year and the beginning of the New Year as his clan members pass through the loop. They must circle three times in one direction and another three in the opposite direction. Then the rooster's throat is slashed and its blood is applied to the grass rope and tree. All are tossed away, except the rooster. It is dressed and becomes somebody's dinner.

Following this ceremony everybody goes back home. In each household, the oldest male or the patriarch performs the religious ceremony for the family. He starts with what is called soul calling (*hu plig*). This is to bring the souls of every family member back to their respective bodies, for if the soul is no longer with the body, the body succumbs to sickness or even death. By reuniting the soul with the body, the health of every member of the family should be restored. Hmong people believe that money, animals, and crops also have souls. So their souls, too, are called back into the house.

This is also a time to renew altars, which are home to the various religious entities. The most common altar is the suka (*xwm kab*). Suka is the unifying spiritual entity that all Hmong people have. Some people do not have suka. Instead, they have shengkha (*seej khab*). There are other altars such as the one for shamans (*thaj neeb*) and herbal spirits (*thaj dab tshuaj* or *yum vaj*). These altars have to have the decorations replaced and incense holding urns washed. A chicken is also offered to each to renew the worshipper's commitment to these guardian spirits.

During this ceremonial phase of the New Year, many chickens are butchered to prepare for the feast marking the end of the year. Sticky rice patties known as joua (*ncuav*) are made and offered to the ancestral spirits. Offerings to the ancestors are made in what we call laida (*laig dab or ntov phab ntsa*). This is also a time to set personal standards for the coming year. Everybody is to be patient and avoid all conflicts, ill behaviors and bad deeds. It should be a joyous occasion.

When all the ceremonies, cooking, feasting and cleaning are done, the head of the household takes a stack of religious papers and sticks them to various parts of the house — to tools and to large objects around the

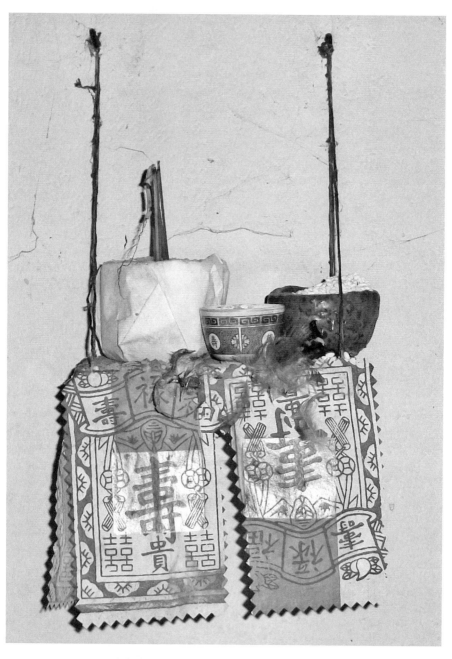

An altar for the spirits of medicine (*thaj dab tshuaj or yum vaj*). The power of herbal medicine is both natural and supernatural.

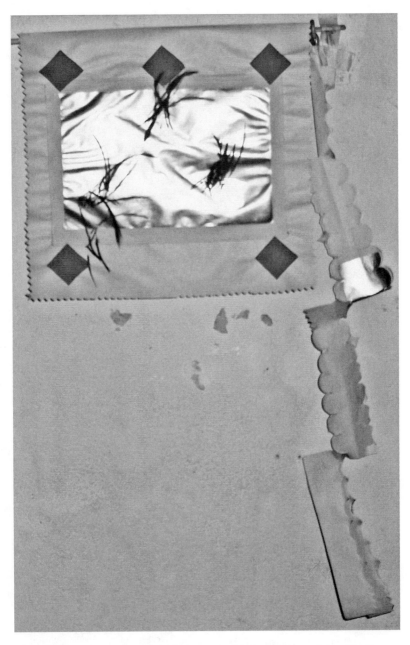

This is the emblem for suka (*xwm kab*), the lead guardian spirit of the house. The middle is painted gold (*ntawv kub*). Metallic color (*ntawv nyiaj*) is an acceptable alternative.

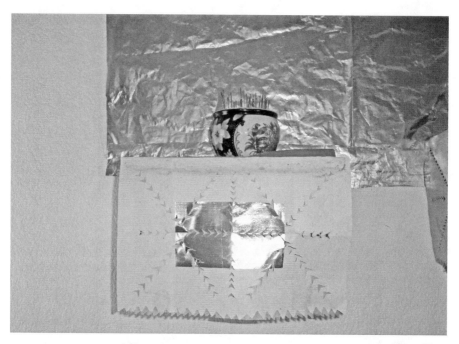

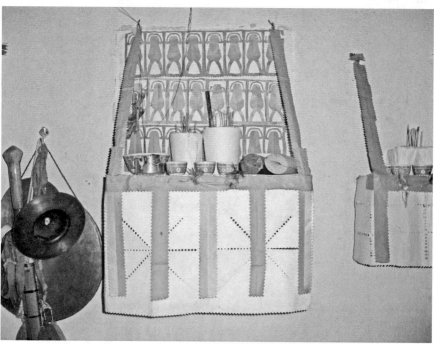

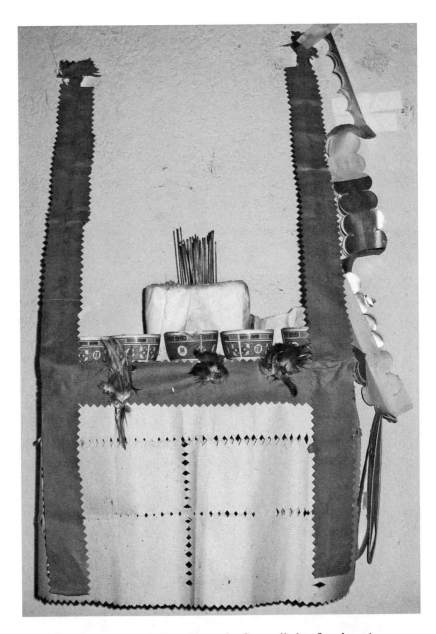

Above: An altar for the kherkong (*khawv koob*) usually has five shot-size containers called peexue (*pib txwv*). This is where the spirits of healing reside. *Opposite, top:* An altar for shenkha (*seej khab*), a different version of suka. There is only one bowl to hold incense sticks in place. *Opposite, bottom:* Altar for a shaman who is not a full-fledged shaman (*tsis tau tsa thaj*). The character designs against the wall are called mozeng (*moj zeej*). Shaman tools such as the gong and sword are visible.

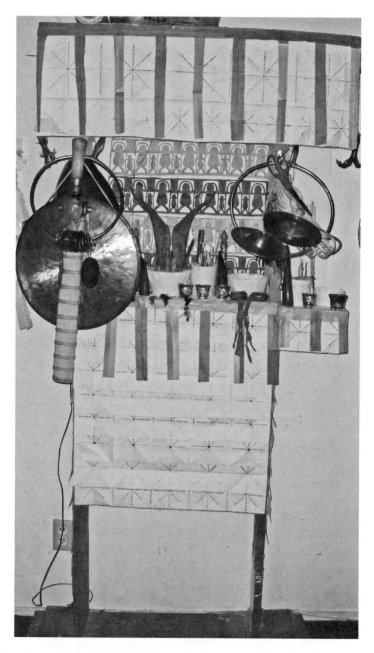

This is a typical altar for a full-fledged shaman. On the altar are shaman gears, including the metal rattlers, gong, and sword. The emblem for a true shaman are the horns of a ram sitting on the incense holder. On the right side is an extension of the altar. This is the medicine altar. A shaman combines his medicine altar and shaman altar into one.

house. This is called fongyeng (*foob yeem*). This is to mark the halting of all tasks and activities for the year and the beginning of the resting period, which is three consecutive days. For the remainder of the night, nobody is allowed to do any work, not even household chores, until dawn.

During the night, the men gather in one house and reminisce about the year that has just passed. They talk and drink into the night to welcome the dawn of the New Year. This is also a time when elders pass skills and knowledge on to the next generation. As they celebrate into the early morning hours to welcome the New Year, they listen to animal calls. Be it from a domestic animal or one in the wild, the first call signals the arrival of the New Year, and is known as "open the New Year" (*qheb xyoo tshiab*). The kind of animal signaling the New Year foretells events to come. If the night is all quiet until roosters crow in the wee hours, it is a good blessing for the New Year. If wild beasts such as tigers and wolves should be heard, they are signs of bad things to come in the New Year. If domestic animals such as horses and pigs should be the ones making noises in the pre-dawn hours, the coming year should be a prosperous and fruitful one. The interpretation of each animal call might have slight regional differences.

The next day is the first day of the first lunar month. The first three days of the New Year are resting days (*hnub caiv*). No one is to go anywhere or do any work. Traditionally, New Year celebration begins on this day and continues through the three resting days. As soon as people start going back to their daily routines, the celebration ends. In places where there are lots of people attending the celebration, New Year can go on for more than a week.

During these first few days of the New Year, Hmong people traditionally spend time with family and friends. Some will visit friends and families in the nearby towns. Some invite families and friends over to dine. Young people often seek out potential soulmates in surrounding communities. For the elderly, this is a great time to visit friends and reminisce about the past. Overall, it is a festive time.

Many events and games occupy people's time and attention during the New Year celebration. An event still popular in Laos today is bull fighting. Bull fighting involves two full-grown oxen or water buffalo brought together by their owners to clash with each other. A popular activity for males of all ages is wooden top competition (*ntaus tuj lub*). Wooden tops range in size from that of an egg to a grapefruit. A strip of narrow cloth tied to the end of a stick is wound around the top. When the string is unwound, the top spins very fast as it is released. This game is played in two teams of an unlimited number of players on each team. One team releases its tops, and members of the opposing team try to hit them with their own tops flung from afar.

New Year is a time for people to show off their accomplishments of the past year. Some show off their children in bright, colorful new clothes. Hmong women often dress their children up and take them to the New Year celebration. This is an annual social event where the whole community gets involved. It is a time for parents to show off their most prized possessions — not just the children, but also clothes, jewelry and talent.

It is also a great time for people to meet each other. The leaders of the community designate a central location with a wide open space for people to gather. This outdoor gathering place is called the New Year field or "ground thirty" (*tshav peb caug or tshav qaib*). During the days of the resting period, people of the community converge at ground thirty to socialize and meet other people. Single people flock to the New Year celebration compound to seek out a potential wife or husband. Without many spectacles or attractions, single men and women toss balls with each other and sing traditional folksongs. Parents take this opportunity to scout for brides for their sons and grooms for their daughters. Overall, this is nothing more than a social event that is free, harmless and safe.

In the small towns throughout Asia, New Year is still low profile and safe as originally intended. In the Western world, however, the New Year celebration has become more than just a gathering place. In large towns such as Fresno, California, New Year has become an international affair with multitudes of spectacles and vendors. Organizers put in a lot of time and money to put the celebration together. It can cost hundreds of thousands of dollars each year for a week-long celebration, from renting the location to paying for security. Vendors' fees and admission fees are collected to offset the cost. Vendors offer a variety of food and products. Activities during these events include talent shows, concerts, carnival rides, and beauty pageants. Ball tossing at the New Year celebration is becoming a thing of the past.

Traditionally, New Year celebrations have been held at the convenience of the community, either at the end of the 12th lunar month or the following month at the latest. However, all New Year celebrations were held no more a month apart. In Hmong communities throughout the Western world these days, New Year celebrations do not always happen at the same

Top: The marketplace across from the makeshift food court at Fresno New Year, December 26, 2009. *Bottom:* A makeshift stage at Hmong New Year celebration in Sacramento, California, on November 26, 2009.

People gathered at the Hmong New Year in Sacramento, California, on November 26, 2009.

time. From late September through December, Hmong New Year celebrations are being held in different towns at different times. Some towns even have more than one celebration. Sacramento, California, for example, has two different New Year celebrations on separate occasions.

New Crop

The new season of cultivation usually starts during the sixth lunar month. It falls in May when the rainy season starts in Southeast Asia. The main staples in the Hmong diet are corn and rice, along with a variety of fruits and vegetables. The first crop harvest warrants an offering to the spirits of the ancestors (*laig dab*). Offerings to the ancestors start with cucumber during the month of July or the eighth lunar month. It entails gathering a few sizeable cucumbers which the patriarch offers to the spirits of the relatives who have passed away. It is customary that this offering take place before anybody can eat any cucumber.

The next crop in line is corn. Hmong families usually plant a small patch of sweet corn (*pob kws cauj*) and a large field of dent corn called slow corn (*pob kws taj*). When the sweet corn is ready, a large batch is picked. This first batch is boiled, and an offering is made to the ancestors. The dent corn is usually left in the field until dried. Then it is harvested and stored for long term use throughout the year. Dent corn is sometimes used as a rice substitute, otherwise it is primarily used for feeding chickens and pigs.

The new crop celebration is a feast during the first rice harvest. Traditionally, each Hmong family plants a small patch of rice that matures faster and earlier than normal. This type of rice is called bleachau (*nplej caug*), meaning early rice. This variety of rice plant has shorter stalks. The texture of the rice is coarser and the taste is blander, but the liquid extracted from it has a wonderful aroma. When prepared properly, this is probably the best meal Hmong people have throughout the whole year. Families that are well off usually take great care to make sure the new rice harvest (*mov nplej tshiab*) makes a great meal every year.

The new rice harvest meal is prepared well in advance. What goes well with the new rice are boiled fattened capons or big fat neutered roosters (*lau qaib sam*). Some people slaughter a pig for this event, but nothing beats boiled chicken.

In preparation for this occasion, several young roosters are raised until they start to crow, when they are about four to five months old. The roosters' testes are surgically removed. I have vivid recollections of rooster castration. Because I was the only boy in the family, my father would spit-fry rooster testes for me for breakfast — he always castrated his roosters in the morning. The capons, or castrated roosters, are fed with corn and rice for another six months, after which they should be plump and tender.

Early rice is harvested when it turns gold. The stalk may still be green. The rice grains are separated from their stalks and roasted in a giant wok until they are dried enough to be dehulled or dehusked in a pestle. The dehulled rice is boiled until soft and drained. The juice is saved. The drained rice is steamed until completely cooked. The sweet, pleasant aroma is wonderful. All the while, the capons are slaughtered and dressed. They are chopped and boiled in plenty of water. Lemon grass is added for flavor. A nice meal should have a pot of boiled chicken with a thin layer of oil floating on top to lock in the heat. This may sound plain, but for Hmong people it is one of the best meals of the year. That's why it is offered to the ancestors before everybody can start eating. It is the most anticipated feast year after year.

The new crop celebration is a private family feast to which all beloved relatives are invited. Closely related relatives who do not get invited to such a feast will remember the slight for a long time. Certain families are never privileged enough to have such a feast. Families that do not lead an agrarian lifestyle also do not have such a feast, because one cannot just use store-bought rice and chicken to prepare for a new rice feast (*mov nplej tshiab*).

Name Changing

Another tradition is the changing of a man's name. When a boy is born, he is given a kiddie name. Normally, this is single syllable such as Neng, Chong, Tou, etc. This name is to remain in effect until there is a need to change it or when he is married and has one or two children. At this point in his life, he should be in his late teens or early 20s, and he is considered a man. A mature name (*npe laus*) is given to him. To properly change his name, his father-in-law (the wife's father) is invited to his home to institute it. If there is no father-in-law, or he lives too far away, then the closest relative of the wife will do. Special preparations are needed for this occasion.

Before a man can have his name changed, he must prepare a set of burial clothes (*ris tsho laus*) for both his mother- and father-in-law. For Green Hmong, a special embroidery called teng kia (*teem kiam*) is also given to the in-laws. Once everything is set, a messenger is sent to ask the father-in-law. Normally, the messenger would personally go to the in-laws' home and ask, but now a phone call usually does the job.

The father-in-law usually brings a special gift to the name-changing ceremony. Usually, such a gift should be one with sentimental value as opposed to something expensive. My father gave my brother-in-law a silver bar as a gift on a similar occasion.

When the in-laws arrive, they usually bring a spokesperson to make talking easier. The son-in-law should also have a relative in charge who knows how to conduct such a ceremony. At this point, the father-in-law is called to sit at a small table and is given a drink. Then he is officially asked to select a new name for the son-in-law. A large domestic animal, usually a pig, should be at the ready. The pig is shown to the in-laws before being slaughtered, and the father-in-law gives some money to the son-in-law as a gesture of respect and acceptance of the offer.

This is considered a fairly elaborate or important ceremonial service so all relatives should be present. It is said that the more people at the name changing ceremony, the more likely the name will stick.

Sometimes, the father-in-law will ask whether or not his son-in-law favors the name to be given. In either case, this is a huge undertaking. Some people can afford it. There are some who never have the capability to do it. For those unfortunate souls, they either find another way to earn an adult name or just keep their child name forever.

When the name is selected, the pig and a pair of chickens are used in the soul calling (*hu plig*). The animals are slaughtered and a meal is prepared. There are no restrictions on the types of dishes that can be prepared on this occasion —fish, chili pepper, vegetables and anything else can be eaten at this ceremony.

Another sizeable pig is also slaughtered to honor the father-in-law. It, too, needs to be shown to the father-in-law. This pig is also cooked so as to be feasted on at the same time.

Once the table is set, the elders are called to sit at the table first. They are honored (*pe*) and then each guest ties a string to the son-in-law and everybody wishes him well and calls him by his new adult name for the first time.

During the course of the feasting that follows the string-tying ceremony, there are many rounds of drinking that should be conducted. Each round of drinks has a name. The first one is called soul-calling. Then there is the name-changing round. There is a string-tying round, and so on. Oftentimes, liquor is used and people do get drunk at these ceremonies.

At the conclusion of the ceremony, a hindquarter of the pig is given to the father-in-law to take home for ceremonial purposes. When he gets home, he uses the packed meat to prepare a feast of his own and invites his relatives to come join. He then tells his relatives that his son-in-law has a new name and they should call him by his new name.

Home Restrictions

I once had a friend who thought that Hmong were the most superstitious people in the world. I felt defenseless — Hmong *are* superstitious. Hmong believe that when something terrible is going to happen there are signs. Such signs can be in the form of dreams, visions, or an unexplainable phenomenon. When such a sign appears, there are measures you can take to avoid what is destined to happen. One of the things you can do is to restrict the home (*caiv*). Nobody is to go in or out. No strangers are allowed to come in. During such a time, a small branch with green leaves is placed at the door on the outside. Usually, a mat with six-sided holes is placed behind the leaves. This is equivalent to the traffic sign "DO NOT ENTER."

What are the signs that warrant a home restriction? Let's start with dreams. Hmong believe that a dream foretells the future. There are specific interpretations for various dreams. Oftentimes, sad and nasty dreams foretell good things to come. Happy dreams are bad dreams. A dream about severe natural disasters is indicative of the grave sickness of a family member. Seeing giant trees falling in your dream means an elderly person close to you will pass on. Dreaming of receiving money, bleeding and having opium are always about tears, losing money and heartaches, respectively. Dreams of animal attacks are signs of bad health or injuries. For example, when you dream of vicious wolves attacking you, it means you will become sick, perhaps with the flu, and so you should rest (so) and take care of yourself. My cousin Po Ka Cha dreamed that his uncle fell down a rocky cliff. A few days later, his mother died. He was only 5 years old at the time. Dream interpretation is backward sometimes, but Hmong people take dreams seriously.

Visions of abnormal phenomena are reasons to stay home. Certain visions are indicative of bad things to come. When you have a vision of ghostly figures or a badly decomposed corpse, be careful. You will have to deal with a death or funeral in the near future, though it may not be you personally. You should, however, still take a period of home confinement. This type of vision is the ghost of things to come (xyw). Hmong believe that when something catastrophic is going to happen its ghost appears first. Hmong funeral rites include the case of the powerful Hmong prophet Shao (Saub). Right before he succumbed to evil forces, his death ghost came in the form of a giant snake and a huge tiger seen near his house. Perhaps he should have stayed home for a few days and not have fought the evil spirits.

A phenomenon that Hmong people take seriously is the sudden appearance of maggots or housefly eggs. When these appear unexpectedly or in unexpected places, there will be death in the family. Housefly eggs are normal on rotting meat, food that has been left uncovered for a long time, on unattended wounds, etc. Unexpected appearances can consist of housefly eggs on someone's clothes, perfectly good food, bedding, living areas, fresh meat, freshly slaughtered animals, etc. The same goes for maggots. This is especially true when there is no decaying organic matter around. In the early fall of 2002, I woke up very early to go hunting with my father. I found more than a dozen maggots crawling on the kitchen floor. I looked into the trash can and there were no maggots. In fact, the trash didn't even smell bad. There were no crevices or holes the maggots could have come out of. I swept them up, dumped them into the trash and took the trash out immediately. Later that day, when we were up in the mountains hunting, I received a call that my cousin Blia Lia passed away that morning. When it comes to these types of phenomena, Hmong people usually take drastic measures to pacify their minds. This includes a day of rest for everybody. No one is allowed to go out of the house no matter what. Such vivid phenomena, however, are often followed by the inevitable.

Monuments and sturdy structures are believed to be the spiritual protectors or deities of the living, especially those of higher social status. When these things crumble without cause, there will be severe consequences. Usually, a leader of the community will part. In 1977, my family lived in a refugee camp near a small town called Seven Mango Trees, Thailand. Without warning or apparent cause, the radio tower at the hospital fell. My uncle said, "This town is going to lose a leader." I thought it was silly for him to make such a bold prediction. Sure enough, less than a month later, the mayor, Kanam Xi, died unexpectedly while still in office. Was it just a coincidence? Who knows. Perhaps taking some measures such as placing the mayor on home restriction might have made a difference. After all, he died from alcohol intoxication.

Home restriction is also warranted when a shaman deems it necessary. When a shaman has expelled evil spirits from a home, he usually tells the residents to restrict the house and confine themselves to the house for three days or more. That is to avoid the expelled evil spirits from re-entering the house with or in the form of a stranger or following a person from that house back inside.

Hmong people take home restrictions seriously. That's why when you are about to enter somebody's house, you should always ask, "Is your house restricted?" (*Nej puas caiv los tsis caiv os?*) Usually, people will tell you if you can go in or not. On rare occasions, people will take it offensively if you don't know when you are not supposed to enter their house. Entering someone's house when you are not supposed to is a punishable offense, especially when the house is visibly marked with green leaves clipped to the door or next to the door. When you see green leaves clipped to the outside of somebody's door, do not enter — even if the residents say it is all right to enter. In some cases, Hmong people will tie a hexagonal mesh (see illustration) somewhere outside the door. When green leaves are clipped to this mesh, it is a sure sign to not enter.

Clan Blessing

The clannish way of the Hmong people has its advantages and disadvantages. One disadvantage is that it divides people. Another disadvantage is that there are taboos within each clan. There are numerous advantages of the clan system.

The human survival instinct tells people to think of themselves first. The family is secondary. The clan or extended family is next, followed by the community at large. Now that leaves very little room or time for the good of all Hmong people as a whole. Ever wonder why Hmong have no country of our own?

The advantages are that being clannish allows people to know where they stand when it comes to relationships, political support, and moral support. In the Hmong world, where there are no Motel 6's or McDonald's to be found, as long as you can find a family with your last name, you will always find first class hospitality. People can be total strangers, but if they have the same last name they have an undeniable bond — there is an unexplainable level of trust and respect for each other.

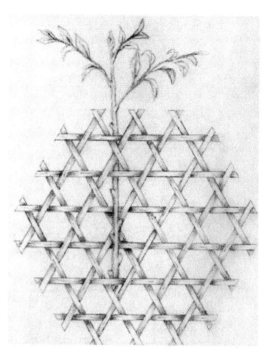

A hexagonal mesh Hmong place outside the door to indicate home restriction.

That is being Hmong—this is the Hmong brotherhood (*kwv tij*). I met an old woman in a small village in southern China called Shateng (*Sam Theem*). She was the only Cha there. Right away she made me feel like I was significant. She insisted on me going into her house to visit her humble home. As I entered the home, with its dirt floor and cramped living quarters, she introduced me to her children as an uncle—as if I was a long-lost relative. That's what being clannish is about.

The 18 clans (better known as Vang-Cha-Seng-Lee or Vang-Cha-Lee-Seng [*Vaj Tsab Lis Xeem*]) have been the key to establishing trust and hope in every community. This is a group of elders who provide guidance and conflict resolutions for Hmong people as a whole or between people of different clans. Such a group is sometimes established, but it can be assembled on a need basis by simply calling on several elders with different last names. The three last names do not mean that they are the top clans. When these three last names are mentioned together, it represents all the Hmong clans. And, of course, there are more than 18 clans of Hmong in the world. There is confidence, strength and power in Vang-Cha-Lee-Seng.

Throughout history Hmong have always called upon the 18 clans to resolve problems. In every major city across America, Hmong establish an organization of 18 clans. This is central to the community. Representatives of the 18 clans are usually people who are highly respected members of each clan. Thus, people usually respect what this organization stands for.

There is supernatural power in the 18-clan or Vang-Cha-Lee-Seng system. It is believed that when a body of people has the power to resolve problems in the natural world, it also has the power to resolve problems in the supernatural world. When there is a major religious function, it is important to have as many clans represented as possible. When a child is frail and sickly and nothing seems to help her recover, the parents usually look to the 18-clan unit or Vang-Cha-Lee-Seng for spiritual support in what is called clan bless (*thov xeem*). In clan blessing, the parents go to a member of every clan available and ask for their blessing or spiritual support. Usually a strip of cloth and some rice is given to the parents. The cloth is either sewed together with those from other clans on the back of the child's shirt or simply woven into a rope and tied around the neck. The process is quite elaborate and extensive.

At any rate, clan blessing is a long-standing tradition that is tied to our religious beliefs. It is an inter-clan support that Hmong provide each other.

Superstitious Taboos

There are things certain people don't do. People avoid them because of superstition, but those who defy them face real consequences. These taboos range from avoiding eating certain food and animal organs to personal conduct. The causes of these restrictions can be traced back to grave misconduct many generations back. The consequences of not abiding by these restrictions can range from going blind to horrific death. Described below are some of the most common restrictions recognized by large sectors of the Hmong population.

The most well-known taboo is one where every male member of the Yang clan cannot eat the heart of any animal. A woman who marries into a Yang family will have to live with this restriction. A Yang girl, however, can eat a heart. According to Yang elders, a long time ago two Yang brothers went to a nyuda ceremony (*nyuj dab*). The younger brother was mute and mentally challenged. As the older brother was busy helping out with the ceremonial activities, the younger brother stood by the fire where the meat and inner organs of the slaughtered cow were being cooked in a giant wok. All the cooked organs were to be offered to the ancestors. When the organs were cooked and taken out to be chopped, they couldn't find the heart. They looked and looked to no avail. The mute was just standing there, oblivious to the commotion around him. The older brother thought his younger brother must have picked up the heart and eaten it. The older brother took the mute to the back of the house, killed him, cut out his heart and dropped it in the wok. It was then used in the ceremony — everyone thinking it was the cow's heart that had reappeared. When everything was done and over with, the actual cow heart was found stuck to the bottom of the wok. The mute was found dead with his heart missing. From that day on, all Yang males are cursed to never eat the heart of any animal. Whoever eats one will become blind.

Chas cannot use a bow and arrow, although cross bows are permitted. It is said that the arrow will pierce a tiger's eyes. We also restrict daughters-in-law from using the dry storage on top of the fireplace (*nthab*). There is no definite explanation for these restrictions — they have been with the family for so long that they are just second nature.

A certain sector of the Lee clan cannot eat the spleen of any animal. This is not widely known, which can create problems for those who are affected. When they are guests at parties, there is no way for them to know if all the slaughtered animal's internal organs have been used in the cooking.

Some Lor and Vang families cannot eat sour fruits with rice. Likewise, they cannot carry sour fruits in their carrying baskets (*kawm*) with their lunch on their back. Those who defy such a taboo often find a snake in their baskets.

Hmong people believe that human breast milk cannot be ingested by weaned children and adults. Breast milk can only be ingested by babies who continually breastfeed. An adult who ingests breast milk, whether voluntarily or involuntarily, will be struck down by lightning. Therefore, nursing mothers must be very careful to not accidentally contaminate food with their breast milk.

There are many clans that restrict a father from entering his daughter-in-law's bedroom. The daughter-in-law is also banned from entering her father-in-law's bedroom. Whoever ignores this restriction will lose their vision.

Polygamy

In the patrilineal world of the Hmong people, a son is highly valued. When a man dies, the family will do everything possible to keep his orphan sons with the family. If a widow should remarry and the children are too young to be separated from her, the children would end up with a new family and maybe with a new last name. To safeguard against this, a younger brother or cousin of the widow's dead husband is forced to marry her. On the evening preceding the burial, the widow and the potential husband are called to the presence of the elders whether or not they both agree to unite. If they agree, then it is announced to the world that the widow is engaged to a younger brother and that all potential suitors should stay clear. In such a case, the widow cannot start dating, even though widows can remain in mourning for months or years.

If the engaged younger brother or cousin should have a wife already, then the widow will become a second wife. This kind of marriage, however, can only take place if the widow agrees to it.

Another situation where a Hmong man would take another wife is when his wife does not give birth to a son. If the wife agrees, he can get married to an additional woman to become his second or third wife.

Polygamy has always been a common practice for Hmong people, but it has become less acceptable in modern times. In parts of the world where polygamy is prohibited by law, such a practice is illegal, so it is strongly discouraged. Even in places where the law turns a blind eye, Hmong men have learned to turn away from the practice because having more than one wife has become consistently problematic.

Less Common Traditional Practices

There are also traditional practices that are unique, but are less common. Some of these traditions include bull fights, not pointing a finger at the moon, and cooking food at gatherings no matter how large the event. These and other traditions are deeply rooted in the Hmong culture. Although they are not discussed here, it does not mean that they are not important parts of the Hmong culture. Furthermore, there are also isolated groups that have their own traditions. Some traditions are becoming obsolete, and others are evolving. For what it is worth, these are the traditions that have helped define our culture for many generations.

5 TRADITIONAL WEDDINGS

When conducting a wedding ceremony, follow the footsteps of a wedding
When conducting a wedding ceremony, follow the trails of a wedding
When conducting a wedding ceremony, adhere to Lialue's doctrines
When conducting a wedding ceremony, adhere to Trumee's art
If there are flowers, let them blossom
If there are fruits, let them grow

(*Noj tshoob taug tshoob qab*
Ua kos taug kos lw
Noj tshoob yoog lis nraim Liaj Lwg txuj
Ua kos yoog lis nraim Rhwv Mis ci
Muaj paj los yeej meem tawg
Muaj txiv los yeej meem txi)

These are the sing-song chant phrases Hmong elders use to empower wedding ceremonial performers to do their jobs. The words remind them to carry out wedding proceedings according to traditions and ask them to perform wedding chants which reverberate throughout nearly every traditional wedding. Hmong wedding traditions are believed to have taken root with the two sons of the siblings who survived the great flood which cleansed humanity. These two sons were called Lialue and Trumee (*Liaj Lwg thiab Rhwv Mis*). They made everything possible that is used during a wedding, including the rules, the chants, the wine, the wedding table, etc. So, during a wedding, following tradition means following the footsteps of Lialue and Trumee.

In today's world, a Hmong girl is likely to dream of walking down the aisle in an elegant white wedding dress to meet her prince charming and exchange vows. Who would not want such a wedding when it has been glamorized so much in movies and on television? In contrast, in a traditional Hmong wedding the bride and the groom are the reason for celebrating, but they themselves are not the center of attention. In fact, going through a Hmong wedding is a daunting task because young people these days have very little idea what is going on except for the fact that there are money and drinking involved. Insight into and knowledge of the traditional Hmong wedding can calm the nerves of brides and grooms to be. More importantly, understanding the true meaning of the wedding proceedings allows people to appreciate a Hmong traditional wedding for its true values.

During a traditional wedding, Hmong people place a heavier emphasis on uniting the two families than on making the bride and groom happy. A marriage is not just uniting the bride and the groom, but is rather about bringing the two families together. Pre-existing quarrels between the two families have to be settled before the wedding can proceed. If there has never been intermarriage between the two families, a fresh start has to be initiated (*tuam choj tshoob*) before the marriage can be recognized. The interaction between the two families is enough to make the bride and groom feel unimportant during their wedding. As if that is not bad enough, before they can be united as one, the bride and groom have to show respect toward and honor members of both families. The bride does not take part in most of what goes on during a Hmong wedding.

A traditional Hmong wedding is quite extensive. Normally, it takes two days and one night to complete. On rare occasions, a wedding can last longer than two days. It is said that one can learn about wedding rituals and chants his whole life and still feel inadequate. No two weddings are carried out exactly the same way. There are always new things to learn about weddings. The way weddings are conducted is constantly changing. Today's weddings are carried out differently from the ones a couple of decades ago. For example, 20 years ago, drinks at a wedding came in two pairs of shot-size drinking glasses or plastic cups. The glasses were passed among the guests from one end of the table to the other. The paired drinks race down either side of the table as two young men constantly fill the cups with alcoholic beverages. Back then, a lot of hard liquor was served. All guests at the table were required to drink the same type of liquor and young people who sat at the wedding table were no exception. Today, in most parts of developed countries, each guest sitting at the table has a pair of drinking glasses which are not to be shared with anybody else. Each guest fills his own glasses with whatever drink he wants (usually beer or soda), drinks them, and acknowledges it to the person sitting down the line. Hard liquor is not used very often anymore. In any case, everybody on the table has to drink out of respect for the bride and groom. Traditional weddings have not only changed over time but also differ from one region to another. The basic concept, however, remains the same.

Every Hmong young man has to know what to do when he wants to get married; it is his responsibility to know how to conduct himself. There are dos and don'ts in getting married and during the wedding itself in which Hmong call the rules of wedding ceremony in the manner of the originators of Hmong wedding, Lialue and Trumee (*Liaj Lwg tus cag txuj, Rhw Mis tus cag ci*). A man who does not know what to do when he wants to get married and does not consult with elders will not only cause his family embarrassment but will pay out more money as well.

There are several things a groom to be has to keep in mind. First of all, only one person from the same family can get married during any cycle of the lunar calendar. In other words, only one person in a family can get married per year. If a son should get married, his brother, sister or parent should not get married until the first day of the first month of the next lunar year—after the New Year celebration. It is said that multiple marriages in the same family within the same lunar year will bring grave consequences. One common belief is that in such a case one of the couples will have a poor and miserable life, or one or both will die prematurely. Hmong people take this seriously.

Another taboo is that two couples should not plan to get married at the same time or on the same night. Sometimes women will plan to get married on the same night, thinking that as friends one cannot carry on when the other has gotten married. This is unacceptable for Hmong people. The same goes for the men.

People with the same last name should not marry each other. All Hmong with the same last name are believed to have come from the same ancestors. For example, a man with the last name Xiong should not marry a woman whose last name is also Xiong. There is nothing morally wrong with marrying into a family with no known common ancestry but with the same last name, and there have been many such marriages. However, for the Hmong, those types of marriages prove to be embarrassments for the people involved.

A man and a woman of different last names can get married—with a few exceptions. The marriages in question are between clans that were once the same but over time evolved into separate clans. Vang(*Vaj*) and Fang(*Faj*), for example, used to all be Vangs. Pha (*Phab*) and Lor (*Lauj*) also have the same origin. Between the more populous clans, such as Xiong, Vang, Cha, Vue, Lor, Moua, Yang, Lee and Thao, however, there are no restrictions. Parents sometimes forbid marriages between certain clans. This is an issue between the families rather than between the clans. Some of the issues may be because of close family relationships, problems in past marriages between the two families, grudges, etc. Hmong people are notorious for bringing up past conflicts between the bride's family and the groom's family during a wedding, which have to be resolved before the wedding can go on. Therefore, parents usually discourage their children from marrying into a family they have had conflicts with in the past so that the marriage will not be spoiled.

A marriage between first cousins of different last names has been a traditionally acceptable, long-standing practice. This is a marriage between the children of a brother and a sister or of two sisters. In fact, such a union has been deemed an honorable deed and is encouraged. It is called a brother and sister's wedding path (*nkauj muam nraug nus txoj kab tshoob*).

Hmong wedding rites have an open invitation. Customarily, the family of the groom always invites the bride's brothers this way:

Traditional wedding chants contain a clause that states:

> If the bride should bear a son, then he cannot be wedded off. If she should bear a daughter, then the bride's brother can bring his son to ask her hand in marriage.
>
> *Yog nkauj nyab nraug vauv mus tu tau hawj keeb kus los tuam ces yuav cia tuav kuv niam kuv txiv tus ncej dab, hos yog tu tau hawj keeb kus xyo mim ces mam tshaj xo nraws rau nus tij kus nus kwv kom nws nrauj nyog tseg qaug lawm ces tseg yog nrauj tsis nyog tseg tsis qaug ces nws ho kwv kaus lis yeev txoj lis nraim nkauj muam nraug nus txoj kab tshoob.*

This is an open invitation that the bride's brothers have the right to take their sons to the sister's house to marry her daughters, and she cannot refuse. Conversely, the sisters' sons can also marry the brothers' daughters. A marriage of this nature can take place when the children have come of age, and if they are attracted to one another. It can also be a marriage that is pre-arranged when the bride and groom are still small children. In such a case, the children continue to live with their respective parents until they come of age and a huge wedding will be carried out to bring them together for the first time. This is usually when the biggest Hmong weddings are held.

A big Hmong wedding is not one where lots of people are invited and celebrities are in attendance. A big Hmong wedding is one where there is not just more eating and drinking, but more traditions are involved and many wedding chants are performed, which means that the wedding will last longer. Big weddings are not exclusive to arranged marriages. How big a wedding can be depends on how a marriage is initiated. It also depends on the status of the woman. Besides an arranged marriage (*qhaib*), the groom can also go to the girl's parents and relatives asking for her hand in marriage (*nqes tsev*). Marriages of this nature can also involve the full extent of Hmong traditions.

On the opposite end of the spectrum are the weddings of widows or divorced women. Women who have already had a wedding cannot have another full-fledged traditional wedding. The status of the man has no bearing on how the wedding proceeds. A man can be married as many times or at any age and still have to comply with whatever wedding the bride's parents demand.

The average traditional Hmong wedding (*tshoob tog qws*) consists of four major parts. First, the bride and groom unite. Second, she is inducted into his family on the third morning of their union. This is also the day to send the wedding crew to the bride's family. Third, there is the grueling wedding at the bride's family home. The wedding concludes with the groom's family.

The wedding of a divorced woman or a widow is just a brief, one-time event, and is quite easy in most cases. In such a wedding, the groom needs to be represented by a go-between who is knowledgeable and can talk to the people who are responsible for the woman. This person must be a divorcee or widower himself. The go-between will personally come in contact with the responsible party of the potential bride and talk to them regarding a possible marriage. A small amount of money is usually paid to the bride's guardian or people who have been taking care of her. A small feast is also in order. Then all her belongings are handed over to the groom, and they are married.

Traditionally, a divorced woman has to be divorced by a certain community leader or multiple elders. In the Hmong villages and towns of Southeast Asia, people who have the capacity to do that are the leaders of the village (*hau zos*). In parts of the world where Hmong people do not have a town of their own, such people would be the elders of the community (*kev txwj laus neeg*). When a man is interested in marrying a particular divorced woman, his representative (*niam nug txiv nug*) has to approach the leader or an elder. He has to find out if her divorce is final and if the man he represents can marry her. If so, he invites the woman and her guardian, usually her birth parents, to the leader's house. Then, he offers some snacks and drinks to the elder and her guardians. He tells them that so-and-so (who has to be present) wants to marry the woman. They tell him how much money they want the man to pay for all the services and care they provided for the woman. The amount can begin at several hundred dollars, but can be no more than several thousand. Once that is settled, the groom has to prepare a meal. A whole freshly slaughtered pig is usually sufficient. In the end, they will hand over her belongings and send her off with him. If she has children from her previous marriage, it is usually dealt with during the divorce proceedings. Children who live with her will go with her to live with her new husband. He is now responsible for their well-being. If the children are young, they can take the surname of their adopting father. If the children are old enough to understand what is going on, then they usually keep the surname of their biological father. In either case, when the children grow up and get married, the adoptive father is obligated to take care of everything.

A widow is usually obligated to stay with her deceased husband's family. When a man wants to marry her, he has to approach the clan leader with a representative — basically in the same manner as for a divorced woman. They are dealing with the former husband's family because when she married into his family, she became a member of that family. Her biological parents are no longer a part of her life. If she has children, they belong to her deceased husband's family. Usually, all the boys, no matter how young, are to stay with the closest relative of the deceased husband. The girls are negotiable because a daughter will eventually marry into a third clan, so she may go with her mother to live with her new husband. Traditionally, only if the girl is old enough to be separated from her mother would the family fight for her. The truth is, if a fatherless child is an asset then the relatives of the father will fight to keep him or her; otherwise, he or she is awarded to the mother when she remarries. A motherless child always stays with the father.

During the wedding, the bride's family is usually left out of the proceedings. After the couple has gotten married, they will have to go to her family. There, they will prepare another meal and invite all the relatives to her parents' house. A representative of the groom then announces to the family that the couple is now married. He introduces her new husband, who kneels to every relative that shows up to show his respect for them. This is the traditional wedding for a widow.

If a man is not informed about these traditions, and he takes the bride home just like a woman who has never been married before, the wedding is usually treated as an actual wedding in which the woman is marrying for the first time. That is not only more time-consuming and more expensive, but it goes against tradition. As such, it is wise for a young man to consult with a knowledgeable elder when he wants to get married.

A man can be married many times, but when he marries a woman who has never been married, it is just like his first time all over again. The difference is just the way his family will receive him and his bride when he brings her home. Whether it is the groom or the bride who has been married before, Hmong people believe that the spirit (*xyw*) of being a divorcee or widow travels in front of them. Family members and friends who are not divorced or widowed should not cross their path or welcome them on their journey home together for the first time. Whoever greets them in their path on their way home to be wed or to their wedding will intercept this unfortunate spirit and become divorced or widowed. So, when a man gets married for the second time, the reception party is usually not as large or as enthusiastic as the first.

For a woman who marries for the first time, getting married can be a difficult and lengthy process. The man normally brings her home by mutual agreement or, on rare occasions, by force. This is traditionally a nighttime event, but there is nothing wrong with taking a wife home during the day either. It should be done on a waxing moon (*hli xiab*). At any time during the process of bringing a wife home, strange and unusual occurrences are bad omens. Some of the things that should not happen during such an occasion include wild animal calls, death, accidents, encountering a snake, or the mention of death. If unusual things should happen, the groom has to try it again at another time. My cousin, Chai Lue Cha (*Nchaiv Lwm*), made many attempts to marry a girl he had been courting for a long time. After three attempts to bring her home with a bad omen each time, he gave up. To this day, he still talks about how regretful that experience was for him.

In bringing a wife home, some people resort to force. A woman can be literally carried home to be wed (*zij poj niam*). Whether she agrees with it or not, when she has entered a man's house, there is no going back. On rare occasions, a woman still gets away, but in such a case, her purity is spoiled and her reputation is tarnished. Often, when a girl is kidnapped in this way, she literally has to fight for her life, because her fate is being determined for her. Every mother who sees her daughter being carried away in this way will do everything within her power to free her daughter without seriously injuring or killing the men involved. The father and brothers, on the other hand, would be reluctant to participate out of respect for the men in question, for every Hmong man knows it is part of the Hmong culture. A woman in such a situation will fight tooth and nail until she is carried past her soon-to-be-husband's doorsteps. No matter the outcome, a girl can be forced to get married, and it still happens in remote parts of south and Southeast Asia today. More often than not, a girl who seriously does not want to be married by force usually gets away from it, because it is common that marriages of this nature have grave repercussions.

A woman can sometimes be forced by her parents to marry a particular man. This usually happens when the man does something to offend the parents or the spirits of the house. I have seen many girls forced by their parents to marry an acquaintance because they were out on a date late into the night. Another common way to get forced into marriage is when the girl gets pregnant out of wedlock. Getting caught sleeping with a girl in her bed is another ticket to a forced marriage. In any case, a forced marriage is a custom that still persists in the Hmong world.

Another method of taking a wife is to go to her house with two go-betweens or maykong (*mej koob*) and ask her parents for the bride's hand in marriage. This is the honorable way. This is the traditional way for a man to show his future wife that he cares about her and her parents' wishes. Every Hmong parent dreams of having an honorable daughter that will get married in this way. Hmong people say such a marriage brings honor to the family (*tau ntsej muag*), and it used to be the only way to get married. However, this is the most costly way to get married, and only people who are financially well-off can afford it. That is because during the process of asking her parents permission to wed their daughter, the groom has to offer money to the potential bride's parents to pacify their hearts. Usually, the parents do not settle for a small amount of money, so the total cost can add up to more than twice that of a regular wedding.

The most common way of getting married these days is for the bride to agree for the groom to just take her home; or, better yet, she just follows him home (*tshoob coj los yog tshoob raws*). This is more acceptable for the groom's family, and the eventual wedding is a lot smoother. This by no means happens only between people who know each other very well. More often than not, naive girls will say yes to men they hardly know, especially in the mountains of Laos, Thailand, Vietnam and China.

Throughout history, Hmong women have not had much choice in how they will get married. Men, on the other hand, seem to have many options and choices, depending on how deep their pockets are. They choose their own path. In fact, Hmong men can even choose to be married to as many wives as they want. That does not mean that men have it easy though, because men face many challenges. First of all, the slightest misconduct by a man can end up in his being forced to marry a woman he never thought he would want to be stuck with for the rest of his life. A man also has to be out there actively courting a potential mate, otherwise he will end up being an old man without a wife. No reputable Hmong woman is going to approach any man. Most importantly, in parts of the world where self-subsistence is the norm, a man is solely responsible for his family's welfare, so getting married is a tough choice to make.

Whatever the reason, forcing a man into marriage often spells a disastrous future. For both men and women it gives new meaning to the phrase "I see my life flash before my very eyes." But, of course, this is the nature of the Hmong culture, where principle and family pride take precedence over personal well-being and individual happiness.

So what happens after a man brings his bride to his doorstep? Once a woman is brought to the man's door, all the bad luck and bad omens are cast away by taking a rooster and waving it in circles over the bride and groom (*lwm sub*) as they stand next to each other outside the door facing inward. Then, the couple goes inside the house. The groom has to kneel in front of his parents or guardians asking them for help. He will then be instructed to kneel in front of the various spiritual deities of the house and the ancestors. The older brothers will also be honored. The next thing to do is to send a messenger to the bride's parents' house to inform them that their daughter has gotten married. This is called fee saw (*fi xov*). Traditionally, this used to cost nothing but one pinch of finely chopped dried tobacco leaves. This is still the case in parts of Laos and China. In certain parts of the world, however, money is involved. The exact amount of money needed to fee saw varies from region to region. In the United States, for example, it is normally $320. This money is a token of good faith from the groom to the parents or guardians of the bride, indicating his seriousness in wanting to marry the bride. The breakdown of the money is as follows:

$100 for the father (*txiv lub khaub tsho*)
$100 for the mother (*niam lub khaub tsho*)
$60 for the relatives (*ntaus tsiaj tsis paub faib hno los yog muab rau niam hlob txiv hlob niam ntxawm txiv ntxawm nus tij nus kwv*)
$20 for the clan leader (*tus tsawb tshoob*)
$20 as a pinch of tobacco (*ib kab yeeb*)
$20 to go with the message (*lub xo*).

When the messenger arrives at the bride's parents' home, he offers tobacco to the parents and all adults present — two pinches of tobacco or two cigarettes each (*tsab ib kab luam yeeb*). He then goes on to give extra doses of tobacco to the father as an extended offering to the ancestors (*poj yawm txwv txoob*), the paternal uncles and their wives (*niam hlob txiv hlob niam ntxawm txiv ntawm*), the maternal uncles and their wives (*niam dab laug txiv dab laug*), the paternal aunts and their husbands (*phauj yawg laus*), and the bride's brothers (*nus tij nus kwv*). He offers a last set and tells them that he is there to relay a message about their daughter, indicating her name. She has been taken home by a certain man (mentioning his name and his parents' names) to be wed. She is in a safe place and they should not worry or look for her. He then asks the parents to call for their relatives and the clan's cultural leader (*tus coj tshoob coj kos*). On rare occasions, the father receives the message himself without calling anybody else. Traditionally, the clan leader or another clan elder is called on to receive the information.

When the clan leader arrives, the messenger immediately offers him two cigarettes and relays the message referring to the bride's and groom's names and their parents (*Ob niam txiv hu li no tus tub hu li no coj nej tus ntxhais hu li no [qhia kom txhua lawv cov npe] mus yuav ua nws poj niam lawm es kom niam thiab txiv txhob txhawj txhob nrhiav, nws mus nyob muaj chaw lawm*). Then they might ask if the groom is really marrying her. In extreme cases, they might call the bride on the phone to confirm if what they have been told is true and whether or not the bride intends to marry the man who has taken her. Often, the parents will be upset, but to be polite they remain silent and let the clan leader do the talking. If the clan leader receives the news without objection, the messenger hands over the money, breaking it down as mentioned above along with a shee cheng (*siv ceeb*). If they accept all these tokens then a wedding date is set at the convenience of both families. If the bride's parents should become hysterical and irrational, the messenger can just tell them that he is only a messenger. If they have issues to settle, they should wait until the wedding. Traditionally, the messenger does not need to kneel to the parents of the bride and her relatives. Hmong people believe that only the groom and his best man should kneel. Those who are just helping the groom out are in no position to drop to their knees on his behalf, except for his younger brothers and cousins.

For the first three days of the union, the bride is not to do any work. Visits from the parents and relatives are also prohibited. She may not go visit her parents either. She may, however, go in and out of the house and run light errands. The husband should get her new clothes to start their new life together. During this period, the groom has to plan and get things in order for the wedding with the help of members of his family. Often times, his older brothers and father will make all the preparations, especially to ensure there is money for the wedding. Most importantly, the groom has to ask two maykong (*mej koob*) to represent the family to conduct the wedding. Traditionally, the groom has to go to their houses, personally ask them, and kneel (*pe*) to them in order for the maykong to help.

On the morning of the third day, the bride is expected to start working. On this day, a ceremony is held to induct her into the groom's family. Two chickens and an egg are used to call her soul (*hu plig*) into the groom's house. A freshly slaughtered pig is often used to prepare for a short ceremony and a feast. The slaughter of a cow for this purpose sometimes happens, but it is rare. Extended family members and friends are invited to the festivities. When the food is prepared, an offering to ancestors and spiritual deities of the house is made (*laig dab*) so they will protect her and to acknowledge her as a member of the family. Before everybody starts eating, speeches and well wishes are in order. In parts of Southeast Asia and the Western world, family and friends tie yarns or cotton threads around the bride and groom's wrists as they utter words wishing them well. The purpose of this ceremony is essentially to introduce the bride to members of the groom's family, his friends and ancestors.

At the conclusion of the ceremony, and if the wedding is set for the same day, which is customary, the crew sets out to do the wedding. In modern times, where it proves inconvenient and weddings are usually set at a later date, the bride and groom are to visit her parents on this third day. A visit requires a maykong to take the bride and groom to see her parents. No preparations are needed. On this first visit, the only ceremonial ritual is for the groom to kneel to the immediate family members and ancestors upon arrival. The maykong informs the parents that the couple is there to visit. Then he leaves them there to spend the night. On the next morning, the bride packs her clothes and goes home with the groom after breakfast.

Whether the wedding at the bride's parents' house is done on the third day or on a later date, the preparation for the wedding is the same. A wedding crew needs to be assembled. A wedding crew includes the maykong (one for Green Hmong and two for White Hmong), the bride, the groom, a bridesmaid (*niam tais ntsuab*) and the best man (*phij laj*). When requested by the bride's parents, additional party members are needed. These include a kussue (*kav* xwm), who takes charge and oversees everything, a chue (*tshus los yog tshwj kab*), who does the cooking, and a checher (*ce cawv los yog tub tuav txiaj*), who oversees the drinks. The wedding crew starts at the groom's home with some basic preparations and rituals.

In all weddings the maykong needs to carry an umbrella. A black and white striped strip of cloth called shee cheng (*siv ceeb*) is tied around it with a slip knot. It is carried to protect the spirits of the bride and groom. In some regions, an apron (*sev*) folded and tied into a loop is also carried to accompany the umbrella. This is called sheng (*seev*). The umbrella represents the bride and the sheng represents the groom. The lead maykong carries the sheng and the other carries the umbrella. These are to be carried side by side by each of the maykong from start to finish during the wedding. The bride, the bridesmaid, the groom, and the best man are to wear new and decent clothes. Traditionally, they wear Hmong clothes. In some parts of the world, the bride and bridesmaid wear Hmong clothes but the groom and the best man may wear casual or semi-formal clothes.

The ceremony to send the wedding crew off (*tsa mej zeeg sawv kev*) is usually very simple. It starts with dining followed by a short ceremony. This is how the ceremony is usually done. A table long enough to accommodate all the male guests is set and only meat is served in small plates spread across the table. The number of plates must be even. The crew sits on the upside of the table, the rest of the wedding guests are on the down side (closest to the main door). A round of drink is initiated to empower the wedding crew (*thov mej zeeg*). During this round, the maykong and his crew (except for the bride and groom) are honored and empowered to represent the family. The males of the groom's family kneel to them to initiate them one at a time. The bridesmaid usually elects a male representative to sit in her place at the table. The phrase used to honor them can attest to the fact that the family relies on them to help conduct the wedding as they put their personal jobs or obligations on hold and come help the groom. However, they also ask that though the family does not have good food for them to eat nor good wine for them to drink (only a plain thank-you) that they patiently carry out the task on the family's behalf ([*txiv tuam mej koob*] *e, tias yuav vam koj mus leg tshoob leg kos coj lub ntsej lub muag mus ntaiv hnub ntaiv hli los twb pam tsis muaj zoo kab phaj tus ntxuag rau koj lub xub ntiag los thov koj ua siab ntev pab mus leg plaj tshoob kom nto txheej kev kos kom nce ntxhee no mog*).

Usually, a responsible person of the groom's family will say this as the young male members of the groom's family kneel two times each to the individual members of the wedding crew. With a modest response, each of the honorees will stand up, receive and respond to the effect that the family has high hopes for them, but they do not know much and they still need the help of the family to complete the task (*tsis pe os, nej vam vam kuv mus pab leg tshoob leg kos los cav tsis paub dab tsi li thiab*). The crew normally thanks the family for honoring them in return.

Then the wedding crew is sent off (*tsa mej zeeg sawv kev*). The departing party is now switched to sit on the down side. Another pair of maykong (*txum mej koob hauv tsev*) sits on the upside facing the two departing maykong. These two will hand the umbrella and sheng over to the maykong who are going to leave for the bride's side of the family. This is to empower them to speak and make decisions for the family. In addition to the umbrella and sheng, the money to be used at the wedding is handed over at this time as well. After a round of drinks, the crew bid farewell. The best man and the groom pay respect to everyone by kneeling to the relatives and spirits, and they leave for the bride's side of the family. The clan leader and the responsible parties for the groom will follow at a later time when the wedding has begun, which can be hours later.

The procession is important. The lead maykong (*tuam mej koob*) takes the helm. He is followed by the other maykong (*lwm mej koob*), kussue, chue, checher, best man, groom, the bride and bridesmaid. This is the same order they will travel when coming back from the wedding.

Additional things the crew has to take with them to the bride's side of the family include at least three whole chickens with feet and heads intact. These chickens can only be boiled until fully cooked. A small knife with a sheath, a small bottle of cooking oil, some salt, one or two pairs of spoons, and two packs of steamed rice are among the things to pack along. A large blanket tightly folded with attached strings is to be carried on the back by the best man or the groom if short-handed. Of course, alcoholic drinks are always a part of wedding ceremonial services, so they must be brought along. In the past, when people were more isolated, a live chicken and a sizeable pig were needed for the next day as well. Two of the boiled chickens and one pack of rice are to be eaten along the way (*qaib noj sus*). The third chicken (*qaib npws poj*) and the other pack of steamed rice are to be taken to the parents of the bride. They will be offered to the ancestors of her family.

Midway in the trip to the bride's family, the crew stops to eat (*noj sus*). Hungry or not, everybody has to eat even if it is just a few bites. Before anybody starts eating, however, the lead maykong holds a small amount of rice and a piece of meat in a spoon in one hand and a small cup of drink in the other hand. He then takes a few steps in the direction they are traveling in and offers the food and drink to the spiritual guardians of the land (*daig dab su*). This is to invite the spirits to dine with the crew and to ask for their blessing. Then the crew eats. The chicken feet are to be saved and taken to the bride's parents to show that they ate along the way.

At the bride's parents' home, the wedding crew always enters through the back door (*qhov rooj tag*). Normally, the crew will just enter the house. On rare occasions, the family would have their two maykong, called resident maykong (*txum mej*), stand by the door with a small stand in the doorway with drinks on it. There will be plenty of spectators inside the house feasting, drinking and waiting to welcome the guests. They literally block the doorway. This is called opening door-bridging walls (*qheb roog tuam ntsa*). In such a case, the groom's maykong, now called guest maykong (*plhov mej*), will have to be knowledgeable about wedding chants in order to get through the blockage. Otherwise, it is going to take time to get inside, and there will be lots of drinking involved. The guest maykong have to chant the appropriate wedding chants to open the door, thank the parents for the generous offering and pair up the wedding crews from both sides of the families. The bride's parents usually ask the groom's parents to send maykong who are well-versed (*tub txawg*) when they plan to block the door in such a manner.

Once inside, the lead guest maykong instructs the groom and best man to kneel to the house spirits and relatives telling them that the crew is there to do the wedding ceremony. The bride and her bridesmaid are to change into more comfortable clothes. The maykong hand the umbrella over to an elder of the house. The umbrella and sheng are to be hung on the wall next to the spiritual altar (*hauv plag*). Before sitting down, the guest maykong have to offer a pair of cigarettes to each and every adult on the bride's side of the family that is present as well as extend them to close relatives who are not there and to the ancestor spirits (*poj koob yawm koob*). The crew can now sit and wait until all the important members of the bride's family have arrived, if they have not already. It is customary that dinner be served before the wedding ceremony can begin. At dinner, chili, eggs or fried food are to be avoided. Ducks, white chickens, and wild game are never to be served at weddings. Appropriate food for such occasions are boiled pork and boiled chicken. Some people don't even eat vegetables during a wedding. The food that is served during such an occasion is a reflection of how well the bride's parents receive their guests, and meat with steamed rice is good. Hmong people believe that what we eat becomes us, so piercing and bitter food make for unfruitful and bitter relationships. As for ducks and white chickens, they are believed to be polarizing food in that people who eat duck and white chicken on special occasions end up being permanently separated. The offering of chopped tobacco or cigarettes is merely a gesture of goodwill. This tradition can be traced back many generations to when tobacco smoking was quite common and offering tobacco was the appropriate thing to do when trying to start a conversation. So a wedding dinner should be decent but plain. The wedding proceedings begin at the conclusion of dinner.

To initiate the wedding, the bride's father or clan leader has to introduce the resident maykong to the guest maykong. Then the guest maykong asks the resident for a small table which is suitable for four people. Some people would invite the parents and elders to join them at the wedding table, but more often than not, it is just the four maykong. In either case, it all begins with three rounds of drinks for formalities and the dealings begin.

There are specific issues to be brought up at the beginning of a wedding. First, the guest maykong have to tell the others that they represent the groom's family, and that they are there to conduct the wedding. The following are subjects of inquiry by the guest maykong:

1. improper conduct by the groom during courtship (*kev txhaum txheej*)
2. unresolved issues between the two clans (*lus txeej lus xuam*)
3. existing pre-arranged marriage for the bride (*muam phauj dab laug cuam tshuam*)
4. whether the messenger informed the parents of the groom's intended marriage properly (*fi xov raws kev cai*).

If any of the issues is problematic then both sides have to come to terms and resolve it. These used to be major sticking points that Hmong people have had to deal with in the past. As of late, people avoid bringing these issues to the table in order for weddings to proceed smoothly.

The actual terminology for a man to get married is literally "buy wife." Buying a wife is what it is perceived to be, but it is no more than a token of generosity or a demonstration of the groom's commitment to the bride to the family of the bride. The use of money as a gift or token of good faith from the groom is just a matter of convenience; other means have been used in the past as well. The actual monetary dealing during a wedding centers on the following, where a certain amount of money is allocated for each:

1. the grandparents (*poj/yawm tsiag zov kwv*)
2. the older sister(s) (*qhwv niam laus hauv caug*)
3. the closest relatives (*yaj ncos cob txheeb*)
4. bridging the two families (*tuam choj tshoob*)
5. the authorities (*nyiaj khaib nom*)
6. the bride price (*nqe mis nqe hno*)
7. the feast preparation (*ua noj*).

Each of these has its own set price which differs regionally. There is also room for negotiation. During the wheeling and dealing, the four maykong are to go between the two families negotiating all these prices without the families having to come face-to-face. Normally, the groom's family stays outside and the bride's family stays inside the house away from the table. The maykong will help to not only facilitate but to pacify the two parties. The biggest part of the deal is the bride price, which varies significantly from one part of the world to another. Traditionally, it is a set price agreed upon by the 18 clans under a certain jurisdiction. In the United States, it can range from $5,000 to $10,000. In certain parts of the world where the living standards are lower, this price can be as low as one silver bar, approximately $150 in U.S. dollars. A universal rule on how to deal with the regional differences is to accept the norm of the land where the bride's parents reside.

As a common practice, the bride's family would make higher than acceptable demands. The groom's family counters with a lower amount. In the end, the bride's parents would normally drop the price down a little. Sometimes this bride price is negotiable, sometimes not. Currently, in California the asking price is about $7,000. Are we bargaining the price of a bride? Yes. It appears to be no different from bargaining for a car or a cow, but that is part of a long-standing tradition.

Notice the even numbers in the bride price. It is believed that where possible, all things should be paired, as the newlywed is a couple. To keep that number even means the couple will remain together forever.

When the wheeling and dealing aspects of the wedding are done, the rest of the traditions are merely symbolic gestures. In the days of old, the guest maykong would hand over the live pig (*npua luam xim*) and chicken (*qaib dab ciaj*) to the bride's family. These days, however, giving the bride's family money in lieu of the live animals is more practical. Additionally, the knife with the sheath (*riam dab*) and all the materials packed in the carrying basket are handed over to the resident maykong. To wrap up the deal, the maykong will sweep the table (*cheb rooj*). This is initiated by the resident maykong as he places five equal piles of money (usually $2) at each corner of the table and one in the middle. The guest maykong then add twice the amount to each pile. At the two corners in front of the two guest maykong, the resident maykong will place the maykong fee (about $60) on top. The guest maykong then place two times the amount at each corner of the table in front of the resident maykong. They each take the pile of money closest to them. This is called mayzeng wearing belt (*mej zeeg sia siv*). The pile in the middle is given to the people who will chop up the chickens, set the table and clean up afterwards.

By now, it is usually late in the night. The final order for the night is that four boiled whole chickens (two from the bride's side and two from the groom's side of the family) are brought to the table and the maykong offer them to each other as tokens of appreciation from both sides of the family. It also signifies the conclusion of the ceremonial part of the wedding. These chickens (*qaib qhe tsiaj*) are meant for the maykong only. More often then not, however, the maykong will invite everybody to join in. At every step of the way in the proceedings described above, there is a wedding chant (*zaj tshoob*) to go along. Nowadays, most of the time, the chanting is skipped.

When the wedding ceremony has concluded, it is customary for the wedding crew to sleep at the bride's family's home. The bridesmaid sleeps next to the bride. This is to safeguard against the bride doing inappropriate things, such as running off in the middle of the night to bid farewell to an ex-boyfriend. The rest of the wedding crew will sleep wherever the host family has prepared a place for them to sleep. Where it proves more convenient, however, they may sleep anywhere they want until morning.

The celebration takes place the next day at the bride's parents' home. Traditionally, a large pig is slaughtered and prepared for feasting. A well-mannered groom will help with all the preparation of the food as should the best man, chue, and checher. Here, the meat is also prepared quite plainly. Traditionally, the meat will have no spices. Fancy dishes are off limits. A wedding is usually not a place to get good food.

Two different tables are set to accommodate the guests. One is dedicated to the parents, uncles and aunts (*xyuam tsum*). This is one for all the honored guests who often are the elderly men and women. Here, a man representing the bride's side and one representing the groom's side of the family will be the hosts. They can proceed at the same pace as the main table or on their own. The main table (*sam tsum*) is where all the wedding crews and guests sit and dine. The parents of the bride and the groom should never participate in the main celebration part which is described below. Hmong believe that by eating and drinking at the table at this time, the parents dig into the wealth and prosperity of their children. The bride and her bridesmaid also do not take part in the festivities. Women and children may take part in the celebration, but they usually do not get involved because there is a lot of drinking of alcohol.

If there are kussue from both sides of the families, they guide the guests through the celebration. Otherwise, the maykong will lead. Once the table is set, the kussue and lead maykong from either side sit at the head of the table. The other two maykong sit at the opposite end of the table. If there is only one table set up, then a representative of the groom's father and a representative of the bride's father are to sit next to each other beside the lead maykong. The special guests, including the uncles of the bride, sit at the upside of the table. The groom, best man, two male cousins (one from the father's side and one from the mother's side or a son of one of the parents' sisters) sit on the down side of the table. The bride's paternal cousin sits next to the maykong, the groom sits next to him. The maternal cousin is next, followed by the best man. The rest of the seats can be filled by anyone. The maykong and kussue are responsible for making sure all adult guests are invited to join the celebration. Only when every adult guest has a seat and every vacant seat is filled can the festivities begin.

The maykong from both sides of the family will inform everybody of the occasion and set the ground rules. Whether the same sets of drinking glasses traverse the whole table or each person has his own pair, the drinking starts at the head of the table and travels toward the opposing end where the other maykong sit. The head end is the one closest to the kitchen. The tail end is the end of the table on the far end of the house. Here are ten basic ground rules for things you should not do at a wedding table.

1. Do not talk about negative things such as death, divorce or gossip.
2. Do not cross your legs or fold your arms as you sit.
3. Do not rest your arms on the table or rest your chin in your palm.
4. Do not use the term finish (*tas*); use clear (*meej*) instead.
5. Do not open your own can or bottle of drink and start sipping from it. Only drink what is being offered at the table.
6. Do not start trouble when you are drunk — have self-control.
7. Do not just get up from your seat to tend to personal needs. Excuse yourself from patrons on either side of you before getting up.
8. Be attentive. Do not use your cellular phone at the wedding.
9. Do not penalize or correct the maykong for every mistake they make. It is not like they really want to do it in the first place.

10. Avoid stalling the drinking procession, especially when it is your turn to drink.

The ten things a guest at a wedding table should do include, but are not limited to, the following.

1. Guests from the bride's side always use the hand further to the head end of the table to pick up his or her drink. Those from the groom's side use the other hand.
2. Drink the glass closer to the tail end of the table first.
3. Watch your neighbors to either side of you for misconducts.
4. Always inform the person sitting next to you before you drink, specifying the name of each round of drinks.
5. Address the people who hold positions at the wedding by their given roles not their given names. For example, call the lead maykong lead maykong (*tuam mej koob*), not his name.
6. Once you take a seat at the table, stay for the whole wedding. If you must leave make sure there is a replacement.
7. It is proper to inform the maykong of the drinks each time you drink.
8. When it is time to eat, try to eat your fill quickly so the maykong do not have to wait for you to finish before they can clear the table.
9. When it is time to say thank you, do it properly and politely.
10. To correct misconducts at the table, do it through the maykong to prevent confrontations with other guests.

When these unspoken rules are observed, weddings usually run smoothly. This is one of the reasons why although there is a lot of drinking at Hmong weddings, there is hardly ever a fight. Often times, people behave out of respect for the bride and groom and their families. It is believed that misconduct and violence incurred at a wedding is a bad omen for the couple's marriage.

The main wining and dining part of the wedding consists of four to 12 rounds of drinks. It ends with the groom and best man kneeling to every male member of the bride's relatives and her older sisters and aunts and their husbands. Then rice is served and the celebration is over, for Hmong do not consider a celebration complete without a decent meal with rice. Traditionally, dining follows drinking. More often than not, wedding guests are invited to eat before the drinking begins (*noj tshoob*). In such a case, there is no more eating later on.

The basic rounds of drinking are as follows (*xeej caw*):

1. open the door (*qhib roog*)
2. await guests (*tos qhua*)
3. enter the house (*poob plag*)
4. rice and cold water (*mov dej txiag*).

These first rounds are rounds of drinks the bride's family offers to the groom's family. The following are those offered by the groom's family to the bride's side of the family:

5. small-trade (*luam xim*)
6. honor the relatives (*piam thaj los sis laij nyug*).

Each of these rounds can be single (*ib xeej lus ib xeej caw*) or double (*ib xeej lus ob xeej caw*), meaning the drink goes around once or twice per round. If it is single (*tab*), then the drinking goes from one end to the other end of the table only once. If it is double (*txooj*), then the drinking goes from one end to the other end of the table two times.

The round of drinking called rice and cold water is considered a welcoming gesture from the family to the guests. Each and every member of the groom's wedding crew will have to thank the members of the bride's family who is at the table. To do that, each crew member calls out guests to thank individually. The words of thanks may be fashioned in this way: "Thank you, the parents from the other end have not done as we should have, mother and father on this side do not have to but you still prepare food and drinks for us to feast on, so thank you" (*[tuav npe] e, ua tsaug os mog, luag tias niam txiv tom ub twb pam tsis muaj kab muaj ke tuaj los niam txiv tom no tsis cia li haj tseem pam dej pam cawv pam nqaij pam hno rau peb tuaj noj quaj npws haus quaj npws thiab es ua tsaug no mog*). When most of the guests at the table are thanked, one can inform the next person in line and drink. This is usually one of the most important lines every young man has to learn and use during his wedding. The wordings used by different people may vary but the basic idea of the content remains the same and that is to thank the bride's parents and their relatives for their generous hospitality.

The small-trade round of drinks and the one to honor the bride's relatives (*luam xim thiab piam thaj*) are goodwill gestures from the groom's family to the bride's family. These may be the most important rounds in any wedding celebration. So during the small-trade drink, the bride's relatives will have to thank the groom's family before drinking. The saying is very similar to the one above with only minor changes. Before any guest at the table may drink, including the resident maykong, he has to call out each member of the groom's crew and say, "Thank you, the mother and father on the other end have sent in all their livestock and money, but they still prepare a feast and drinks for the bride's family, none of which will be extended back to them for they might be upset" (*[tuav npe] e, ua tsaug os mog, niam txiv tom ub tsiaj tuaj lawm nqha nkuaj nyiaj txiag tuaj lawm nqha nas, nws tsis cia li, haj tseem pam dej pam cawv pam nqaij pam hno tuaj rau peb noj es peb noj tsis feb haus tsis rov tseg niam txiv tom ub tu siab*). In return, the person being thanked would respond to the effect that it is no trouble at all and that the gesture would have been greater if the parents were well off. During these proceedings, the table may seem chaotic because many individuals would be up and chanting their lines of thank-you, each with his own special twist. To Hmong people, this is quite normal.

At the beginning of round six, the guest maykong take the groom and the best man toward the door. He makes them stand on the inside, backs to the door. With their shoes off, they are instructed to kneel to every relative of the bride. Customarily, a mat and blanket are set up by the bride's brothers. The groom's maykong begins directing a few times for them to kneel, and then the resident maykong will direct them with the rest of the relatives.

Kneeling to honor the relatives, ancestors and spirits signifies the groom's respect for them and recognizes them as important members of his newfound family (*pom niam pom txiv pom neej pom tsav*). More importantly, it is the realization of the bride becoming an integral part of the groom. Hmong believe that when the groom places his thumbprint on the ground to honor the spirits, the bride can no longer double-cross her husband without consequences. For example, if the bride should commit adultery, it is a sin (*khaum*).

Kneeling is a long-standing tradition for Hmong. The groom and best man stand upright, side by side. When instructed to, they bend down, planting both knees on the floor, keeping their toes on the ground. Simultaneously, with fingers folded into a fist and thumbs extended slightly, they plant the thumbs onto the ground. Normally, the upper body needs to be lowered by bending the arms outward at the elbows. During a wedding, however, the groom and the best man will have to do literally hundreds of these strenuous kneelings, so it is acceptable to not have to lower the upper body and just keep the arms straight. The physical demand is great enough to cause a sweat — at which time, the bride should wipe the sweat off her husband to show that she cares about him.

When the groom and the best man are done, they come back to the table and wrap up the last round of drink. To conclude, the maykong would announce that there will be no more drinks (*cawv mus cawv tsis tuaj lawm*), but ask everyone to not get up for rice will be served. This is when rice and chunks of boiled meat and lard are brought to the table. Everybody dines. During the dining, everybody can introduce themselves to the groom, best man and the bridesmaid. This may be the part where the groom and bridesmaid are offered the most drinks, if the bride's family is extensive. In certain parts of the world, like the United States, the eating is done at the beginning of the celebration, so eating at this time is only for the groom, best man and the bride's brothers. Even so, they should still make each other eat until full. In either case, they have to discuss their relationship (*sib zeem*); of course, alcoholic drinks are used to put the exclamation mark on the newly established kinship. As this is happening, it is time for the bride and her bridesmaid to get dressed and look pretty for the journey back to the groom's house.

At this point, wedding guests may leave. For the close relatives of the bride, however, the next phase of the wedding can be quite emotional. That is because it is time to send the bride off to be a part of the groom's family. It is time to bid farewell. For some, it is goodbye forever. This phase usually has two parts. The first is the sharing of a few words of wisdom with both bride and groom from her uncles and brothers and handing over all the gifts and money the bride's relatives are giving her (*pom sam*). The second part is to send the groom's party home (*tsa mej zeeg sawv kev*).

There are two rounds of drinks dedicated to sending the groom and his crew home. Traditionally, the table is reset and the seating is rearranged. As in the beginning, only meat (*ntxuag*) and drink are set on the table. Both the resident maykong are situated at the head table on the up side and both the guest maykong sit directly across from them. The groom and first man sit next to their maykong. Next to the resident maykong are the clan leader, and uncles and brothers of the bride who will officially bid farewell to the bride. Two people need to sit at the end of the table to receive the rounds of drinks. The lead maykong starts off with the announcement of the round of drink dedicated to the vows and advice to the bride and groom. When the drinks reach each person on the up side of the table, it is that person's turn to talk to the bride and groom.

The resident maykong starts. The responsibility of the lead maykong is to commend the bride to the groom. The message is relayed through the guest maykong, but it is directed at the groom, his parents and his clan leader. This is called paw sha (*pom sam*). The purpose of paw sha is to inform the groom that the bride is now his wife and it is his responsibility to take care of her. To the parents of the groom, the bride is now their daughter-in-law (*nyab*) and they should instruct and treat her accordingly. To the clan leader, the bride is now part of his clan and he should watch over her. The maykong usually starts by detailing the gifts that are to be handed over to the bride and groom. Usually, the maykong would start like this:

> Companion (this is how maykong address each other), at this time we are their cane to wade through water and companion to pass the forest. We have completed the wedding, and now one side gets money, the other gets a person. Still, we need you to take a message to the parents on the other side and their clan leader. They say, if the parents want a daughter-in-law that brings nine cows and ten horses or one that brings nine suitcases and ten sets of clothes, they should have married into royalty. They want our daughter and the parents on this side are poor peasants. The parents grab into Heaven only to retrieve dust and grab into the earth only to retrieve charcoal, so they cannot give anything to their daughter and son-in-law to begin their lives with. The money and clothes to be given to them are as follows [state what the amount of money and items are]. Buy the pot and not the nest, so the parents only get the girl's four feet and hands, for parents on the other side are not to be upset. (*Kwv luag, luag tias tav nov peb ua luag cwj dua dej ua luag luag mus dua zoov. Plaj tshoob leg nce txeej kev kos leg nce ntxhee, luag ib tog tau nyiaj ib tog tau neeg los tseem yuav vam neb coj lus mus rau niam txiv tom ub. Neb coj mus hais rau niam txiv tom ub tus tsawb tshoob. Luag tias niam txiv tom ub ntshaw tus tau cuaj pha kaum tsoos, cuaj nyug kaum nees, nws tsis mus yuav nkauj nom nkauj tsw, nws ntshaw raug niam txiv tom no tus ntxhais, niam txiv yog tub ruag tub u ua lub neej tuaj qab tsag. Niam txiv ces tsuab pem ntuj los yog nkhawb tsuab pem teb los yog tshauv xwb lauj. Niam txiv muab tsis tsheej ib yam dab tsi rau ntxhais vauv coj mus chiv peev ua neej, nws me nyiaj phij tsab tsoos phij cuam ces tsuas muaj li no xwb [qhia kiag cov nyiaj thiab tsoos]. Luag hais tias muas hub tsis muas zes muas tau nkauj nyab plaub txhais taw tes xwb los kom niam txiv tom ub tsis txhob tu siab no nawb mog.*)

This is essentially to send the message to the groom's parents that the bride's parents are poor, and they cannot offer much for their daughter and son-in-law to start their lives with. All the gifts are itemized and money counted before handing over to the guest maykong to take home to show to the groom's family. There are a few essentials that responsible parents have to give to their daughter. The most important thing is enough money to buy a bull. This is called an animal mouth (*ib lub ncauj tsiag*), which really is a head of cow. Frankly, this is a sacrificial bull the parents give to their daughter, for when she passes on she can take it with her to the spirit world (this will be discussed in more detail in the chapter on funerals). Secondly, they need to give her some casual clothes to wear on special occasions (*tsoos tsuj tsoos npuag*) and some traditional old clothes (*tsoos laus los sis tsoos maj tsoos ntuag*), which are made of coarse natural fibers to be worn when she passes on. Thirdly, all her belongings are given to her at this time. All these are to be acknowledged and verified by a guest maykong, who is responsible for taking it to the groom's house to show to them. Of course, everything will be given to the bride and she is to keep it. Except for the clothes, all gifts and money belong to both the bride and groom. The money and the clothes are for them to keep until the end.

Next up is the part where the bride is commended to the groom. Sometimes, the lead resident maykong does this part, but it is the responsibility of the paternal uncles. They are the ones who have the capacity to marry her off. It is believed that the power to wed is invested in the uncle — a responsibility the parents themselves cannot assume. Below is an example of how the bride is commended (*lus cuam tshoob cuam kos los puas yog nkaw lus*) to the care of the groom in traditional Hmong weddings. If an uncle is not available, the maykong, the clan leader or the bride's brother may perform this task. If it is done by the bride's brother, simply change "our daughter" to "our sister" (*peb tus nkauj tus muam*). This is also relayed through the guest maykong, but is directed at the groom and his family. The actual statement is rather lengthy, but the following is the gist of it:

> The groom is capable, that is why he marries our daughter. Now she is the wife of the groom. He has to take care of her. She is grown up but only physically. The groom and his parents have to teach her everything they want her to do as long as it is deemed acceptable by society. If she still cannot do what they desire, they may bring her back to her parents to help teach her. If

the bride is proven to be unfit or if she commits adultery and the groom no longer wants her, the parents will refund his money. On the other hand, if they do not show her what they want her to do and if the groom does not watch over her and anybody accuses her of wrongdoing without any substance, the parents will take legal action against the groom. In such a case, the groom's money will be lost. Please take it to the groom, his parents and their clan leader. (*Nraug vauv nws muaj ob ceg qab thiaj hnav tau lub ris yaj pws, nws muaj rab laj lim plab plaw thiaj haus taus ntim kua txws, nws muaj rab laj lim plab plaw thiaj tuaj yuav tau niam txiv tus tub tus ntxhais mus ua nws poj nws sev. Zaum no dej ntshiab ces ntshiab lis liaj rau nruab nkhob, cawv ntshiab lis liaj rau nruab nee, peb ua niam ua txiv mej koob mej zeeg muab tus ntxhais cuam lis zus saum tshoob saum kos rau tus vauv coj mus ua nws poj nws sev, yog nws poj niam. Txij hnub no mus, niam txiv tus tub tus ntxhais yog nraug vauv thiab niam txiv tom ub neeg lawm, kom nws yeej meem saib yeej meem xyuas mus. Niam txiv ciaj toog tais tsis taus thiaj muab rau nraug vauv ciaj hlaus tais, yias tooj hau tsis taus thiaj muab rau yias hlau hau, peb ua niam ua txiv tswj tsis taus thiaj muab rau nraug vauv coj mus tswj. Nce toj yeej meem soj nqes hav yeej meem kav. Yog tias niam txiv tus tub tus ntxhais tsis tsheej tsis kiab es mus nrog luag plhoj luag twv, kom nraug vauv muab txab muab ntawm tawv plab. Luag tias loj zog tau niam txiv tus tub tus ntxhais tes qaij taw ntxee coj rov tuaj rau peb ua niam ua txiv yog tias peb kho tsis tau ces nraug vauv las npua rog nyob nram nkuaj hos nyiaj txiag nyob qab tsuas qhuav. Hos yog tias nraug vauv coj niam txiv tus tub tus ntxhais mus thoob xib nws tsis npuj phav xib nws tsis thi, nce toj nws tsis soj nqes hav nws tsis kav, tsis saib tsis xyuas, tso tus ntxhais rau kab theeb tim puad, tes tsis qaij taw tsis ntxee yog lam yawb txab hiam meem, tsis muaj los tias muaj tsis tau los tias tau, niam txiv tus tub tus ntxhais noj hno ntxuag kua muag, taug kev nrog suab dab quag lub moo ncha txog peb ua niam ua txiv. Yog hais tias cua tuaj nruab roob ces cia nrog cua tshoob, yog cua tuaj nruab ha ces muaj cai niam txiv yuav nrog nraug vauv yuav cai no nawb, es hais li no rau nraug vauv thiab niam txiv tom ub tus coj noj coj ua.*)

In a sense, this is the bride's family's vow to the groom and his family that the bride is now his wife, but they should not mistreat her. He has the fortitude to marry her and he has to have the ability to take care of her and protect her. If the bride should commit an infraction against their marriage and he has evidence of it, he needs to bring her back to her family. Responsible members of the family will help to mend the marriage. If they are not able to fix it, they will return the money the groom paid for the bride. On the other hand, if the groom should neglect his wife and accuse her of misconduct without substantiation and the bride should shed tears, her parents have the right to seek legal retribution. It may be evident that during the wedding a bride and a groom do not exchange vows, but they are indoctrinated and an uncle commends the bride to the care of the groom and his guardians. There is more substance than if only the bride and groom offer each other vows, because the responsible parties of both families also enter into the marriage contract.

If there is more than one family member speaking to the groom and bride, only the first relative can present this part of the speech to give the bride away. The rest of the relatives will only give words of advice to the groom and bride. One of the responsibilities of the paternal cousin who is paired up with the groom during the celebration is to ask the bride if she still has any belongings, debts or pictures of male friends. If she does, they have to be returned or thrown away. This first round of drink called paw sha can go on for hours.

The last round of drinks is to send the guests home (*cawv sawv kev*). This is usually when the wedding chants are sung. The chantings are to formally ask for the umbrella (*taij kaus*), cleanse the house (*cheb plag*), bid farewell (*mej koob sis faib kab*), thank the bride's family (*ua niam txiv tsaug*) and establish the foundation for continuing marriage between the two families (*cog ncej tshoob*). More often than not, wedding chants are skipped, and the crew heads home.

In addition to what was packed on their way in, the bride's parents would have packed double the number of spoons, a hind quarter of a pig and half a dozen pork ribs (*sawb nqaij*) for their return trip. These are to be handed over to the crew by the kussue or secondary resident maykong while the bride's belongings change hands between the lead maykong.

The wedding crew also eats midway through the trip back. When they get home, the groom's family can block the door just like at the bride's house. That is, however, quite rare. At the groom's home, more feasting and drinking are in order. A table is set up the same way as it is at the bride's family's home. Except for the bride and her bridesmaid, all members of the wedding crew need to sit at the table just as they did before. They sit on the down side of the table. Two people (also called maykong) will sit across from the maykong. The first round of drinking is for the maykong to hand over everything to the family and report to them (*pom sam*) how much money they spent and what the bride's family has told them. Everything is to be put away, but the umbrella and sheng are to be kept intact for three days before they can untie them.

The second drink is pia tha (*piam thaj*) for the maykong to take the groom and best man to kneel to all the spirits, ancestors and relatives much like they did for the bride's family, only this time it is to the groom's relatives. For large extended families this can be a grueling task.

The third one is called circled wine (*koos cawv*). This is to conclude the ceremonial aspects of the wedding. Encircling the drink means the drinking goes to the other end of the table and circling back through the other side of the table to where they began.

Lastly, both maykong, kassue, chapa, checher, best man and the bridesmaid are switched over to the up side of the table for the last round of drinks. This is, once again, to thank the wedding crew for their service. A token of appreciation for these people includes a certain amount of money and a rib each, brought from the bride's family. Each of the maykong may have kept the money given to them by the bride's family's maykong the night before; however, additional money may be given to each of them here as well. The amount of money given to each differs regionally. In the United States, for example, this amount can run between $60 and $120. The rest of the crew will get around $20 each.

For this last round of drinks, when the wedding crew is situated, a pair of glasses filled with drink is given to each person. To show that the family appreciates their services, a few words of thanks are said to them as the young men of the family kneel twice to honor them one by one. Once the drinks are in their hands, an envelope with the maykong fee is given to the lead maykong. The envelope is handed to him, followed by the rib. When the money envelope is offered, it is referred to as a leaf of paper for the heart (*ib nplooj ntawv ua dej siab dej ntsws*), and the meat is referred to as a fish (*ib tug mi ntses*). The person in charge can then tell each member of the wedding crew that the family has relied on him to represent them at the wedding, that he used his face to shield the family from the burning sun and the glaring moon lights. However, the groom's family cannot even offer him a good meal or a good drink to honor him, so thank you. (*Koj [tuav nws lub npe] vam vam koj mus leg tshoob leg kos, coj lub ntsej lub muag mus ntaiv hnub ntaiv hli, twb tsis muaj zoo kab phaj tus ntxuag los ua koj ib los tsaug, tsuas ua ib los tsaug qhuav qhuav xwb mog.*) As these words are directed at the maykong, the young men kneel to him twice. Repeat the process for every member of the wedding crew. After the crew is thanked, the last round of drink is over, rice is served, and the wedding is officially over.

Meanwhile, back at the bride's family, the celebration ends when the visiting wedding crew leaves. However, the two resident maykong and those who took an active role in the wedding ceremony need to be thanked as well. There is a proper way to thank them. A couple of rounds of drinks are in order, so another table is set much like what takes place at the groom's house. The people to be thanked are seated in this order: kussue, maykong, family representative, chue, checher and the male cousins who paired up with the groom and best man. This time, the father of the bride can and should join everybody at the table. The drinks, maykong fee and rib are offered in the same manner as is done at the groom's house. The words to thank them are quite similar to what is said to the wedding crew at the groom's house except the part where they use their faces to block the sun and the moon and simply indicate the fact that the family relies on them to help conduct the wedding. Normally, the person saying this does not kneel — only the young men would line up behind him and kneel. The festivities, again, conclude with a meal that includes rice.

During a wedding, the groom usually takes a humble and passive role. More often than not, the father or clan leader of the groom takes charge of making sure the wedding goes smoothly so the groom will not have to worry about anything. Therefore, a young man who does not have a responsible father or relative to help him will feel the void in his heart during his wedding. Furthermore, without a clan leader to spearhead the wedding, it is rather difficult to carry out the wedding as both families place a greater emphasis on the clan leader than the bride and groom themselves.

The bride is rather inactive during the whole wedding; yet, ironically she is the reason for the celebration. However, it is a tradition of a male-dominated society.

Every step of the wedding has an accompanying wedding chant (*zaj tshoob*), though these days, the chanting is usually not performed. The traditional maykong would normally take the easiest way out and not perform wedding chants unless requested by the parents or clan leader of either family. That is because it is the role of the maykong to pacify both families, and so they will make every effort to diffuse ill-will and unreasonable demands from either side. Furthermore, the lead maykong from the groom's side is burdened with the responsibility of getting the wedding crew back home safe and sound. As tradition dictates, any maykong will have to be a guest maykong sometime. So maykong are quite sympathetic toward each other, and most of them do not make it difficult for one another by making the other chant every step of the way.

It is the responsibility of both families to make sure there are no mishaps associated with a wedding. There should be a responsible individual who stays sober to oversee the proceedings and the well-being of the guests. If a guest should become drunk and start trouble, someone has to calm him down. Transportation arrangements should also be available for guests who have had too much to drink. It is believed that misconduct and mishaps at a wedding foretell misfortunes in the future of the marriage. So it is crucial that weddings are carried out without incident.

Traditional Hmong weddings may seem intimidating and chaotic to outsiders, but when the basics are understood a wedding can be a rather meaningful and pleasant experience for everyone involved.

6 TRADITIONAL FUNERAL SERVICES

You the family of mourners, you bow to Heaven and you get Heaven to protect your head. Your parent dies, you bow to your parent and good things will come to you.

You bow to Heaven and you will get Heaven to lead. Your parent dies, you bow to your parent and you will get to eat amongst others.

You kneel diligently behind the fireplace, Heaven sees and Heaven calls, elders and royalties see, for you they will extend love.

You kneel diligently beneath the drum, Heaven sees and Heaven praises, elders and royalties see, for you they will shed tears.

Nej tsev txoog npoj xyom cuab, nej xyom ntuj ces tau ntuj ntoo. Nej niam nej txi tuag, nej xyom nej niam nej txi ces nej yuav nrog luag tau zoo.

Nej xyom ntuj ces tau ntuj coj. Nej niam nej txi tuag, nej xyom nej niam nej txi ces nej yuav tau nrog luag noj.

Nej xyom kim lis ntsoov tej qab cub, ntuj pom ces ntuj qhub, liaj nog teb tsw pom ces luag thiaj nrog lawm nej hlub.

Nej xyom kim lis ntsoov tej qab nruag, ntuj pom ces ntuj qhuas, liaj nog teb tsw pom ces luag thiaj nrog nej los lub kua muag.

These are the verses chanted to the descendants of an elder who passes on as a call for them to kneel to their parent or grandparent as a way to show respect and honor.

The Meaning of Death

Hmong treat death as the most important event in a person's life. Death is a time of transition for the human soul, for the body may have perished, but the soul lives on. That is the premise of Hmong funeral rituals.

A soul is said to begin its predestined journey from Heaven, the realm of the ancestors, into the life of the host body. Everything that a person does in life and everything that happens to that person has already been written in a script carried in a palm of the individual's hands. For a man, it is in the left palm, and for a woman, the right. In the other hand is the inscription of his or her spouse. In other words, life is a series of events that has been predetermined. The year, month, day, and time of birth foretells a person's life. The timing and the funeral rituals help determine the life of the host body of the soul in the next life. As my father always says, "A person that has suffered enough through life should die on a good day. With a good funeral and a good resting place, he or she will have a better next life."

So when is it a good time to die? The answer is: No one knows for certain and no sane individual would want to plan his or her own death. However, a daylight hour with a waxing moon on a day of a powerful yet good-natured animal on the Chinese zodiac calendar makes a good departure time according to Hmong popular belief. It is believed that the soul rides the zodiac animal into the spirit world. Daytime allows the soul to see on the journey into the spirit world. A waxing moon signifies good fortune in the next life. The nature of the zodiac animal determines the nature of the host body of the next life.

The timing of a person's death cannot be controlled, but the funeral rituals and burial site are controllable factors. That is why Hmong people take great care of our deceased and are very selective of burial sites. The slaughtering of domestic animals and burning of incense and money papers during the rituals are part of the preparation for the soul to journey into the spirit world.

An elaborate funeral shows that a person has had a successful life. It also better prepares the soul to enter the spirit world and the next life. The rituals resolve all conflicts and debts a person may have. It removes all obstacles the soul may face during the journey. It also paves the way for the soul to journey into the spiritual world with dignity. Some say the rituals guide the soul right into the womb and into the next life.

To understand why funerals are the way they are, we need to understand the agrarian lifestyle of the Hmong people that led to these traditions. With a lack of education, Hmong people did not understand the physiological and biological functions of the human body. Hmong cannot comprehend the fact that when a person dies, everything shuts down. Because of this, Hmong have a tendency to think that a dead person can come back to life or, worse yet, transform directly into another form of life such as a tiger or dragon. Of course, every culture has scary tales of the dead coming back to life as monsters, and Hmong people are no exception. Compound that with the eerie silence of village life, without bright lights and electricity, and death is a bone-chilling experience. In China and Southeast Asia, a corpse does not get cleaned up and embalmed with formaldehyde. Considering the humid climate in these regions, a corpse can be dripping with decay fluid and crawling with maggots within hours of death. The stench can be nauseating. This can make a death in the family all the more traumatic. So when there is a death in a small village, all the villagers gather and stay up day and night throughout the entire service to comfort each other and keep survivors company. Traditionally, a family would get this kind of support from the moment a person is gravely ill until at least three days after burial.

In the agrarian lifestyle of the Hmong people in the high mountains of China and Southeast Asia, natural resources are limited. Water has to be carried from a distance, rice has to be de-hulled, animals have to be butchered for food to feed the guests, firewood has to be gathered, and even lanterns have to be refueled every so often. There is a lot to do during a funeral — even more reason for the whole community to come together at that time. These are the reasons why Hmong have the saying, "When others die, you die with them, so when you die, they will die with you" (*luag tuag yuav tau nrog luag tuag, yus tuag luag thiaj nrog yus tuag*). This means that a person who helps others in times of need and in times of death will receive help in return under similar circumstances. During a funeral service what looks like a circus in full swing is actually all the friends and relatives coming together to comfort, pay respect, and help run errands so rituals can run smoothly.

In a world where opportunities for advancement or improving one's socio-economic status are limited, Hmong believe in luck and spiritual support. They believe that a good funeral and strategic burial site will trigger praises from elders and improve the life of the deceased in the afterworld. In return, the descendants will lead better lives. After all, the deceased become the ancestor spirits who are worshipped, so when the ancestors are better off in the spiritual world, they are in a better position to help the living.

The funeral rituals also serve as an education for both the living and the deceased. This is still the popular belief among members of the Hmong community, even in the Western world.

A death in the family is a devastating phenomenon. The relatives of the deceased are so traumatized that their minds usually do not function well. The house spirits are also traumatized, so all altars are immediately covered with white papers when a person dies in the house. This is to shield the spirits from all the commotion. When somebody dies, it is common for the loved ones to cry and wail to express their emotion and grief. It is the traditional way of mourning and expressing their love and affection for the deceased. Mourners who know the rules are very conscientious about their personal conduct with respect to traditions, and they show gratitude toward guests and helpers properly. While the close relatives are mourning, distant relatives and friends are busy making plans and preparations. In small remote Hmong villages, the whole village needs to be mobilized every time there is a death in the village. Oftentimes, friends and relatives from nearby villages are summoned to help. In the modern-day global community, family members can fly in from other countries in a matter of days to help. Refrigeration and embalming, which keep the deceased in good condition, help buy time for family members from far away who wish to participate in this final farewell. When Mai Vang passed away in Fresno, California, in 2002, her body was kept in the morgue for nearly three weeks until her daughter, Mao Vue, flew in from Phonsavan, Laos, to say good-bye to her.

In the Hmong world, there are personal and family responsibilities and obligations people always strive to fulfill. These obligations become crucial at the time of death. A man's responsibility is to pay the bride price for every son he has. In return, each son is obliged to provide his parents a head of cattle and a set of clothes when he passes on. In addition, the financial burden of the funeral rests on all of the sons' shoulders. Those who do not live up to these obligations are judged by the court of public opinion. It often results in ridicule and curses. In parts of the world where money is hard to come by, a funeral service proves to be financially burdensome. That is why the elders always advise young people to "use some [money], but save some."

It is normal for Hmong people to expect a lengthy and elaborate funeral. A funeral can last anywhere from a day to a week depending on the age of the deceased, availability of funding and resources, and the types of rituals performed. Essentially, the basic underlying function of a funeral is to guide the soul of the deceased to the spirit world and beyond. The more elaborate a funeral is the longer it takes.

The preparation for a funeral starts early for Hmong people. For a girl, preparation begins when she gets married. At her wedding, her parents usually give her a silver bar and several sets of clothes. Some of the clothes are to be worn when she passes on. The bar of silver represents a head of cattle to be butchered during her funeral. A man has a lifetime of preparations. As a young man, there are basic skills and knowledge that he needs to acquire so he can help others so when it is his turn, they will return the favor. This is called exchange work (*pauv zog*). Furthermore, as he grows up, he needs to get married and have lots of sons so that when that fateful day arrives there is somebody to hold his head. Dying in a caring son's arms means just as much to a Hmong man as it does for a child to be born into the arms of loving parents. This is partly why every Hmong man has to have at least one son. Throughout life, he needs to save enough money to take care of his final expenses and have a wardrobe on standby, for who knows when and how a person will part from this world.

Another aspect of self-preparation involves personal relations with others. Both men and women have to show love and care toward all relatives, especially the brothers of the wife and the sisters of the husband. They are a person's closest lifelong relatives. The reason these relations are so close is that parents will perish and won't be there to the end. Children are expected to love their parents, but they do have their own lives. Siblings are lifelong friends who are expected to watch over each other and pat each other to the grave (*plhws rau qhov hleb qhov ntxa*). (Hmong people show love and affection toward children by gently stroking the hair from the top of the head to the side with their palms. We also wipe and brush foreign particles off the body and clothes. This is something Hmong people often do to their loved ones before burial as well.) Having siblings to see one another through is one of the reasons why Hmong parents have so many children. It is also why siblings need to treat each other with decency, if not love and care. There is a saying, "Eat with love and drink with giving" (*noj sib hlub haus sib ce*), which simply means be inclusive of and generous to each other. A good example is when a person has a family gathering with feasting involved, he or she must invite all the relatives, especially the brothers and sisters. Love and caring is carried out in both good and bad times. When somebody in the family is sick or there is problem in the family all relatives have to share the burden and help in any way they can. Where there is love and caring throughout life, when a man or his wife dies relatives will continue to support unselfishly to the end. A funeral is a lifelong preparation for Hmong people.

When a person is dying, it is important that the closest relatives are there to witness his or her last breath in what Hmong people call "see life" (*pom siav*). The deceased is said to leave good fortune (*hmoov*) for those who "see life." For Hmong elders, it is inconceivable to imagine writhing through those last few moments of life without a loved one to comfort them.

A person cannot die inside the house of a family that does not share a common ancestry or, as Hmong people call it, "share the same spirits" (*thooj dab koom qhua*). Because every Hmong house is a religious sanctuary, allowing an outsider to die in the house is a crime against the house spirits. In fact, a daughter who has gotten married becomes an outsider, and she cannot give birth or die in her own parents' home even if she is divorced or widowed. So when a person who is not an immediate member of the family is dying, Hmong elders will take him outside even if it means that the individual will die without a roof over his head. Perfect strangers can, however, get inducted into the family and become full-fledged family members and then can die or give birth inside the house.

The clothing a person wears at the time of death is believed to be the clothes the soul wears going into the spirit world. In preparation for the funeral rituals, the clothes worn at death are taken off and multiple layers of new clothes are put on the deceased. Many layers of clothes are needed to protect the physical being from the harsh elements of nature (*tiv luaj tiv av*). So it is crucial that a single set of nice clothes is worn during the moment of passing. Besides wearing a decent set of clothes, the dying person needs to be treated well. If the person is elderly, the sons and daughters have to make every effort to try to save her; otherwise, during the funeral ceremony, they will be ridiculed and scolded by others.

Preparations for a Funeral

A funeral can start anytime after death, but the preparations for the funeral start at the moment of death. In parts of the West, like the United States, time constraints and logistics do not allow the rituals to begin immediately. All the paperwork and preparations need to be made prior to the funeral, so there are times when weeks or months have passed before a funeral can be held. Whether the wait is minutes or weeks, the preparations are essentially the same with slight regional differences.

To prepare for a funeral, basic human needs such as food, drink and space are required. Furthermore, there are lots of people who need to be contacted for they are the ones who will carry out the ceremonies and provide manual labor. In the West, food and drink can be bought at the local grocery store and people can be contacted by phone. It is not as simple in other parts of the world where food and water need to be gathered naturally — many human resources are needed. Dozens of people are to be contacted in person and their services requested. At the same time, the family needs to make a formal announcement of what is already known to relatives near and far. Sacrificial animals need to be bought and lined up to be butchered in a timely fashion. These tasks have to be done simultaneously, which is difficult. Only when there are numerous supportive and knowledgeable relatives will things go smoothly. This is the main reason why Hmong tend to congregate in large populations no matter where we live.

In the Western world, the deceased can wait at the morgue for all the arrangements to be made and the funeral home to become available, which allows a more elaborate funeral to be planned. That is why funeral services in the United States can be shortened to two or three days. Hmong people in other parts of the world are not so fortunate as to be able to leave their dead in a morgue for weeks on end, so everything has to be arranged and rituals have to start almost immediately after death. These rituals can carry on for more than ten days, and the corpse can become badly decomposed before burial time.

The people who help out at a funeral can be categorized into two groups: those who are asked to provide manual labor to make the funeral possible and those who are invited to come pay respect or show love (*tuaj hlub*) for the deceased. The first group is usually made up of distant relatives and friends who are less emotionally attached to the deceased. The latter group are the close relatives of the deceased and his or her spouse. The way these people's services are requested is especially important. For the service people, the family of the deceased ask (*thov*) them to help. For the others, it is a two step process. The first step is to inform (*tso moo*) and the second step is a summon (*hu hauv qhua*). All these preparations are done exclusively by the men. Although women play a major role during the funeral itself, the burden is heavily placed on the men.

It is vital to properly ask a fellow Hmong to help out at a funeral service. People have dignity, and they will not waste their time to provide free services that are not valued or appreciated. Two men have to go to the person's home, set a table at the middle of the house, seat that person at the upside of the table, offer him a drink and ask in a humble tone in this manner:

> [Deceased's name] has left us. I have received hardship. We don't know who to ask for help, that is why we come to ask for your help to do [state the specific job]. If you are well, then we beg for your help whether you are available or not. (*Ntuj kawg xub zeb teb kawg xub ntoos, tsis pom qab thov dag thov zog thiaj tuaj thov koj mus pab ua [qhia txoj hauj lwm]. Yog tias koj noj qab nyob zoo ces txawm khoom thiab tsis khoom los yuav thov koj mus pab peb.*)

As these words are said and if the person in question is well or does not have an urgent matter in his family, the two messengers stand up and kneel once. They insist on one round of drink and tell him when the funeral starts so he can show up when his help is needed. Often, a request for service does not need to be so elaborate, especially when telecommunication is readily available. In that case, a phone call is quite sufficient — especially between people who know each other well. Even so, when these people arrive at the funeral home or at the house of the deceased, they are to be officially asked just as would have been done at their home.

For the relatives who are to be informed of the bad news, two people are sent to each person's home, though a phone call can work just as well. The messengers simply inform that person that so-and-so has passed away and for him or her to come "help love" (*tuaj nrog hlub*). Only certain relatives are to be officially summoned to come help love. These are the same relatives who have been informed of the news, only this time they are asked to come bid farewell (*ua qab tu*) to the deceased. These people include a brother of the wife and sister of the husband, whether it is the husband or the wife that passes away. Others include the fathers of the daughter-in-law and son-in-law. A member of the clan is also present in this group of mourners to be invited. These are people who will make sure the deceased is properly tended to and also see him or her to the grave.

Sometimes these people may already be at the home at the time of death and they can be asked to help right away, but the two-step process is still needed.

When each of the helpers (*tub qa tub num*) arrives, a table must be set, and he or she is seated at the upside of the table. Then all the male members of the family, now called sho choua (*xyom cuab*), gather on the opposite side and kneel to him once more. This time it is to give thanks for his help. A phrase such as the following should provide the basic expression of a proper thank-you (*ua tsaug*), though there are much more elaborate versions:

Thank you. It is because of our family of mourners, a family of sickness and death, of ruin, crushed, that you think of our kinship and you are here to help tend to our religious rituals so as to stand strong like a pillar. Someday, if we fare well, we will return the favor; however, if we don't fare well your favor will not be returned. (*Ua tsaug mog. Yeeb vim peb tsev xyom cuab tsev mob tsev tuag tsev puas tsev ntsoog, koj xav neej xav tsav xav txheeb xav ze, koj tso qav tso num cia tso qav tso num tseg, tuaj pab peb nta dab nta qhua ntseg ntws puav tam ncej txawb. Hnub qab nram lub ntsis peb ua neej xws luag ces yuav nco ntsoov koj txiaj ntsha txiaj ntsig, yog peb ua neej zoo tsis xws luag ces yuav nrauj ncua koj tus txiaj tus ntsig rau nraum toj nraum dawm ua tshauv ua thee yaj no mog.*)

Depending on how extensive and elaborate a funeral is planned, the number of helpers can vary. However, the different types of helpers usually remain the same. Having more helpers makes their job easier. The following is a list of the service people who are the backbone of any funeral. The titles in English are translated literally from the titles in Hmong.

1. The kheng performers (*txiv qeej*) play kheng and drum day and night.
2. The chiefs (*kav xwm*) manage all affairs including food service, rituals, take care of guests and conflicts, etc.
3. The cooks (*tswj kab*) clean, chop and cook all the meat.
4. The rice cookers (*niam ua mov* or *niam pam txam*) cook rice and are normally women.
5. The custodian (*tshaj thawj siv thawj*). Traditionally, this role does not exist, but in the Western world an individual is needed to oversee all sanitation needs.

In traditional settings where resources are not readily available the following are needed as well:

6. The casket makers (*txiv txiag*) make the coffin.
7. The woodcutters (*tshaj thawj*) gather firewood for cooking and heating.

8. The water carriers (*siv thawj*) carry water for all purposes.

9. The rice de-hullers or corn grinders (*niam diaj zeb tuav cos*) dehull rice or grind corn.

10. The lantern manager (*ywj kab*) keeps lanterns shining at night.

Another group takes part in the rituals but are not the regular laborers. Members of this group perform the religious ceremonies.

11. The path pointer (*taw kev*) instructs the spirit of the deceased on the journey to the land of the ancestors.

12. The family leader (*cuab tsav*) makes offerings to the deceased, ensures customs are followed and receives donations.

13. The lead fighter (*hau rog*) leads the procession in the ritual of rallying fighters in certain sectors of the Hmong population.

14. The death song chanter (*txiv nkauj*) chants the death songs, which are interludes with qeej during rituals.

15. The lead shochoua (*thawj xyom cuab*) is the family representative in charge who provides directions for the mourners and communicates with the helpers.

16. The tsee xai (*txiv xaiv*) are chanters on the night before burial.

Groups one through ten require a minimum of two and no more than four in each group. Eleven and on are single individuals. These are people who help selflessly without any compensation (except for the tsee xai) for their hard and sometimes laborious work. The only thing they normally get in return is when bulls are butchered. In such cases, they each get a small chunk of meat to take home to their families. There are usually two tsee xai who get paid one silver bar or up to U.S. $1,000 in a country where silver bars are not honored.

The number of relatives to be summoned to aid in the glorification of the deceased during the funeral depends on how extensive the family is. The bigger the family the more relatives are to be invited. All the relatives bearing the same last name as the deceased are considered mourning family members or shochoua, and they don't need to be notified. All other relatives who bear a different last name are to be notified. In a large extended family, that is a lot of people to be contacted. There is a core number of people instrumental in the funeral rituals:

1. The family leader (*cuab tsav*)
2. The brother of the wife (*txiv dab laug*)
3. The sister of the husband (*maum phauj*)
4. The father of the daughter-in-law of the oldest son (*cuas nyab*)
5. The father-in-law of the oldest or youngest daughter (*cuas ntxhais*)
6. The brother of each daughter-in-law (*xov txiv dab*)
7. The daughter and son-in-law guarding the deceased (*ntxhais vauv zov qauv*).

These are the closest relatives outside of the clan. They are invited to come to the funeral on the day before the burial to mourn or pay respect to the deceased. To officially attend a funeral to mourn is referred to as "doing head guest" (*ua hauv qhua*). It simply means to be a guest. This day is called guest appearance day (*hnub qhua txws*). It is said that their presence and show of love provides closure to the deceased and reassures the living that the bond between the families will continue to be strong. It is this comfort and need between people during tragic times that bond Hmong families together and keep them close.

On guest appearance day, all the invited guests arrive with a container holding certain necessities and a long strand of paper on a small tree branch. Food and drink in the container are for the survivors and other guests. A small piece of meat and a pinch of rice are packed separately and offered to the deceased. Paper is to be burnt for the deceased. These invited guests will be greeted by awaiting shochoua on their knees. The guests are to help the shochoua rise to their feet, and together they converge on the deceased. The guests bid farewell to the deceased and offer money and condolences to the family. There are a lot of traditions and rituals involved.

In regions where the funeral starts immediately after death, the helpers are recruited as the funeral rituals are being carried out. In other regions where time permits, all the helpers are reserved well ahead of time and on the day the funeral starts things just start rolling. Either way, prior to the day all the summoned guests arrive these helpers have to be honored (*tiam tub ncig*). When honoring the helpers, a table is set up with steamed rice, large portions of boiled pork ribs, and lots of drinks. All the helpers are seated at the table in the order listed above. Starting from the top, each person is called out by their job title. Each person is handed a drink and a plate with a portion of the cooked pork. The words to thank the helpers should reflect the fact that their services are much appreciated and will be returned someday, and the lead shochoua says:

> It is a burden on you, [title of person drink and meat were given to], because our mother [or father] has parted from us. We don't know whom to ask for help, so we ask you. You abandon your work at home and come help us. You suffer through hunger and breathe the bitter cold. We don't even have a good cup of drink and a good plate of food to put in front of you to thank you. In the future, if you have a son getting a bride or a daughter being wed, and you need our help, our shochoua will come and if we cannot uphold a table's leg or add a dipper of meat broth, we will pick up a plate (meaning to help bus tables). (*Khwv lawm saud koj [tuav tus thawj lwm tub ncig ntawd npe], yeeb vim peb niam [los sis txiv] qaij qaug los mus, tsis pom qab thov dag thov zog thiaj thov koj tuaj pab peb nta dab nta qhua. Koj tso qav tso num cia tom vaj tom tsev tuaj nrog peb nyob nyiaj tshaib yoo nqhis nyiaj no nqus ntsim los peb ua lub neej tsis xws li luag twb tsis muaj ib pib zoo dej ib khob zoo cawv, ib tug zoo ntxuag rau koj lub xub ntiag ua koj ib los tsaug. Hnub qab nram lub ntsis koj tsis muaj tub muab nyab tsis muaj ntxhais qua los tseg, yog koj muaj tub muab nyab muaj ntxhais qua peb cov tub xyom cuab peb tuaj txheem tsis tau sib tug ceg rooj, txhab tsis tau ib tshob kua zaub los peb yuav tuaj nrog koj tshaj ib lub phaj no mog.*)

At the conclusion of these words, all the shochoua kneel to each helper once. The same phrase can be used for each of the helpers with a change in the title and the job description to suit the individual position. When everyone has been honored, all the shochoua are to kneel down and remain in that position until the helpers thank the family for honoring them. They should eat the food that was offered them for a short time. Then they will tell everyone to get up, wish them good luck and a prosperous future and ask them to come join the feast at the table. In the phrase of thank-you above, the part about sons and daughters getting married has a deeper meaning—it really means when there is a death in your family. In addition, the phrase extends an offer that if the sons and grandsons cannot afford to help with money or livestock, they will help to do the manual work. The words used at a funeral are carefully chosen so as to not hint that anybody will have a death in their family in the future or the family of the deceased will have another death in the family.

If the overnight chanting called tsee xai (*txiv xaiv*) is going to take place, then those who are doing the chanting will also be honored on this occasion. The words used to honor the tsee xai vary slightly from the rest. If there is to be no tsee xai, then this concludes the honoring session.

A few essential things that the family must prepare for the funeral include a drum, a crossbow, knives, twine, a paper umbrella, a kettle of warm water, a tiny pot of rice with a hard boiled egg mixed in, and a host of other lesser things. For the cooks, chopping blocks, pots and pans, rice steamers, spatulas, utensils and other food preparation and serving items must be at the ready. The important thing to remember about the family's preparation for a funeral is to make sure all the people who are going to help are lined up and all the essential materials ready to go. This is so that the people who are burdened with the funeral rituals and services are able to do their jobs without stressing psychologically, physically and financially. There is no comfort in conducting any aspect of a funeral, but when everything is well-planned and the family is knowledgeable, the job of the helpers can be much easier. No individual is excited about taking part in a funeral service, and nobody gets paid for their labor. It is the right thing to do to help each other — after all, no one is immune to death.

The drum used at a funeral can be made quickly for the occasion or an existing one can be borrowed. Some Hmong families have what is called a domestic drum (*nruas yug*). Hmong take drums seriously as they are used exclusively for religious and funeral rituals. A domestic drum is a drum that is specially made to be kept permanently with a family for generations. It is treated like a spiritual entity. If the drum is borrowed, there are special rules guiding the borrowing and returning process. Even the usage during the funeral needs special care. Hmong people believe that a drum serves a meaningful purpose in a funeral. It sends the message of death throughout the region and keeps ghostly figures away. In practice, it is played to accompany and provide rhythm for the kheng. The drum and kheng are said to keep the house warm and break the eerie silence of death in the air. So as long as a funeral is in progress, the beating of the drum can be heard day and night.

The actual funeral rituals, however, cannot start until the deceased is wiped down with a wet cloth and death costumes are put on. Hmong have a traditional belief in the body's disintegration back into the earth after death. One who does not totally disintegrate into the soil will not reincarnate. Anything that cannot be broken down naturally should not be put on the deceased or inside the casket. Everything from shoes to headwear has to be made of natural fibers. Even the casket has to be made of solid wood and not synthetic or metal. Women wear dresses and men wear trousers. Women wear aprons and men wear a long red sash around the waist much like they ordinarily do in real life. As for the shirt, women wear regular wrap-around shirts underneath and a larger one with an expanded collar extending out the back on the outside. Men wear normal shirts underneath, but traditionally a large and long Chinese-style robe (*tsho tshaj sab*) is worn on the outside. For both men and women, headwear is a long cloth wrapped around the head with a nicely patterned black and white cloth called shee cheng (*siv ceeb*) wrapped around the outside to secure everything snuggly onto the head. Some men, however, prefer not to have anything put on their heads, because it makes them look feminine.

The feet are the most important part as far as covering the body goes. It is believed that the soul will have to travel through treacherous domains. The feet need to be well protected — otherwise, the soul will not make it to the realm of the ancestors. There are three critical layers of foot covering. Socks made of black cloth are put on first. Over the socks is a pair of cloth shoes called bird shoes (*khau noog*) with pointed toes. Over these cloth shoes is a pair of strap-on shoes woven out of hemp fibers. These are called hemp shoes (*khau maj khau ntuag*). Hemp shoes are not to be put on the deceased until much later when the first ritual is conducted. The clothes worn going into the underworld are a reflection of what is worn in life but are made with coarser natural fibers that are rather dull in color. People are not supposed to try on these clothes while still alive, let alone wear them in public.

It is customary to put many layers of pants or skirts and many layers of shirts on the deceased. Unlike everyday life, clothing articles cannot be put on piece by piece. The pants or skirts are inserted inside one another, as are the shirts. Only the long rope is placed on last. When the layers of clothes are ready, they are put on the deceased. Strips of cloth are tied around the deceased at various sections to secure all the clothes until the body is placed in the casket. Whatever clothes are placed on the deceased cannot be removed, so what needs to go on the deceased has to be put on all at once at the beginning. It is preferable that everything that needs to be done only be done once and never repeated. No clothing article can be added later. Once the deceased is dressed up, the rituals begin. From then on, the clothing cannot be undone or changed.

From the moment of death, it is customary that relatives and friends come to offer to help and comfort the family. They also want to pay respect to the deceased and bid farewell throughout the funeral. Most of them will offer their condolences and contribute food or money to the cause. These unselfish gestures are not to be taken for granted. Male members of the family of the deceased must take each benefactor to the center of the house. Then both the giver and receiver stand next to each other in the cowering position with both hands cupped together facing the wall with the altars. The cupped hands are swayed back and forth away from the benefactor. They perform a thank-you ritual with each uttering a different special phrase. At the conclusion of the saying, the receiver shows gratitude by dropping to his hands and knees and standing right up swiftly once. The giver should not kneel. Instead, he should help the other stand up as he kneels. Women normally don't perform these thank-you rituals. If a woman should be the benefactor, shochoua have to find a male relative of the woman to give thanks to. The words of thank-you have to reflect two important points. First of all, the phrase must contain the words "thank you" (*ua tsaug*). Secondly, a promise to return the favor in the future has to be included. Here is an example of a thank-you:

> Thank you! It is because our shochoua family of death and ruin, you value our kinship, you kindly give to help us resurrect our religious convictions firmly like a pillar. In the future, if we live well like others, we will never forget your generosity. If we don't live like others, then your generosity will vanish like charcoal and ash. (*Ua tsaug mog, yeeb vim peb xyom cuab tsev mob tsev tuag tsev puas tsev ntsoog, koj xav neej xav tsav, xav txheeb ncwm txhua, nyiaj txiag qas ntos tuaj pab peb nta dab nta qhua ntseg ntws puav tam ncej txawb. Hnub qab nram lub ntsis yog peb xyom cuab ua neej xws luag ces yuav nco ntsoov koj tus txiaj ntsha txiaj ntsig, yog peb ua lub neej tsis xws luag ces yuav nrauj ncua koj tus txiaj ntsha txiaj ntsig rau nraum toj nraum dawm ua tshauv ua thee yaj no mog.*)

This means that in the future, if members of the family of the deceased do well, they will be able to return the favor. However, if they become poor, they might not be able to return the favor. During the thank-you ritual the benefactor might simultaneously utter a humble statement such as this:

> There is no need to thank! We relatives don't lead lives like others, we cannot bring anything to help you. We cannot help to hold back your tears, so do not thank. Please stand up! (*Txhob ua tsaug mog! Peb kev neej kev tsav los twb ua lub neej zoo tsis xws li luag, muab yam tsis tsheej yam tsi tsis tsheej tsi, twb*

muab tsis tau ib yam dab tsi tuaj teev tsis tau nej tsev xyom cuab lub kua muag es tsis txhob ua tsaug mog. Sawv!)

Just before the gestures end and the kneeler is on all fours, the bene-factor turns to the kneeler and helps him stand up. Traditionally, a bene-factor is expected to be thanked repeatedly by various members of the family of the deceased. The shochoua can expect to perform this task every time somebody makes a donation — be it money, food, clothes, or an ani-mal. Oftentimes, the object of donation is mentioned in the saying. Most benefactors will resist the idea of being thanked legitimately, but that is just being modest. When pressed, they will participate. If the benefactor is a woman or a person with no knowledge of Hmong culture, a friend or relative of the donor can be called on to receive the thank-you.

As a way to pay respect to the deceased, to honor the words of the ritual and be receptive to the gesture of good fortune from the deceased, relatives of the deceased are to kneel during most of the rituals conducted throughout the funeral. To properly kneel as tradition dictates, a person has to rest both knees on the ground with hands held together holding a stick of incense above the knees and head down low in a crouching posi-tion. That is a very uncomfortable position to be in, but it is the correct way. In contrast, some people would sit with legs crossed and body erect, much like a meditating Buddha. That is a very comfortable position to sit in, even for a long time. This is the wrong position, and it totally defeats the purpose. At any rate, caring descendants of the deceased are usually found kneeling behind funeral ritual performers most of the time through-out the funeral, even at the graveside.

The Journey Home

Funeral rituals start immediately after the deceased is dressed up. It is important that during the first ritual, nobody talks to, cries to or wails at the deceased. It is believed that such distractions will make the soul not want to go or not listen to the instructions and perhaps get lost. For this part of the funeral, the deceased is laid down on the ground or on an ele-vated platform in the middle of the house next to the central pillar where the drum will be hung. In a non-traditional home, the deceased can be laid down at a centrally located part of the house. Some clans have the head pointing in the direction of the main door, but others point in the opposite direction. A paper umbrella and a paper fan are placed near the head of the deceased. A large leak-proof container (bottle) is used to hold the liquor offering. Traditionally, a bamboo container is used for this purpose, which gave rise to the phrase, "If you cannot eat all, stuff them in the gourd; if you cannot drink all, pour them in the bamboo container and take it to share with your grandmother and grandfather" (*noj tsis tag ntim nruab taub, haus tsis tag ntim nruab rag coj mus pub pog pub yawg noj coj mus pub pog pub yawg haus nov tos*). A bamboo container is usually a block of a large bamboo cut with nodes on both ends. The top end is tapered and the node punctured to get into the internodes, which are used to hold liquid substances. Other things needed for this ritual include a live rooster, a kettle of warm water, a red unused cloth the size of a washcloth, a bottle of liquor (wine is acceptable), a large knife, a stack of rectangular cut paper (*xav txheej*), and a pair of split bamboo pointers (*kuam xyoob*). The split bamboo pointer is a block of pinky-size bamboo split in half, an imitation of a split horn. It is important that the bamboo retains a joint in the middle and one end is cut perpendicular while the upper end is cut at an angle from both sides. The tip of the split bamboo pointer is tapered. This is the instrument used to communicate with the deceased. When it is tossed, depending on how the halves land, the split bamboo indicates the rejection or acceptance of offerings made to the deceased. A good example is when food is offered to the deceased and the split bamboo is tossed down. If both halves of the bamboo are either facing up or down, that means no acceptance. The offer or command needs to be repeated. Only when one side is up and the other down would it indicate acceptance.

To begin, the path pointer sits facing the deceased near the head. The relatives kneel on the down side from the deceased. With the split bamboo in hand, gesturing and chanting his or her name, the path pointer starts by asking if the deceased is really dead. When the split bamboo is tossed and confirmed three times, it is official. Death has come. The path pointer chants a memorized set of verses directing the deceased into the land of ancestry (*qhuab ke*). The ritual follows a sequence of events and descriptions of how life comes about, but the basic parts of it are the preparation of the corpse and the journey to the ancestors. In terms of ancestors, it sounds like the forefathers of the deceased. However, the term "ancestors" in this case refers to the new parents into whom the soul of the deceased is going to reincarnate.

An initial order of the ritual is to wash the deceased's face and to feed the cooked rice and egg. The washing of the face is to make the soul forget everything about this life when it reincarnates into the next. Under the direction of the path pointer, a member of the family takes a cloth, soaks it in warm water from the kettle, wrings out the water, and wipes the face of the corpse thoroughly. This part of the ceremony is called face wash (ntxuav muag). On rare occasions, people request that their faces not be washed so they can take care of some unfinished business in the afterlife.

Then, a rooster is offered to the deceased and killed. This is called the pillow chicken (qaib hauv ncoo). A small portion of the dead rooster's liver is cooked very quickly and offered to the deceased. The offering is tossed into a container holding all the food offerings that are made throughout the funeral. The carcass of the rooster is placed in a container which is next to the head of the deceased along with the liquor container, paper umbrella and container of food offerings. The rooster is believed to lead the way to the realm of the ancestors (qaib coj ke) when the soul gets to the dark underworld where it can no longer see. For the most part, the carcass of the rooster gets buried with the deceased.

The journey for the soul into the spiritual world starts by thanking all the spirits of the house and asking them for permission to leave. The path pointer chants a narration of every step. The chanting guides the soul as it backtracks through every permanent settlement the deceased has ever occupied, starting with the most recent and ending at the place of birth. The backtracking is the journey back to the place of birth. At each city, village, or town in which the deceased has lived, the path pointer helps thank all the spirits of the land, paying them dues with paper money. The soul has to pay the regional guardian spirits to thank them because it had used their land and their natural resources. In each case, several pieces of the rectangular spirit papers (xav txheej) are burned to honor the guardians of the land the soul passes through. When the soul has reached the birthplace, it is instructed to recover its placenta, or the silk coat (tsho tsuj tsho npuag). Only when the placenta is recovered can the soul reincarnate again.

From the place of birth, the soul goes to the ancestors. The road to the ancestors is full of obstacles and danger. There are four important things that are pointed out by the path pointer along the way. One is a pair of hemp flip-flops. The soul is told that when traversing through the mountain of caterpillars and spiky worms(toj kab ntsuab dawm kab ntsig), the shoes are to be worn. At this point, the hemp flip-flops are strapped onto the feet of the deceased.

The path pointer reminds the deceased that when traveling through barren land that is hot and dry, the umbrella is to be used. When traveling through the mountains of dark wind and clouds, the fan is to be used to fan away clouds and winds. Then there is the land of darkness. This is where the deceased must follow the rooster, as the sound of the rooster crow can be heard in the dark. The rooster will guide the soul to the ancestors. Eventually, the deceased arrives at the border between the living and the dead. Up to this point, the path pointer's chanting is from the position of leading the soul's way through every step. From this point on, the path pointer only tells the soul what awaits ahead. This is the end of the journey for the path pointer and the soul has to go forward by itself.

This final part of the journey varies slightly from one path pointer to another because there are many versions of this ritual. One version tells the soul to crawl into the ancestor who has a dark face and an open skirt. The other version tells the soul that it will have to traverse through many obstacles and finally come to a forked road. The road will branch into three.

The correct path is the one in the middle where there is clear water to wade through to find the ancestors. In either case, the path pointer directs the soul right into the womb of the new mother the soul is to reincarnate into. At that point in his narration, the pointer bids farewell to the deceased and heads back to reality. He takes a knife and scrapes the tip across the ground between the deceased and himself, uttering words to separate himself from the deceased. Often, the path pointer sings a traditional song to conclude the ritual. Loved ones can now bid farewell by crying and wailing as they see fit.

Immediately following the path-pointing chant, a kheng player takes his turn in sending the spirit to the land of the ancestors. The tones of the kheng instrument speak words of a chant in their own special way. So the first time the kheng is played gives instruction to the soul on how to go to the land of the ancestors. This is called the kheng of death (*qeej tu siav*). The kheng of death starts with the beating of the drum. The main part of the kheng playing, however, is done without the drum. The gist of the death song follows the same pattern as the path pointer's chant with slight variations in the detail. In the case of the kheng, there is a lot of repetition. What is uniform about the kheng of death is that toward the end of the journey there are more details where the path forks into three. The soul must pick the middle road to reach the land of the ancestors. Again, the soul is directed into the womb of the mother in the next life. The kheng of death can take anywhere from four to eight hours to complete, depending on how thoroughly the kheng player is asked to perform.

After the kheng of death, another kheng player will play a ritual sequence to raise the death horse. The horse is not an actual horse but a symbolic term for the gurney that holds the corpse. It is a crude stretcher made from bamboo strips and wooden beams. It is also called the master of shades (*kws txaij kws nraug*). The stretcher is used to hold the corpse during the funeral and to carry it to the burial site. In the West, this stretcher is made for ceremonial purposes only so it is downsized to the point of uselessness. The reason is that the corpse is placed in a casket and taken to the cemetery in a hearse rather than by the traditional means of being carried on the shoulders for miles to the burial site. The death horse is made of two fairly long and strong wooden bars which are carrying beams that two or four people can carry on their shoulders. Between the wooden beams are additional support beams that parallel the long beams. The middle beams are shorter. All these are held together by weaving long bamboo strips between them.

The kheng is played to the beat of the drum continually. The beat and pattern of the drum varies according to the tone and rhythm of the kheng. The kheng and drum played together creates an eerie music.

During this ritual, the stretcher is brought in through the common door and into the center of the house. There the corpse is laid on it, and it is hoisted to chest level along the wall underneath the altars and stakes are placed to support it. Each altar should have been totally covered with a large paper immediately following the death. A pig is offered to the deceased immediately after he is secured on the stretcher. In parts of the world where a casket is used, a miniature stretcher is made and placed next to the casket. The corpse is placed in a coffin, and the coffin is set on a raised platform resting against the wall. Where a funeral is conducted at a funeral home instead of a family home, the coffin is placed against the wall away from the doors and trusted members of the family sit to form a perimeter to shield the deceased from strangers and pests.

Once the deceased is situated, offerings can be made to his soul. Traditionally, a live animal (usually a pig or cow) would be brought into the house and offered to the deceased by tying one end of a length of twine around the neck of the animal and placing the other end in the palm of the deceased. The family leader (*cuab tsav*) takes the split bamboo and instructs the deceased to accept the animal. Then the animal is butchered. The butchered animal is dressed by the family with the cooks' help. When the pig is cleaned it is shown to the chief. He cuts it up. The ribs go to the kheng performers. A hind quarter goes to the owner of the animal. The cooks take the rest, chop it, cook it and serve it to guests and service people. Because traditional funerals run non-stop from beginning to burial, it is critical that food is provided, so there is usually a lot food and drink at funerals.

Once an animal is offered, the kheng is played to legitimize the offering. As soon as an animal is offered to the deceased, kheng performers begin. One plays the kheng and the other beats the drum in a rhythmic fashion to signify with words the offering of an animal for the soul, and so the soul of the animal will accompany the deceased to the spirit world. Hmong believe that the journey to the underworld is cold, lonesome and treacherous. Sending animals' souls, paper money, lots of clothes and other artifacts with the deceased will make the journey easier and will enrich his or her life in the spiritual world.

The song by the kheng performer bestowing the animal offering on the deceased explains who is making the offering and instructs the deceased to take the animal to the spirit world. In the middle of the song, the kheng player turns to the shochoua and tells the relatives and descendants that the deceased blesses them with good luck and prosperity. This is the kheng song for an animal offering (*qeej cob tsiag*). The kheng song for food offering is similar to that of the animal offering. The difference is that a small amount of rice and a small amount of meat is offered to the deceased instead of a live animal. The offering of food is done three times a day for breakfast, lunch and dinner. The animal offering can be at any time. So the songs reflect those differences. In each case, the death song chanter (*txiv nkauj*) can chant the proper accompanying song to reiterate what the kheng song expresses. During these rituals, the relatives and descendants of the deceased may kneel in the middle of the house behind the drum and kheng performers face the deceased with incense in hand. This is to honor the deceased. When the kheng is swayed or the chanter gestures toward the kneelers, it marks the conclusion of a stanza in a song, but more importantly, it bestows blessings from the deceased onto the honorees.

Another important kheng song played several times a day for certain groups of Hmong is called the kheng song to rally fighters (*qeej tsa rog*). Some say this ritual is to keep evil spirits at bay so they will not come to the funeral. According to Chong Leng Cha, a long time kheng player, when Hmong fled from China to Southeast Asia, certain groups had to fight their way out of China. Now, when the soul travels back to the land of the ancestors, some go through these former battle grounds. The spirits of the Chinese soldiers of the past still await such souls. The fighters-rallying ritual builds a fighting force to protect the soul as it travels through the battle fields. According to the content of the kheng song, spiritual fighters are rallied during this ritual, and as the soul gets to the realm of the spirits, these spiritual fighters will drive away the spirits of the land so the soul can claim ownership of the new world.

During this ritual, a kheng player plays his instrument as he walks from one door to the other inside the house. The lead fighter carries a crossbow and a flag, leading at least one other person walking around the funeral home on the outside. Both lead fighter and kheng player time themselves so they always meet each other at the door. As they meet, they swing their feet at each other, blow a horn made of a hollow tube making a "boooooo" sound and shout "woooooo." The process repeats seven or nine times depending on family tradition. At the conclusion of the song, the lead fighter and his crew come inside. Some clans will have a kheng player lead the fighters outside.

While all these rituals are taking place, the chief (*kav xwm*) finalizes the invitation of the closest relatives mentioned above. To do so, he and a companion go to each relative's house and personally invite the relative to come help to show love and bestow honor on the deceased. There is a special way of doing this. Usually, relatives who hold no grudges against the deceased will come willingly. If there are misunderstandings or problems between a relative of the deceased and another relative, that person will not agree to attend the funeral until all issues are resolved. At any rate, these relatives are to arrive at the same time on guest appearance day (*hnub qhua txws*), usually the day before burial. In some cases, among Green Hmong in particular, these guests can show up anytime. What to bring may vary regionally, but the most important thing is for the guests to bring some money, food and wine to be offered to the family and the deceased. Each guest shows up with a representative to take care of the logistics. The guests approach the deceased to express their feelings and to bid farewell. Details of the rituals vary widely, but every Hmong person will have to participate in these rituals during his or her lifetime.

In the evening of the guest appearance day, the representatives of all the invited guests are seated around a table in the middle of the house or funeral home and the chiefs or tsee xai will initiate a discussion of the life and death of the deceased. Often, the tsee xai and the chiefs are the same people. Whether they are the same or different, those bearing the different titles conduct this ritual differently. If the ritual is done by the chiefs, no chanting is done and it is swift. The representatives of the invited guests are asked to voice any concerns or questions they may want to direct at the descendants. Issues to be brought up can range from debt to unsettled family problems; from the number of children the deceased has to the number of cows the children plan to slaughter. All issues brought up have to be resolved. If debt is involved, the children or surviving spouse of the deceased has to honor it. This comes about because Hmong believe that personal issues in life have to be resolved before passing on, otherwise the soul has to deal with them in the spiritual world before it can reincarnate. Life's unresolved issues are much more difficult to fix in the spiritual realm. When all issues are resolved, the family receives the blessings of the invited guests and it concludes the ritual.

If this part of the ritual is conducted by the tsee xai, then it will take the whole night to complete. That is because tsee xai is the theatrical version of the issues settlement described above. Tsee xai refers to two specially selected elders who are well-versed in what we call tsee xai. The name of the trade and the title of the person with the trade are the same. This is a system of chanting which details the life, death, and afterlife of the deceased. An important component of tsee xai is to provide words of guidance for the descendants when they become orphans. Such guidance includes what the survivors should do to get along with each other, love each other, become self-sufficient, good people, etc. Another component of this ritual that Hmong people highly value are the words of blessing bestowed to the descendants to give them a sense of empowerment to become rich and obtain royal status. Hmong people highly value these words of empowerment because they give hope to the descendants of the deceased. Hmong believe that the hope to escape from hardship and the constant struggle to survive can only come from wealth and royalty.

Tsee xai is so extensive that the ritual can last more than 12 hours straight. This ritual can be broken into three major parts, all of which are chanted from memory: the introduction (*qheb phiaj*), guests resolutions (*cwb qhua*) and blessing (*foom kom*). The introductory part informs the guests of the humble life of the deceased and how death occurs. Even though this part takes several hours to complete, it is strictly for formality purposes. The next part is a more extensive version of what is described above and carries great significance for the guests. The tsee xai empowers each of the seated guests to ask questions concerning the deceased and circumstances surrounding the death. Furthermore, it is their responsibility to make sure the descendants fulfill their obligations which is usually for each son to provide the deceased with a set of clothes and a bull. If not, they can demand that such obligations be met.

Some of the seated guests during this ritual are each given a bull to slaughter for the deceased. Who gets to slaughter depends on the gender of the deceased. For a woman, the family leader, her brother, the father-in-law of a daughter and each of the brothers of the daughters-in-law get to slaughter a bull. If the deceased is a man, it would be the family leader, his sister, the father-in-law of a daughter and each of the brothers of his daughters-in-law. These bulls are to be butchered the next morning. Also during this part, an elder (*xeev txwj laug*) settles any debt and conflict the deceased may have. This is to clear the deceased of a problem the soul may have to settle in the eternal life as described above. Hmong believe that if a person owes someone something and does not pay it back, that person will have to come back and pay it off before he or she can reincarnate. Conversely, if someone else owes the deceased something, he or she will have to reincarnate back into a life form that is closely associated with that someone to collect what is owed. Only when the debt is collected will the soul be able to move on. The debt and conflict resolution part is to avoid such complication for the soul. The last part of this ritual is for the relatives to provide words of blessing to the descendants. Then the tsee xai will conclude with their own words of blessing and empowerment.

Traditionally, on the morning of burial, all the paper money is burned. These papers have to be offered to the deceased much the same way animals are. Traditionally, all the bulls are offered to the deceased and butchered on the same morning as well. The offering of bulls, however, varies somewhat from other animals. The bulls can be cattle or water buffalos. These are large animals that cannot be brought into the house. So the offering is made in one of two ways. The first is to extend a long twine from the animal on the outside to the deceased inside the house. The second has the deceased taken outside to meet the bull. People who traditionally do not move their deceased outside to be offered a bull are called Hmong paw (*Hmoob pos*). The word "paw" means soak. In this case, the deceased is said to be left cooped up inside. Some families take the deceased outside to be offered the bull. They are called Hmong chuecha (*Hmoob tshwm tshav*). Chuecha means exposed to sunlight. The deceased is literally taken outside to be exposed to sunlight and open air. When Hmong people migrated to the Western world, we could not bring bulls to the funeral homes nor could we take the deceased to meet the bulls at the slaughterhouse, so the bulls are butchered at the slaughterhouse without being properly offered to the deceased. As such, the bulls are usually butchered prior to the last day for convenience. Furthermore, when they are slaughtered earlier, the beef can be used to feed the guests and service people. This is a new adaptation that is becoming standard tradition.

Traditionally, by the time the rituals on the last day are done, it is past noon. It has been a long-standing tradition that Hmong people do not bury their dead in the morning. Before the deceased is taken to the burial site, the kheng song to begin the journey is played. This is the last song and a very important one. Toward the end of the song, all the bad luck, evil spirits, and ghostly spirits are sent off with the deceased so that the survivors will have peace and good health. When the deceased is carried out the door, the kheng player leads the procession, followed by a woman carrying a torch. Then the deceased is carried out and everybody else follows. The kheng player and torch carrier only go a short distance, then they turn back home as the deceased is taken to the burial site. The kheng player and the torch bearer must go under the stretcher or coffin in order for them to return home spiritually sound.

Often, a grave is dug before the deceased is taken to the burial site. Sometimes people have chosen a gravesite that is far from home and so the grave may not be dug yet. In such a case, the grave has to be dug quickly once the deceased is brought to the site. Hmong do not have professional undertakers, so the relatives of the dead act as undertakers. At any rate, at the grave, it is important for the family members to say farewell. Hmong people highly value sibling love in the form of seeing each other through to the end, which is a literal expression. In other words, it is of utmost importance for a woman that when she is going to be buried, she has a brother there to make sure her clothes are properly fitted and to bid farewell to her. Likewise, a man needs the reassurance of a sister to be there for the same reason. Hmong believe that besides the parents, the closest next-of-kin is a brother or sister.

Before burial, the family leader cuts small slits into the clothes worn by the deceased and says, "If the Chinese want your clothes tell them that your clothes are torn." The casket also gets cut as well. At the same time, the family has to make sure there are no foreign objects left with the deceased. Coins, jewelry and valuables have to be removed. Who knows how long ago these traditions got started, but it did in ancient China where Hmong graves have been consistently robbed. As such, Hmong were afraid to bury any valuable material with their dead. The last order before the burial is the closing of the casket lid. The cover is fitted snuggly then lifted and dropped back on three times warning the deceased that those are the last moments he or she will ever see light. Then the casket is closed. The rooster killed at the beginning of the funeral rituals is placed next to the casket and then dirt is filled in to create a little mound. In the West, the mounds are not allowed, so whatever the undertakers do is accepted. In some cases, the containers holding all the liquid and food offerings are thrown on top of the grave. A bundle of white cloth cut into the shape of spirit money (*ntshua ntawv vam sab*) is hung over the grave. In other cases, the grave has nothing on it.

All the people who attend the burial should go back to the family home. At the house, a burning fire and bowl of water greet the people who went to the burial. Before they can go back into the house, they have to jump over the fire and wash their hands thoroughly. Hmong people believe that evil spirits are afraid of fire. When a person steps over a fire, evil spirits will not follow suit. The bowl of water is there because at the burial people handled the corpse as well as the dirt to cover the grave, and so naturally they need to wash their hands before going back into the house. When everybody gets back from burying the deceased, the shochoua usually prepares something for everyone to eat before they leave.

After the burial and for three consecutive days, rituals and traditions continue. In the evening, several short strings with a small loop on one end are secured onto foot-long sticks. The loop is left dangling. These stakes are driven into the ground along the path leading to the house deep enough to keep them standing. The stakes are slightly slanted away from the house with the string hanging from the top (*nquam nkog*). This is to ward off evil spirits or perhaps the spirit of the deceased. These are left for three nights. Relatives and friends also come to stay with the family for those three nights. They usually stay up all night every night in what is called night guard (*zov hmo*). There is nothing to be done during these three nights. Relatives and friends are just there to keep the family company.

The morning rituals are different from the evening rituals. For three consecutive mornings following the burial, food is delivered to the deceased. This is called breakfast out (*tawm tshais*). On the first morning, three small containers (often made out of bamboo) are taken to the grave. One container holds rice, another holds meat and the third holds warm water. They are left there for the soul of the deceased. The second morning, the ritual is repeated except this time, the containers are delivered halfway between the house and the grave. On the third morning, the food offering is left by the side of the road or trail leading to the house. In all cases, the containers are left hanging from a standing object like a tree. This ritual is to lead the soul back into the house. For some people, the order is reverse.

Every morning for the first two weeks after burial, a seat at the breakfast table, a spoon and a plate are made available for the deceased. His or her name is also called for breakfast. On the third day, rocks are taken to the gravesite and an imaginary outlet at the head end of the grave is created. This practice is called stacking rocks (*txhim zeb*). Some leave it bare (*ntxa suav*). Others stack twigs and tree limbs piled high to cover the entire grave (*tsuab khaub*). No matter how a family is supposed to tend to the grave after death, all final actions to be done to the grave are done on the third day. After this day, nobody is to physically touch the grave ever again. No one should walk directly over a grave, especially that of a relative.

The 13th day following burial is called full cycle (*puv tsug*). It is time to release the soul (*tso plig*). At burial, the deceased is told to spend the first ten days to get acquainted with the underworld and the next three to wait for relatives to come get the soul to visit the old house (the real house the deceased used to live in). Traditionally, the 13th day is the day on which the final ritual is carried out. This is when the soul of the deceased rises from the grave and comes back home to visit before being sent to Heaven to be reincarnated. This ritual starts with some major preparations. All the helpers from the funeral have to be asked to come back to help. All relatives are informed and invited to come observe and help out. This time, it is a planned ritual so arrangements need to be made to ensure that at least one chief, all the kheng players, a cook and the family leader will be there. Chances are, not everyone is going to be able to make it, and their help is not necessarily needed. For this ritual, one additional person is needed. That person is the one who will carry the winnowing basket which represents the physical being of the deceased. Sticky rice cakes, drinks and other items are needed for this ritual as well. A makeshift gate is usually erected near the house over the path leading to the grave. Inside the house, a drum is set up much the same way as it would be for an actual funeral.

When everything is set, a son of the deceased takes a crossbow and an arrow to the grave to retrieve the soul (*tos plig*). If the grave is far, he can go just out of sight in the direction of the grave, but if the grave is close enough, going all the way to the grave is a good idea. Then he shoots an arrow near or in the direction of the grave and heads back home. He walks directly toward the winnowing basket awaiting a few yards outside the main door. Some people erect a makeshift gate, where the basket is placed on the other side of the gate away from the house. In the basket, a couple of sticks are propped up in a half dome shape and a shirt is wrapped around it. At the crest, a portion of the stick is left exposed and a shee cheng (*siv ceeb*) is wound around it resembling the head. Inside is a stack of rice cakes. The soul retriever places the crossbow in the winnowing basket to mark the return of the soul being resurrected on the basket. The soul is then cleaned, fed and brought into the house through the gate by means of the winnowing basket carried by a basket carrier. All the while, the kheng player plays a song to welcome the soul back and leads it into the house. The purpose of the gate is to keep out the wandering spirits of the graves. Only the pure soul is allowed to come into the house.

Once inside the house, the basket with the imaginary soul is carried around the fireplace nine times and placed on a stool behind the fireplace. If a fireplace is not available, a makeshift fireplace has to be made. That is to give the soul a chance to greet the relatives and become reacquainted with the spirits of the house. Then it is taken to the middle part of the house toward the wall underneath the altar. This is where it will sit for the remainder of the ritual.

The first order of business once settled inside the house is the kheng song to release the soul. The kheng is played with less eerie songs accompanied by more subtle rhythms on the drum. Usually a pig is butchered for this purpose, and the meat is offered to the soul. Then lunch is offered and a lot of paper money is burned. By then, it is usually late afternoon. The winnowing basket is taken back outside beyond the makeshift gate.

At this point the soul is sent off on its way to Heaven. The materials in the basket are taken apart. To conclude, the empty basket is rolled forward until it stops and falls over upside down. The soul can now reincarnate into any life form deemed appropriate by the spiritual guardian of the gate to Heaven.

The shirt that was used to cover the basket, the basket and rice patties are picked up by the basket carrier as he heads back into the house. The kheng player and basket carrier are stopped at the door before going inside the house. Here they hand everything, including the kheng, to the responsible party of the family, who awaits inside the door. If the basket carrier is knowledgeable, he is asked to chant a lengthy song. The chanting is to bestow fortune and prosperity to the descendants and relatives of the deceased. That concludes the rituals on behalf of the soul of the deceased.

Traditionally, when an elder passes away in a certain house, the survivors are not to leave that house for at least three years. During these three years, on New Year's day, the family needs to take some food (a boiled chicken and steamed rice), some papers and several sticks of incense to the grave. The food is offered to the deceased and the papers and incense burned. This ritual is said to help the deceased mark the years (*pe tsiab*).

From this point on, the name of the deceased is enshrined with the ancestors and will be recognized as an ancestor spirit that can be called upon on special occasions. It is believed that the soul that joins the ancestors continues to live in the spirit world for many generations. When the soul faces hunger or encounters trouble, it will come to the descendants who are alive for help. A good example of a problem the soul may face is when an animal digs into the grave of the deceased. Hmong refer to this as a destruction of the home of the ancestors. When this happens to a grave of a person who has male descendants, the soul can come to them for help as discussed in Chapter 7 on shamans. If a person leaves no male descendants behind, then the soul will forever suffer the torture of the elements of nature.

For small children and young adults, funerals are not as elaborate as described above. Their lives are not extensive and relatives are not numerous, so there aren't as many rituals to perform, but proper burial is crucial. Infants that have not been given a name are usually discarded without any commotion. To discard is to wrap the deceased infant up very tightly and take him out through a hole in the wall, not out the door. The body of the infant is taken to a safe place and just left there. Usually, people would leave it in a cave or inside a thick bush far from civilization and out of reach of animals. Paradoxically, Hmong recognize life at the moment of conception, yet life is insignificant until a name is given.

People who die unnatural deaths (such as being crushed by a falling tree), commit suicide, or are murdered in cold blood are to be banished from the land of the ancestors and deemed unworthy of being worshipped. Thus, the souls of such people are pointed to the land of anonymity. The names are never to be mentioned or reused again. It is believed that if such drastic measures are not taken, the soul will reincarnate into subsequent generations. The reincarnated will suffer the same fate. So, Hmong people should be aware of the importance not only of leading lives that are highly ethical, but also of leaving this world in a natural and non-sinful manner.

7 Belief System

Hmong spiritual faith is difficult to explain because there is no structure or written evidence to consult. There is no supreme religious leader like the Dalai Lama or the Pope to provide guidance. Leading authorities in this field are the individual religious leaders within each extended family. This makes it very challenging to remain consistent and authentic. There is no systematic means to describe the action of individual practitioners. People rely on personal experience and testimonies to validate their faith. It is difficult to be objective about religious beliefs, because different religious leaders and shamans may have different interpretations of the various aspects of Hmong religion. Information in this chapter is drawn from common practices, testimonies, rites, wedding chants and legends. This chapter is far from a complete summary of Hmong religious faith.

Many years ago I worked with an older and very traditional East Indian woman. On one occasion, she sneezed. I said, "Bless you!" just to be courteous.

"No thanks," she said, "I am blessed already." I was dumb-founded as other co-workers stared at me and giggled. I did not know what else to say. Being an English learner and a new immigrant to the United States, little did I know that the expression "bless you" was in reference to the Christian God, and I was imposing it on a Muslim.

It is said that religion is the root of all good and all evil. This is no exception in Hmong culture. Religion has kept Hmong together, but it has also caused irreparable harm. For instance, the heavy reliance on the community's help to complete religious ceremonies has made it very challenging for Hmong people to be loners, so relatives and friends stay in close proximity to each other. In recent years, many individuals and families have converted to Christianity. The ideological differences between the traditional faith (*kev cai qub*) and the new faith (*kev cai tshiab*) have torn families and communities apart. This is a new development in the Hmong world that would have been unimaginable less than a century ago.

There is no documentation that Hmong people have ever gone to war for religious reasons. Religion is a private matter for Hmong people. We do not impose our religion on others. We also do not dispute the existence of other religions and the power of their supreme beings. In fact, Hmong are quite open to other religious faiths.

Hmong religion bears heavy influences from Confucianism in China, Buddhism in Southeast Asia and Christianity in the West. Great and different influences have molded our religious practices. At its core, Hmong religion is unique and there is no written documentation of its ancient beginnings. It is an amazing thread that has allowed Hmong religion to survive for thousands of years. There is a common foundation that has not shifted through the ages — the practice of ancestor worship, though I have witnessed changes during my own generation.

Religion is sacred, and we keep it among ourselves. Hmong people feel strongly about personal beliefs. In fact, it is quite difficult for Hmong to just adopt each other's religious rituals even if they share the same last name. A person of a different ethnicity will find it very difficult, if not impossible, to pick up Hmong religion and its practices. This may sound awkward, but it is the reality of ancestral worship. The worshipped ancestors are unique to each individual family.

Hmong do not preach or hold public debates on religious matters, but we often discuss it amongst ourselves in order to find kinship. If two strangers with the same last name should find that their religious rites are performed similarly, they can immediately conclude that they have the same family roots. They can call each other brothers or sisters because they are said to "have common ancestral spirits" (*thooj dab koom qhua*). Religion is not only a means to connect people with the supernatural world, but it helps to reconnect lost relatives in the natural world.

Hmong religion does not revolve solely around ancestral spirits. We believe that there are spirits all around us. The single most descriptive term to define Hmong religion is animism — the belief that natural objects and phenomena have souls that exist apart from their physical bodies. Although the most revered spiritual entities are the souls of the ones who truly gave us life, our parents, animism welcomes the blessing of other righteous spiritual deities. Be it God, Buddha, Confucius, or Allah, Hmong people acknowledge their existence and power. It is common for a Hmong person with traditional beliefs to seek out the divine intervention of a Buddhist monk or Catholic priest. We believe that all righteous deities are saviors, and they will not fault a virtuous person. This is part of the reason it is quite easy for Hmong to convert to Christianity.

Like other religions, we acknowledge a righteous, supreme, supernatural being in Hmong religion. The one who holds the ultimate divine power in the Hmong world is Heaven (*lub ntuj*). Its literal translation is "the sky." The way Hmong people speak of Heaven is that it is not a being, but is more like a place, referred to much like a thing. It is like a place because supernatural beings dwell in it. It is a being in that it can hear, feel, see and instruct. The sky includes all the spaces above ground beyond what the eyes can see. It has authority over all good and evil beings in both the natural and supernatural worlds. Heaven is virtuous, righteous and impartial yet it is not something Hmong people worship. Hmong either respect it or fear it. Its unscriptured divine rules are to be followed strictly. Violators will face swift and stiff punishments. The sky is accessible to any and every one — believers and non-believers alike. A divine intervention can come in the form of miraculous and unexplainable occurrences from this authority.

Heaven covers the Earth (*nriaj teb*) much like a roof covers a house. Heaven and Earth came into being simultaneously. How Heaven and Earth came about is not clear. Legend has it that the Green Lady or Gao Jua (*Nkauj Ntsuab*) and the Rodent Man or Dhao Na (*Nraug Nas*) wove the Earth and Heaven. However, wedding and funeral rituals demonstrate that Earth and Heaven formed by themselves out of nowhere. There is no consensus on the creation of Heaven and Earth.

At the beginning, there was a virtuous being named Shao (*Saub*). He was a man, but he possessed great powers. He held the power to create life according to shamans (*puj saub siv yis tsim noob neej*). In wedding rites, Shao is said to have had the power to stabilize the extreme turbulence in the world when it was first created. He knew everything, and he could foretell the future. He was a savior of the human race.

Legend has it that all living creatures and supernatural beings were created at the same time. One thing that is consistent in all facets of the Hmong culture is that in the beginning, the natural world and the supernatural world were but the same. Supernatural beings and living creatures co-existed on Earth and they could interact with each other. Only when conflicts arose did Shao separate the supernatural from the natural, making the supernatural world and its beings invisible to humans. The spirits, however, can see the living. Despite the separation, the natural and super-natural can still affect each other. Humans, for example, can unknowingly cause harm to supernatural beings. Supernatural beings, on the other hand, can do anything they want to natural creatures. Hmong people believe that spirits can see and humans are blind in the supernatural realm.

There are many ways supernatural beings can cause harm to people. When a human inadvertently violates a spirit's personal space or bumps into a spirit, she can cause distress or harm to the spirit. In return, the spirit can cause pain or sickness for that person. An evil spirit, on the other hand, can just seize the soul of a perfectly innocent individual, causing her to become ill. In other words, evil spirits prey on vulnerable human souls. Any encounter with the supernatural needs to be rectified; if it is not, the condition can become grave, and it can lead to death.

Heaven is relentless and unforgiving in its pursuit of righteousness. Wrongdoers are destined for stiff punishment. The fine line between right and wrong is determined by Heaven. It reigns supreme over everything and everyone in both worlds. Forces of good and evil are confined to its divine rules. When injustice is done and it is beyond human beings' ability to resolve it, the sky can be called upon to bring justice, because Heaven is all-knowing. In the case of an unresolved murder, a relative of the victim can burn a bundle of incense and bunches of spiritual papers for the soul of the victim. At the same time, the family can call to Heaven to help bring justice. Justice, then, is at the mercy of Heaven, and it will prevail. The murderer will be punished. Heaven's punishment can range from physical or emotional suffering to death. Hmong believe that Heaven's punishment does not end with death. The soul can also be subjected to consequences in the afterworld. If that is not enough, one will have to endure a harsh life in the next life when being reincarnated to the natural world. Thus people who have miserable lives would often say, "I must have done something bad in my first life, and now I am paying for it in this life." Individuals who are born with abnormalities often accept their fate as a punishment stemming from previous lives.

Heaven is wide and broad. It can see, hear and notice everything that goes on underneath it. Even when there are no witnesses to an evil act,

Heaven still knows about it. Hence, Hmong always say, "Heaven is above, Heaven sees" (*ntuj nyob saud ntuj pom*). So, to the ordinary Hmong, Heaven is to be feared. Heaven's laws are, for the most part, common sense. People with high moral and ethical values are respectful of Heaven. Evildoers are fearful of the long hands of Heaven. Below are examples of what constitute unethical deeds a person or spirit should not do:

1. steal, rob or commit extortion
2. take a life without justification
3. (a man) be intimate with a married woman
4. (a woman) commit adultery
5. physically or mentally torture a living being (be it animal or human)
6. disrespect or mistreat older siblings, parents, elders, or handicapped people
7. violate the personal space or properties of supernatural beings
8. (weaned children and adults) ingest a woman's breast milk
9. purposely destroy valuable property such as a house or crop
10. cast an evil spell on or harm innocent and defenseless people
11. dare Heaven
12. lie to cause harm or pain to others.

These are just some of the immoral things people can do. It is not coincidental that some of them sound like the Ten Commandments, for many moral and ethical values are universal.

Certain Heavenly laws conflict with modern-day societal laws, especially in the West. Hmong believe that all living creatures can be consumed by living beings for the purpose of sustaining life — a human being can kill any living being, except other humans, for the purpose of consumption. A person may slaughter as many cattle as he can possibly eat, but no more than that. If he can eat only one cow, than he must kill only one cow. At the slaughterhouse, however, a man might slaughter thousands of cattle and not eat them himself. This, according to Hmong belief, is unethical. In today's civilized society, pets are not meant for human consumption and adultery is not punishable by law. These, among other things, are contradictory to Hmong beliefs, and make it difficult for Hmong people to adjust in the Western world. This is one of the reasons why Hmong people have such a hard time abiding by all the laws in the United States. Even so, Hmong consider themselves just and ethical people.

Heaven and its divine laws are simple to comprehend, but the structure is rather complicated to visualize. According to shamans, the spirits of the sky (*dab ntuj*) exist at different levels and in different parts of Heaven in a hierarchical fashion. Both virtuous beings and opportunists dwell in this same sky. Starting with the virtuous spirits, there are the spirits of the four corners of the earth (*xwm fab puaj meem tuam thawj zeej, xab fab xwm meem tuam ncws zeej*). These are the spirits that hold the sky in place. Higher up in the sky dwells the spirit of lightning or Thor (*yawm xob*), the Pleiades constellation (*txhiaj txiv mim*), and the ruler of the sky (*faj tim txij kuj nyab txaim los yog huab tais ntuj*). Somewhere toward the top of the sky is the originator of life (*nkauj kab yeeb tsim noob neej*). The realm of shamanism is also up toward the top where the shaman supreme spirit (*txoov vaj neeb*) resides. In another part of Heaven lies the realm of the spirits of the dead or ancestors (*poj yawm txwv txoob*). Such is how Hmong envision the structure of Heaven.

In Heaven there are also evil spirits. Most notorious is Thurnyong (*ntxwg nyoog*). He is the originator of all evil. According to legend, Thurnyong's wife gave birth to all the evil forces in both the natural and supernatural worlds. Then, there are the lesser of the evil dwellers of the sky such as the spirits of the hands and feet of the sun (*dab hnub tes hnub taws*), the spirits that consume the sun and the moon (*dab noj hnub noj hli*), the wind of death (*moj lwg kaw cua*) and others. These evil spirits can affect humans and make them sick if humans come in contact with them.

It is believed that there are nine levels of Heaven (*cuaj tshooj ntug*), and spirits roam at every level. The human soul can wander into any and all realms of Heaven including the land of the ancestors. Somewhere up there in Heaven lives the immortal savior of all living things Hmong refer to as Shao (*Saub*). Legend has it that at one time Heaven was very close to Earth, and Shao was among all the living creatures so any living creature in distress could go seek out Shao, for he had answers to everything and for everybody. For various reasons, Heaven distanced itself from Earth, and Shao went with it. This means we can no longer visit him. Nowadays, the only way to reach Shao is via the messenger shee yee or the shaman (*siv yis neeb*). A person who claims to have psychic power is often referred to as "Shao." A shaman who is innovative is referred to as being Shao (*ua saub*). Shao is just one of many spirits that dwell in the nine realms of Heaven.

It is rather difficult to have a holistic understanding of Hmong religion, because we don't have a bible or a supreme holy priest. Furthermore, there are no temples or churches where religious services and teaching are carried out on a regular basis. For the most part, individuals are left to discover it for themselves. More specifically, every Hmong home is a shrine. All spiritual functions center around the house. There are house spirits (*dab vaj dab tsev*) that dwell in major parts of the house. So where are the spirits inside the house? Knowing what a typical Hmong house looks like would help in this case, because the most important aspects of Hmong belief are in plain sight inside a traditional Hmong home.

Figure 7.1 is a frontal view of a typical Hmong house. In the case of some mountain dwellers, the foundation of the house may be leveled, but a house is usually built on uneven ground. The left side is on the upside

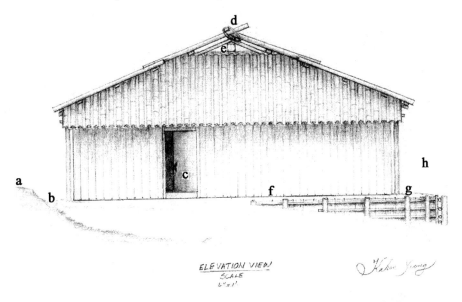

Figure 7.1: The Frontal view of a typical Hmong house. (a) upside (*qaum tsev*) (b) house drainage ditch (*kwj tse*) (c) front door (*qhov rooj txuas*) (d) the crest of the house (*ru tsev*) (e) ventilation (*qhov muag tsev*) (f) side porch (*mom kaum*) (g) rear porch (*qab khav*) (h) lower side (*qab tsev los sis qab tsib taug*).

and the right is on the lower side of the house, which is always toward the lower part of a hillside. The front door is always on the side.

The front of the house is where most of the daily activities are carried out. The front entrance or front door (*qhov rooj txuas*) is the most common entry into the house, though it is not considered the main door. A guardian spirit protects the front door and guards against evil spirits entering the house. It also keeps the souls of the dwellers inside the house from leaving the house without their host's body.

Figure 7.2 shows a cross-section of a typical Hmong house with an inside view from the far end of the house. This is a view of the kitchen and living areas of the house with the front door in the far wall. The fireplace and the oven have guardian spirits (*dab qhov cub qhov txos*). The main cross beam (*nqaj nthab*) runs horizontally across and through the middle of the house. This is where all the ancestors (*dab niam dab txiv*) dwell. The main post at the center of the house, ending pillar (*ncej tas*), holds great significance in Hmong religion. There is a guardian spirit that dwells here. It is believed that when this post is cut down the whole house crumbles. When this guardian spirit is toppled, all the other domestic spir-

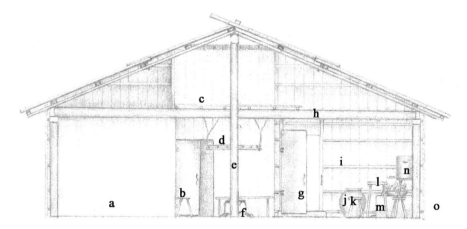

Figure 7.2: Cross-sectional view from the far end of a traditional Hmong house. (a) bedroom (*txaj*) (b) sitting bench (*qab txiag*) (c) dry storage (*nthab*) (d) drying rack (*tsuav ntxaij*) (e) central pillar or ending pillar (*ncej tas*) (f) fire place (*qhov cub*) (g) front door (*qhov rooj txuas*) (h) main cross beam (*nqaj nthab*) (i) kitchen storage racks (*txee*) (j) water storage jar (*hub rau dej*) (k) dining bench (*tog noj mov*) (l) dining table (*rooj noj mov*) (m) wood oven (*qhov txos*) (n) rice steamer (*tsu cub mov*) (o) upside of the house (*qaum tsev*).

its are thrown into disarray. This is where the drum of death is hung during funeral services.

Also in this figure are tables and benches for sitting and dining. The shelves on the wall are for storage of pots and pans and utensils. There are no bathrooms or closets, and the floor is usually bare dirt.

From the fireplace to the rice mortar is open space as illustrated in Figure 7.3. This area is a multipurpose room. All affairs that require space or a gathering of people take place here. The religious altars are placed against the wall on the upside. There are several different types of altars. The rice mortar is also an object with spiritual significance (*dab qhov cos*). The guest bed is usually used for storage of equipment when not being used so it is usually left bare. In large families, the guest bed is turned into a bedroom to accommodate members of the family. The crest pillar and far beam are almost identical to the central pillar except they are on the far end of the house. This pillar and beam do not hold religious significance as they provide structural support only.

From the top view in Figure 7.4, the floor plan clearly indicates where everything is located relative to each other. The main cross beam is next to the central pillar (#8), but it is drawn slightly off to the right to show the location of the post, which is centrally located. The rooms surrounding the fireplace are bedrooms. The box on the lower right is a guest bed (*txaj qhuas*). If the house is big enough, the rice mortar is set up inside the

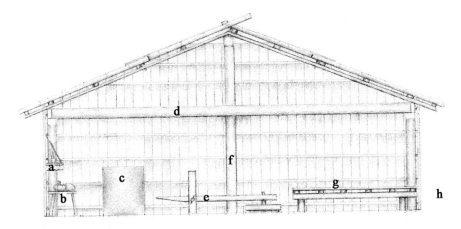

Figure 7.3: (a) altar (*thaj*) (b) work table (*rooj ua num*) (c) storage basket (*phawv*) (d) far beam (*nqaj tse*) (e) rice mortar (*cos*) (f) crest pillar (*ncej ru*) (g) guest bed (*txaj qhuas*) (h) lower side (*qab tsib taug*).

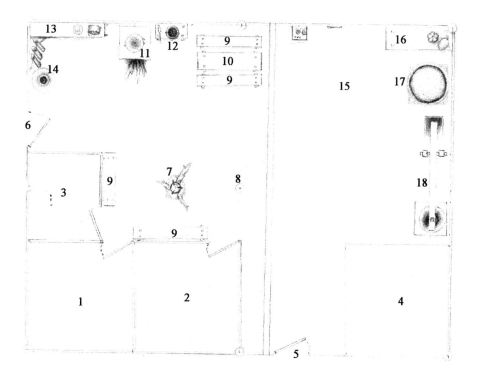

Figure 7.4: Floor Plan of a Typical Hmong House. (1) master bedroom (*txaj loj*) (2) bedroom (*txaj*) (3) bedroom (*txaj*) (4) guest bed (*txaj qhuas*) (5) main door (*qhov rooj tag*) (6) front door (*qhov rooj txuas*) (7) fireplace (*qhov cub*) (8) central pillar (*ncej tas*) (9) sitting bench (*qab txiag*) (10) dining table (*rooj noj mov*) (11) wood oven (*qhov txos*) (12) rice steamer (*tsu cub mov*) (13) kitchen storage racks (*txee*) (14) water storage jar (*hub rau dej*) (15) open area (*tas los sis hauv plag*) (16) working table (*rooj ua num*) (17) storage basket (*phawv*) (18) rice mortar (*cos*).

house; if not, it can be set up outside. The top right corner is usually for temporary storage of field materials such as animal feed. On the bottom wall there is a door. This is the main door (*qhov rooj tag*). The literal translation is "final door" or "ending door." This is the door that holds spiritual significance. The spiritual guardian here is called tsiameng (*txhiaj meej*). This is the guardian of reputation. The middle section of the wall toward the top is where all the altars are located. There are different types of altars. Each family must have either sheng kha (*seej khab*) or suka (*xwm kab*). Sheng kha is an altar with a small bowl filled with rice or corn to hold incense. Suka is a paper with a thin gold or silver lining and a bundle of papers. Additionally, there is an altar for the shaman spirits if there is a shaman in the house. The shaman altar is larger, and it has threads connecting the altar to the top of the main door. Another altar can be set up for kher kong (*khawv koob*), the spirits of healing. Another common altar is called yuva (*yum vaj*) or dachua (*dab tshuaj*) and is for the spirits of medicine. There can be one to six different altars hanging on the wall of any household. As the saying goes, each takes its rightful place in the house. Together, they are called domestic spirits (*dab nyeg*). The ancestor spirits are called parent and grandparent spirits (*dab niam dab txiv poj yawm txwv koob*). The rest of the domestic spirits are called house spirits (*dab vaj dab tsev*).

These domestic spirits are worshiped in different ways and at different times. They are all renewed on an annual basis during the New Year ceremony. The details on how each is worshipped also vary from family to family and from clan to clan, but the name and the basic principles of the religious functions are the same.

There are different types of rituals honoring the ancestors. These rituals bear the same names for all Hmong people; however, the way they are carried out varies from one family to another. It is the nature of these ancestor worshipping rituals that defines Hmong religious conviction. These rituals include niuda (*nyuj dab*), dathong (*dab roog*), buathai (*npua tai*), bualong (*npua loog or npua laus*), and laida (*laig dab*), which is more commonly known as wall splatter (*ntov phab ntsa*). These are usually conducted by the religious leader of each extended family, except for dathong and laida. For these rituals, a domestic animal is usually offered to the spirits. The animal is slaughtered and the meat is cooked. The cooked meat is offered to the ancestors. Ultimately, the meat of the slaughtered animal is turned into a feast for family and friends. It is the process and the names of the ancestors that define the differences among various families. During these rituals, attendees are to speak only Hmong, and they are not to eat any of the ceremonial meat until the rituals are completed. As a rule of thumb, when attending Hmong religious functions, avoid eating any food until the elders tell everybody to eat.

Each ritual carries a slightly different significance. The way each is carried out and why it is performed also varies. Niuda is a ritual directed at the spirit of the father or mother of the oldest male member of a family. If a member of a family is sick, and if it is determined that a niuda needs to be done, that ritual is carried out. Another situation that warrants such a ritual can occur when there is a grave situation in the family. Then the ancestor is called on to provide spiritual support or guidance. In such a case, a niuda will have to be done when the situation improves. A niuda is an offering of a bull to the ancestor in thanks for his or her divine intervention.

Bualao or bualuong is the ritual where the oldest male member of the family performs for the spirits of the grandparents. The conditions calling for this ritual differ from clan to clan. In the Cha clan, when a member of the family has a litter of piglets with one of them having a white stripe completely encircling the mid-section of its body, it is the sign for bualao. Generally, the said piglet is raised to maturity and it is used in the ritual. The ritual is usually performed by the clan religious leader. Usually this ritual requires the pretend playing of an artificial bamboo reed pipe (*qeej plhaub mag*) and beating a fake drum. Then the pig is offered to either the grandmother or grandfather and is slaughtered. The meat and internal organs are boiled and set in a row of 13 plates laid in a straight line across the middle of the house. The religious leader calls to the spirits to dine. In religious rituals liquor is offered first as a courtesy. Once the offerings are completed everybody eats, and that concludes the ritual.

Laida is performed more commonly and frequently. This is merely a call to the ancestors to join a feast or a food that is significant. Laida is often carried out during weddings, the celebration of a newborn, new crop, New Year and more. This ritual takes place when the food is prepared and right before it is served. Meat that is used for laida has to be boiled in water without any vegetables. A bowl of rice and a bowl of meat are placed at the dining table. Several spoons are placed in the bowl of rice. Chairs are placed around the table, and the male head of the household or the religious leader calls the ancestors and the house spirits to dine. To conclude, a spoon of rice and meat along with a cup of wine are taken outside and offered to the spirits of surrounding land features, such as the guardian of the town and the spirits of the mountains and rivers. Laida is a practice that every man has to know how to do.

The key to religious rituals in the Hmong world is consistency. Each type of ritual has to be performed the same way every time. Rituals of this nature include niuda, bualong, suka, xiameng and laida. These rituals form the core of Hmong religion, and they are commonly practiced on a regular basis, though from family to family and clan to clan the details and language differ slightly. The rituals are common practices across all sectors of Hmong society except among those who have converted to Western beliefs.

When these rituals are performed properly, the spirits will protect the souls of the living. They will also protect the reputation, luck, wealth and health of family members. If ignored, these guardian spirits will not protect the family. They can also barter the soul of a family member to evil spirits, making that person become sick. In essence, religious rituals are beneficial when the practice is consistent with tradition. In other words, religious rituals are to be performed the same way the forefathers have done. If the procedures are changed or the spirits are neglected, it is considered a violation of religious rites. When that happens, the spirits a man worships can work against him.

Every Hmong man has to perform certain religious rituals. Minimally, a man must be able to call the soul (*hu plig*), conduct suka rites (*txi xwm kab*), tsameng (*tsa txhiaj meej*), and laida (*laig dab*). The rest are to be performed by the religious leader or a shaman when it is deemed necessary. Each clan can have only one religious leader. A religious leader is often carefully chosen by a predecessor. As a Hmong man, however, one has to know certain things.

The religious leader is referred to as the spirit father (*txiv dab*). He is like the clan's spokesperson to the ancestors—the equivalent of a priest. All members of the same clan in the same town or village who have a common ancestor have only one religious leader. There are many reasons why there is only one. The primary reason is for the clan to maintain religious consistency. Too many spiritual leaders will increase the chances of the rituals being changed over time. When there is only one spiritual leader, it creates a family interdependency. The whole family remains together because everybody depends on just one person to perform the important religious rituals.

The spiritual leader is responsible for several rituals. He presides over niuda, buathai, datuong and laida. When there is a religious decision to be made for the good of the clan, he has the final say. He is also responsible for passing on the religious knowledge and family history to the next generation. For the most part, the religious leader of the clan is responsible for the religious functions that involve the domestic spirits (*dab nyeg*)—the spirits inside the house. Outside the house, however, it is a different story.

Outside the walls of the house are permanent fixtures that are a part of typical Hmong dwellings. These features relate to the traditional agrarian life style of Hmong people. Though geographical features have religious implications, not all are significant. Knowing the spiritual significance of the various physical features found in nature allows a person to have a greater understanding of the Hmong spiritual world. From just outside the walls of the house to the wilderness, there are important features of great spiritual significance.

Areas surrounding the house include walking paths, animal shelters, storage sheds and play areas. These are places where people can fall or be frightened and suffer injuries that can have grave spiritual consequences to the soul. These areas are places a shaman would address during rituals. For example, a child could slip and fall in the chicken coop and have his soul become lodged in the ground. The shaman would have to go to the chicken coop and recover the child's soul. Then, through a ritual, the soul would be reunited with the child's physical being. Therefore, keeping the area surrounding the house clean and hazard free is spiritually sound.

Beyond the immediate vicinity of the house, there are trails, roads, bushes, swamps, rivers, lakes, mountains, fields, and other natural land features where the wild spirits (*dab qus*) dwell. Smaller natural objects such as trees, ant hills and boulders can also have spirits living in them. These spirits live among us as we conduct our daily activities. They are not necessarily evil, but when their personal spaces are violated or they are disrespected, they can cause the violator harm. The violator's soul will be seized, and the person becomes ill.

Hmong people believe that in order for human beings to live in harmony with wild spirits, we must first be acquainted with one of them. Therefore, a spirit of a certain natural landmark is chosen to be honored as the village or town's spiritual guardian. This is like forming an alliance with a wild spirit. A large tree or a huge boulder, for example, can be selected to watch over a village as the guardian, or originator, of the village (*xeeb zos*). There is a process to selecting and honoring a guardian spirit. Furthermore, all the religious leaders of the town or village have to agree because once a year it must be visited and offered spirit papers and a chicken or pig. Such a guardian spirit will protect the people from other wild spirits.

Hmong people have names for the various spirits of the wild: the rulers of the land (*peev nom peev tswv peev teb peev chaw*); spirits who guard the land and animals in the wild on the surface and just above the surface of the land (*sab vaj thwv xeeb*); and guardian spirits from beneath the surface of the land and in the water (*looj vaj thwv tim*). These are the caretakers who tend to the land, mountains, bodies of water and all the creatures in the wild. They are like the owners of the land and animals. These are spirits that human beings need to treat with courtesy. If respected, they are good spirits. If disrespected, they can be evil. When Hmong travel to new territories in the wild and eat, we always invite the spirits of the land and water to eat with us. A pinch of rice and a piece of meat in a spoon is placed on a log or rock, and these guardian spirits are called to come eat. When Hmong people go hunting and shoot a game animal, we also burn spirit papers and offer food to honor these spirits. These rituals are meant to please the spirits in the hope they will protect us. These spirits may be virtuous, but they can be detrimental if humans disrespect them.

In the wild, there are also spirits that are naturally evil, and humans should avoid them altogether. Evil spirits include spirits of the grave (*dab toj ntxas*) and wanderers of the spirit world (*txawv yaj txawv yeeb*). There are many dwellers of permanent land forms, such as the water dragon (*looj seej looj ki los yog dab ntxaug zaj*), which can dwell in any large body of water including large ponds, lakes, deep river channels, and the ocean. Other evil spirits dwell in swamps and springs (*looj tswb looj seej*). The most notorious of them all are family-oriented spirits that oftentimes appear in the form of rats. They are called zao spirits (*dab ntxaug*).

There are evil spirits that are always on the prowl for vulnerable women. These are called sesheng sekui (*xej seej xej ki*) and must be avoided altogether. These are lonesome spirits that are out to court potential mates from the human realm. A similar group of evil spirits is called mong sheng mong kui (*mooj seej moon ki*), and they try to control people's minds. People who are affected by mong sheng mong kui will lose their minds and become delusional.

These are just some of the spirits with names derived from the Chinese language. Oftentimes, ordinary people will hear them being mentioned in a shaman's rituals without knowing their significance. Shamans, however, have to know these spirits by name to be able to communicate with them, for they are evil spirits who will seize the souls of people who are spiritually vulnerable.

There are also ghostly figures whose names are more familiar to the average person. These are dwellers of the wilderness such as the shape shifter Hmong call pawzong (*poj ntxoog*). Hmong believe that pawzongs provide supernatural protection to white tigers. Hmong people usually envision pawzong in the form of a small girl with long hair, fully clothed. People have made claims of having shot and killed pawzong that have taken the form of foul smelling cats or weasels. Another powerful evil spirit in this group is called pinyouvai (*phis nyum vais*). The name comes from the Laotian name meaning fast-lifting evil spirit. Evidently, once it has been disturbed in the wild it will make a lot of noise but will rarely show itself. Sometimes pinyouvai can cause physical harm or death to human beings. These are just some of the more notable evildoers Hmong have come to believe in.

Spirits have supernatural powers that can hurt or kill human beings. Human beings, on the other hand, have the power to produce material goods and spirit money. The value of the papers depends on how they are stamped and cut. Different occasions call for different types of paper to be used. Spirit money is paper cut into specific shapes and offered to the spirits. When these papers are burned, the fumes become money in the spirit world.

There are five basic types of spiritual papers. Satheng (*xav txheej*) are the rectangular papers cut into stacks and punctured to form circular emblems. These are used universally, for all occasions. The only problem is that they are not worth much. They are like United States coins in real life. The second type of spiritual paper is a paper bundle (*ntawv ntshua*). The bundles have three or four folds strung into a bundle with three leaves each.

The bundles are normally used in religious ceremonies and are valued as real money. They can be used to settle debts with both evil and virtuous spirits. The third type of papers is called the death paper bundle (*ntshua ntawv tuag*). The death paper bundle is burned strictly at a funeral as an offering to the soul of the dead. This type of paper is made of many layers stamped and cut into many folds. Still another type of paper is burned to release the soul of the dead. This is called paper to release the soul (*ntawv tso plig*). These are burned during the second stage of funeral services — during what is called the soul-release ceremony. These are carefully cut into many connecting hoops. The last type of spirit papers are the ones resembling a boat. These are yakao chengkao (*yaj khaum ceeb khaum*). The fumes of yakao chengkao, Hmong believe, turn into silver and gold bars in the spirit world. They can be used in any and every ritual from shaman rituals to funeral rituals. The paper has to be layered with a silver or gold coating as a reflection of how Hmong people value silver and gold.

Top: Yakao chengkao (*yaj khaum ceeb khaum*). *Bottom:* A death paper bundle. This is a completed bundle that, when lifted, it extends to about five feet long, with many leaves and shapes dangling.

Spiritual papers are usually made from natural fibers. Hmong used to make these papers from tree bark or young and tender bamboo trees. In today's world, however, these papers are commercially produced and sold in stores. In using these papers, there are certain unspoken norms or clichés that Hmong strongly believe. The most important of all is that spiritual papers cannot be made and burned without a legitimate reason. When a lot of papers are burned without dedication to a specific spirit, the papers in the spirit world have no owner and so they will seek closure or restitution from the person who burned the papers to begin with. The consequences are usually severe. Additionally, these papers have to be made properly. Otherwise, they will be worthless — much like counterfeit money in the real world. Another belief is that spiritual papers cannot be made and left unused. The paper itself can be made, but to stamp and cut it into form is not acceptable. It is believed that having lots of spirit paper lying around will prompt a need to use it. Spirit papers play a special role in Hmong religion in that they serve as legal tender in the spirit world. Spirits are believed to have the capacity to spend money like humans do. That is why when a person dies, Hmong people burn a lot of spirit papers for his or her soul.

What is a soul? A soul (*plig*) is the spirit that lives in the body to keep the body alive. It is like an invisible body double that resides in the body. As a spirit, it is immortal. The soul can detach itself from the body both voluntarily and involuntarily. The soul has a mind of its own, and it can be influenced by the host body, other people and external forces. The soul of a young girl will be sad when her parents do something to show that they do not love her. An example of such action is when they purposely lock her out of the house. Her soul gets depressed and the girl is said to experience a shy plee (*sais plig*). As a result, her soul will wander off and the girl will become withdrawn. If this drags on, she will become ill. Henceforth, the soul is perhaps the most delicate element of Hmong spirituality.

Hmong people believe that every living creature has a soul. Every sizeable object that bears a shadow has a soul too. The soul is delicate and vulnerable. A human being, though, has three main souls called plee (*plig*) and many lesser souls called ju (*ntsuj*). Some of the lesser souls are closely associated with different parts of the body. The majority exist in the form of other organisms in the spirit world, along with the ancestors. They all need to be in the proper place for the body to maintain homeostasis. When a soul is out of place or harmed, the physical being becomes sick.

The soul is immortal. It can re-associate itself or be reincarnated into another host body. The new host body need not be a human or animal. A soul can reincarnate into any living being. When a soul has entered the body of a fetus, the host body becomes ill. The moment the new host body is born, the former host body perishes.

Ju (lesser souls) do not get reincarnated. They just become lost when the host body perishes, like domestic animals when their owner is gone.

The exact number of Ju a human has varies according to different shamans' interpretations. According to Kou Chai Vue, a well-respected shaman in Sacramento, California, there are 12 ju mainly associated with the different body parts. Kou Shue Cha, my father, believes that a human being has 32 ju. Shamans refer to ju as different living organisms or common real objects in their practice. This will be discussed in the section under shaman. If a ju is out of place, that part of the body becomes weakened and the whole body becomes ill. When all the ju are in their proper places, the body is well.

Closely tied to the body are three souls or plee (*peb tug ntsuj peb tug plig*) and several ju that are essential for the body to be alive. The souls do not reside in a particular part of the body. As for the ju that are closely associated with the body, they remain attached to the body. These ju include our shadows (*ntsuj duab ntsuj hlauv*), ju of the hands and feet (*ntsuj tes ntsuj taw*), ju of the body (*ntsuj xub zeb hlauv xub ntoos*) and so on. These are the more important spirits of a person and the core of Hmong belief. When a person is still alive these souls are indistinguishable from each other. When a person dies, his soul parts from the body. One of them becomes the ghost or guardian of the grave. Another one returns to the land of the ancestors and it is the one to be worshipped. The third soul gets reincarnated.

A host of different mishaps can befall a person's soul depending on the spiritual state of the host body. The soul can be strong if the person is in good physical and spiritual health and its souls are less susceptible to harm. For a person who is not in good spiritual and physical health, the soul is vulnerable and the slightest brush with an evil force or a frightening situation will bring harm to the soul and illness to the physical being. A person can sustain a physical impact such as a fall and lose his or her soul (*poob plig*). As a result, the soul must be called to reunite with the body immediately. When the soul becomes separated for a long period of time, it becomes lodged in the ground (*zwm luaj zwm av*) — a literal translation. This really means that the soul has sought out a new host body in the vicinity of detachment. When this happens, the soul will be difficult to retrieve. So when a soul is separated from the host body, it is very important that the soul be called to reunite right away.

There are many ways the soul can be reunited with its host body. When a woman gets into a car accident, for example, her soul can detach itself during impact. It would not be able to come back to her body on its own. She cannot do it herself either. Someone else has to call her soul (*hu plig*) and reunite it with her body with a simple ritual of scraping and calling to the effect. If this is not done right away, the woman can become more frail or sick. In this case, a shaman has to go directly to the physical location and call the soul to come back and reunite with the body (*hu plig qheb thwv*). At this point, a chicken, incense and spirit papers are needed to complete the ritual. If it should drag on until the woman becomes bedridden, her soul has entered another life. When that happens, only a shaman can perform a shamanistic ritual to retrieve the soul by using the soul of a pig to swap her soul (*ua neeb hloov ntsuj los sis ua neeb nqes hiav*). If none of these steps are taken and the soul gets reborn, the woman dies.

The key word to a person losing his or her soul is fright (*ntshai los sis ceeb*). A body may take a major impact, but if the person is not frightened, the soul does not become separated. An impact can be very subtle, yet when the person involved is terrified, his or her soul is likely to become detached. In most cases, Hmong people who are conscientious about these issues do the soul-calling ritual after every major incident just to be safe. My four-year-old daughter has seen enough of the ritual that she calls her own soul every time she trips and falls.

A physical impact is not the only way to lose a soul. The soul can voluntarily leave the host body. It has feelings. It can feel happiness and sadness. When it is happy, the soul stays with the body. If it becomes depressed, it can wander off. When the soul goes astray, the body becomes sick. When a soul goes as far as to find a new host body or residence, or reincarnates into another being, the host body becomes bedridden. When the new arrangement for the soul has become permanent, the host body dies. That is why spiritual intervention is important for Hmong people when a person gets sick.

In the hierarchical spiritual world, some spirits are more powerful than others. Evil spirits possess the power to prey on human souls. They will take a soul as their property, slave, or spouse. Virtuous spirits normally do not possess human souls, but when the physical being violates such spirits, they will use the soul as collateral to make the violator sick until the conflict is resolved. In any case, grave consequences await the physical being if a soul is disregarded when possessed.

In essence, a human being has multiple souls. Some are more critical to life and death than others. For this reason, the soul plays an important part in Hmong religious belief.

Another important part of Hmong religion is shamanism. Shamanism is sometimes mistaken as the Hmong religion. The truth is, shamanism is not our religion: though it plays an essential role, shamanism is not the most important aspect of Hmong spiritual belief. A shaman is like an ambassador from the real world to the spirit world. He or she travels the spiritual world as a savior (*ncig ntuj cawm seej ncig teb cawm lam*) and is therefore able to intercede on a person's behalf.

According to Hmong legend, a long time ago humans and spirits were still able to see each other, and there were a lot of conflicts between them. Human beings were constantly at war with evil spirits. As the war raged on, the two sides went to see Shao. Shao told each side to choose a substance to throw at each other. Humans picked rice hulls and the spirits chose wood ash. So they went at it. When the smoke cleared, the rice hulls did not do much damage to the spirits. The humans, on the other hand, were blinded by the ash and they could no longer see the spirits. Spirits continued to be able to see human beings and interact with human beings. Since then, the natural world and the supernatural world have been separated. The natural world that humans can still see became known as yang cheng (*yaj ceeb*). The dark realm of the spirits became ying cheng (*yeeb ceeb*). This is essentially the yin and yang of Confucianism.

Ever since then, human beings have not been able to see spirits or enter into ying cheng until death. But the war between humans and evil spirits never stopped. As the savior of all living beings, Shao gave spiritual advice and knowledge about how humans could continue to fight evil spirits. Unfortunately, Shao was overwhelmed, and he went to Heaven. Some legends say evil spirits stole his son. Others say Heaven and Earth were very close at one time, and Shao was accessible to all living beings, but Heaven distanced itself from Earth in response to the devious actions of human beings. Shao decided to go with Heaven, distancing himself from Earth beyond human's reach. In any case, when he was departing Earth, Shao cast his supernatural power back to Earth. His power landed on certain plants and those plants acquired medicinal properties. He also threw his fighting weapons back to Earth. Those who picked up his weapons continued to use them, imitating Shao's tactics of fighting evil spirits. These Shao imitators hooded themselves and called themselves Shao Shee Yee. Today, some Hmong continue to wear a cloth veil over their heads and shout "Shao Shee Yee" and chase away evil spirits. These individuals became known as shamans (*yaj saub siv* yis).

Shamanism originated in China. Hmong have practiced shamanism for many generations, though for how long is debatable as there is no record of its beginning. All shamans cover their heads and faces with a red or black cloth. They use a gong, split horn and rattlers. The gong is used to rally the spirits and empower the shaman to go into a trance. The split horn is the tool to communicate with the spirits. There are two types of rattlers. One is a doughnut-shaped, bronze rattler, which the shaman wears around his fingers. The other is a large, round iron ring with oversized flat washers on it. When a shaman performs his ritual, he carries one or more rattlers and jumps or bounces up and down on a wooden bench. He chants in a rhythmic fashion. Every shaman performs in front of an altar where the shaman spirits reside.

Shamans have great respect for each other, and they depend on one another for help (*yus khawb tsis tau yus nrob qaum*). When a shaman is sick, he cannot perform the rituals to cure himself. He has to depend on other shamans to help him. Generally, every shaman follows the same spiritual path (*cuaj tug txiv sua kaum tus txiv sua chaws ib lub dawm*). After all, they serve the same purpose with the same objective of fighting the evil forces of the supernatural world and curing the sick.

Shamans can be classified in three categories: the original or ancestral shamans (*Neeb Txwv Feej*), Shee Yee shamans (*Neeb Siv Yis*), and maid shamans (*neeb poj qhe/neeb xua nplej*). There are slight differences in the way each shaman performs, but their functions are the same. The different types of shamans can be identified by the bench they use. The bench of an ancestral shaman is knee high, short, wide, and rigid. The ancestral shaman refers to his bench, which is his mode of transportation, as a flying horse (*nees huab cuas*). A Shee Yee shaman uses a longer, narrower, and more flexible bench that is either high enough to sit on with both feet dangling or low enough to jump on and off of with ease. A Shee Yee shaman performs his ritual mainly from the bench except for occasionally hopping off and right back on. To a Shee Yee shaman his bench is an air ship (*nkoj huab nkoj cua*). That is because Shee Yee shamans came about in the early 1900s when the French brought fighter planes to Southeast Asia. A maid shaman would use just any sitting-bench. This type of shamanism is performed exclusively by women.

Maid shamanism has not been very popular and is practiced rarely. I have known only one maid shaman who passed away in 1993. Maid shamans had a humble beginning. It is said that once there was a rich family with an old female servant. The family lived in isolation, so a shaman was hard to find. When a child got sick, the family could not get any help, so the master asked if the maid knew how to perform the shaman ritual. She said she did not know how, but she had seen it done before. The man made a deal with the maid that if she were to perform the ritual and cure the child, he would set her free. So she took him up on the offer and sure enough the child recovered. That was how maid shaman came about. Maid shamanism is similar to the traditional shaman style but sometimes the rituals are performed without a gong and metallic rattlers. It is often performed beside the fireplace, often using variations on the more traditional forms of shamanism.

In the spirit world or ying realm, there are good spirits and evil spirits. The good spirits are saviors, but sometimes they can act devilishly if impeded or violated. Evil spirits always harm the souls of living beings. When the soul of a human being falls out of place, is seized by evil spirits, wanders off, or has been harmed, the body suffers in the form of pain or illness. If left untreated, the body perishes. In any case, when a person is ill due to spiritual reasons and one shaman cannot cure it, another can. That is why when a person is gravely ill, multiple shamans are summoned to perform.

Each shaman's journey into the spiritual realm takes slightly different twists and turns depending on several factors. First of all, a shaman usually imitates his master. Secondly, a knowledgeable shaman uses what appear to be psychic and supernatural powers. Some shamans use a learned psychic ability called shaiyai (*saib yaig*). Those who do not have that knowledge will use the split horn (*kuam*) to communicate with their shaman spirits to determine the course of action. A shaman can also change course by calling upon immediate instincts. It is like a change of plan in the real world due to new information or telltale signs exhibited unexpectedly by someone or something. Usually, a shaman will evaluate the circumstances that caused the illness as well as the symptoms of the illness to figure out what is wrong spiritually.

The important part of the shaman's ritual involves his going into a trance when he enters into the spirit world and communicates with the spirits. A shaman closes his eyes and shuns all commotion in the real world. To communicate with the real world, he uses shaman language to send a message to those assisting in the ritual. In communicating with the spirits he uses paired and poetic verses. It is common for shamans to use informal

Mandarin to communicate with spirits. Usually, a shaman will introduce himself to the spirits as a mediator with credentials and good intentions. This can be summarized in a shaman's own words when dealing with spirits during a ritual:

> I am, if not a master, a disciple. I am Shao Shee Yee, who travels Heaven and Earth to resolve conflicts. I travel Heaven to heal and the Earth to rescue. The palms of my hands hold the scripts of shamanism. I settle problems in the spirit world without animosity, and I settle problems in the human world without ill will. So listen to me.
>
> (*Kuv tsis yog xib hwb twb yog thwj tim. Kuv yog yaj Saub siv yis neeb ncig ntuj tu plaub ncig teb tu ntug. Kuv ncig ntuj cawm seej ncig teb txawm lam. Qab teg tuav ntawv neeb qaum tes tuav ntawv yaig. Kuv tu yaj plaub tsis muaj tshawj, tu yeeb plaub tsis muaj chim. Yib huj yib hais*).

Before a shaman resolves a conflict between the spirits and humans, he uses these words to make clear that he is a peacemaker, and he has credentials. In cases where a shaman deals with evil spirits, he usually asks that some money be placed on the altar during the ritual. This way, while negotiating with the spirits, he can tell them that he was paid to broker a deal or to resolve the problem and he is not the parties involved.

During the ritual, a shaman describes his actions and moves his body and limbs to gesture actions. A shaman claims to possess magical power provided by his shaman spirits or spiritual subordinates (*qhua neeb*). These powers only work in the supernatural world. Some shamans admit that they cannot actually see or feel any power. Others are profoundly touched by the experience. They can feel, hear and see things happening during their performances. Many years ago, my father was doing his shaman ritual to help cure an aunt. As any shaman would normally do, he closed his eyes during the performance. He said that during the ritual he had a vision of a bright light that looked like a door opening up and a human figure going through it. He was not able to stop the image from leaving. He said when he opened his eyes the vision was gone. A few days later, my aunt passed away. Other shamans have also described countless mysterious experiences.

A shaman shakes his metal rattlers during his ritual performance as a gong is beaten rhythmically to drown out his voice. These are the tools used to accomplish certain tasks at hand and to rally the shaman spirits. The large metal loop with a series of flat, round rattlers is called shaman scissors (*txiab neeb*). This tool has many uses. It is commonly used to raise a fallen soul, ward off evil spirits and round up scattered souls. A shaman sometimes uses a sword. The sword is used to battle evil spirits. The dough-nut-sized rattlers are used, among other things, to carry the souls back to the host body. Without the proper gear, a shaman cannot perform his rit-ual.

In the spirit realm, a shaman can travel anywhere. Distance is no object. Each jump or bounce on the bench translates into huge strides in the spirit world. The supernatural world is parallel to the natural world, but for the most part it is imaginary. There are nine levels of the super-natural world. The ground level seems to resemble the floor within the perimeter of the house. A shaman's altar has threads linking the top of the altar to the top of the main door. Holding these threads together are three stocks of bamboo cut with some roots and branches intact. The first bam-boo is at the top of the altar. The second bamboo is secured to the central post of the house just underneath the roof. The third bamboo is tied to the main frame above the door on the inside of the house. From the base level, a shaman can also travel to any place on Earth. A few jumps on the wooden bench and he is there, regardless of the distance. For instance, a shaman can perform his ritual in the United States to repair damages done to an ancestral grave in Laos.

There are certain routes that shamans travel along. The path through which a shaman travels into Heaven and its nine levels follows the threads referred to as the threads of shamanism (*sab neeb*). These threads extend from the top of the altar to the tip of the main door resting on top of the bamboo stocks described earlier. The first level (*nyuj vab thawj tom*) in a shaman's supernatural realm is at the bamboo stalk on top of the shaman's altar. A second bamboo stalk tied to the central pillar represents the second level (*nyuj vab lwm tom*). The third level (*nyuj vab xab tom*) is at the door. From the third level, the shaman can travel to every corner of the spiritual world, presumably the different levels of Heaven. Beyond the third level, each shaman has his own imaginary path. The first three levels, however, are consistent for every shaman.

At the third level of Heaven, a shaman can travel to other levels and realms. There are some commonalities between shamans beyond this level. There is the path to the shaman cliff (*tsua neeb*). Another path takes them to the realm of the ancestors (*poj yawm txwv txoob*). Still another path is the path of the dead (*kev ploj kev tuag*). There is also a path to the originator of life (*niam nkauj kab yeeb tsim noob neej*). There are some consistencies among shamans, but there are some differences even in the way shamans envision the realms of Heaven. Although there is a basic understanding and visualization of what the spirit realm is like, the details are the products of individual interpretations.

For a shaman, the primary objective is to save the human soul. As mentioned earlier, each person has many ju and souls. A shaman is always pursuing one soul or another in his ritual. There is no telling which is which, but shamans associate a human ju with tree stumps and rocks (*ntsuj xub zeb hlauv xub ntoos*), snakes and frogs (*ntsuj nab ntsuj qav*), dogs and bears (*ntsuj dev ntsuj dais*), bamboo and trees (*ntsuj xyoob ntsuj ntoo*), butterflies (*ntsuj npuj npaub hlauv npuj npaim*), chickens and ducks (*ntsuj qaib ntsuj os*), deer and wildebeasts (*ntsuj nyuj cab hlauv nyuj kaus*), etc. Most of these lesser souls are associated with the different parts of the body. It is the job of a shaman to bring all these souls and ju to their proper places so the body can have peace.

Besides pursuing lost souls, a shaman seeks peace and harmony between the spirits and the physical world. A shaman reinstates the balance of spiritual health, and the physical being is able to obtain physiological well-being. In a household where evil spirits overpower the good spirits, a shaman can also assert his power to rid the house of evil spirits and empower the good spirits. When a body is possessed by an evil spirit, a shaman can purge the evil spirit. Souls that wander off or are being reincarnated into another being can also be returned to their host body by a shaman. These are just some of the tasks that a shaman is responsible for. In essence, a shaman is a spiritual healer who solves all kinds of problems in the supernatural world and between the natural and supernatural worlds.

A shaman usually resolves issues with words. In some cases, spirit papers, sticks of incense and animals are used. Spirit papers are the monetary notes of the spirit world. Incense represents tobacco as a gesture of goodwill. In more serious cases, sacrificial animals are used to help resolve the issue. There are many ways animals are used in a shaman ritual, but the main purpose is to use the souls of the animals to uplift (*txhawb*) and protect (*thaiv*) the soul of the sick person. In addition, the soul of an animal can be used to replace the possessed soul of a sick person (*hloov*). The animals commonly used are chickens, pigs, ducks, goats, cows, pigeons, and on rare occasions dogs. The use of dogs in shaman rituals has placed Hmong shamans at odds with Western laws. On many occasions, Hmong shamans have gone to jail for such practices, so in recent years shamans have adapted by using clay models or stuffed animals. The use of live farm animals has also stirred trouble over public health concerns, so many shamans resort to carcasses of animals that have been slaughtered and dressed at the slaughter house. The clean animal carcasses are brought whole into the house to be used in the shaman ritual. These are some of the adaptations that Hmong have made in the Western world. In remote parts of Southeast Asia Hmong people still perform as we have traditionally for many generations. The things shamans do to help cure the sick can be financially costly at times, but usually the primary cost is for the feast that follows the ritual rather than the ritual itself.

So how does one become a shaman? Traditionally, becoming a shaman is often not a matter of choice. Rather, it is a matter of being chosen. It also depends on ancestry. If shamanism does not run in the family, a person will never become a true shaman. If it is learned and performed without being chosen, then it is not genuine or authentic. Shaman spirits run in the family in that when a shaman passes on, his subordinate spirits (*qhua neeb*) go back to the imaginary rock walls of shaman spirits (*tsua neeb*). The spirits of the deceased are to be worshipped by the surviving sons. When the sons die, the grandsons normally do not worship the grandparents. Some people say the spirits of the grandparents come back to haunt their grandsons in the form of shaman spirits (*dab neeb los tshoj*). The grandsons or granddaughters are chosen to be shamans. Others say when the shaman dies, his shaman spirits go back to the wall of shaman spirits until the descendants of the dead shaman come of age, at which time the shaman spirits come back to those descendants. At any rate, a person usually becomes a shaman when chosen, and sometimes through learning.

When chosen, a shaman-to-be becomes sick — often without any apparent physiological ailment. He or she might dream of riding a red horse while fighting with evil people or zombies. Symptoms may include shivering, stiff jaws and shaky arms and legs. When this happens, an existing shaman can pave the way for the new shaman to discover himself and become a true shaman. No one can become a shaman independently. It has to be passed down from an existing shaman to his disciple. The disciple will imitate the chants, motions and ways of the master shaman. Even with a master shaman providing guidance, a new shaman achieves full credentials in two stages. The first stage is to practice every night to gain control of his newly acquired power, using a single-board altar that is set up for the spirits (*dai thaj*). After several years of consistent performance and after having learned everything there is to know about shamanism, he or she can prepare for an indoctrination into full shamanship. At this time, the master and the pupil will perform together to bring the rest of the shaman spirits to a multi-level altar (*tsa thaj*). Once in place, the new altar needs to remain in place for at least three years before it can be moved. The shaman spirits or subordinates live at the altar and go with the shaman during his ritual. The spirits also accompany the shaman when he is not performing, so he has his shaman spirits with him at all times.

These days, shamanism is no longer being practiced in China because Communist rules prohibit it. In Southeast Asia and the Western world, people nowadays often associate illness with physiological causes. Young people are more likely to seek out a doctor than a shaman when they become sick. Only when medical doctors fail to come to a conclusive diagnosis are shamans consulted. As a result, shamanism is being performed less frequently.

Shamans are sometimes accused of casting evil spells on people to make them sick. This used to be quite common in the Hmong world when sudden illnesses and unexplained death occurred. For example, a man can have throbbing chest pain and die within hours. Hmong often attributed that to an evil spell. It was cases such as this that have tainted the reputation and caused the death of many shamans in the past. What would make Hmong people accuse a shaman of casting an evil spell might just be a suspicion followed by a fortune-teller's confirmation. Fortune-tellers (*saib yaig*) play a big role in Hmong spiritual belief.

Predicting the future and validating the past have been integral parts of the Hmong belief system for a long time. People who claim to have psychic power are constantly being sought out to provide religious, health and personal guidance. In fact, Hmong religion is built on a belief in the efficacy of second guessing what spiritual beings are trying to communicate to the living. Both shamans and fortune-tellers do quite well at meeting these needs for Hmong people.

The most prevalent tool in fortune-telling is the chicken. A chicken is certainly a guiding light for Hmong. Hmong people believe that a chicken knows everything. Be it personal well-being, impending death, or safe travel, a chicken can foretell the future quite reliably. How it works is very simple, but the chicken has to be young, for older chickens have feet that are too rigid. A chicken the size of a pigeon is ideal. Before the chicken is slaughtered, a lit stick of incense is swirled over the chicken's head. At the same time, the chicken is told what the problem is and what kind of answer is being sought. Then the chicken is slaughtered, dressed and boiled with the head and feet intact. As the chicken is being cooked, the feet are kept from touching any part of the pot that it is being boiled in. When the chicken is half-cooked, it is taken out to be read. The feet, the tongue, skull and thigh bones are the commonly read parts of a chicken. These parts of a chicken hold clues for things to come.

The signs in these parts of the chicken can be quite evident if the reader knows what he is looking for. How the chicken's toes come together is an indicator of how things will unfold in the future. The feet can show both positive and negative things that will happen. Different people may have slightly different ways of interpreting the signs on chicken parts but there are some commonalities.

It is a universal belief that the left side of a chicken pertains to the males of the family whereas the right side refers to the females. These are indications of the respective sides of the families. Furthermore, a male animal refers to the female side of the family and a female refers to the male. This is usually the case when a pair of chickens, normally a pullet and a cockerel, is being used. As an example, during New Year ceremonies a pullet and a cockerel are usually used to call the souls of the family. Any positive or negative signs that show up on the cockerel pertain to the mother and daughters of the family as well as relatives of the mother. Likewise, signs on the pullet pertain to the sons and husband as well as his side of the family.

Boiled chicken feet are most commonly inspected. There are some basic signs to look for when reading chicken feet. When the toes of a chicken are curled up and pinched together excessively, there is sadness in the family or the person in question is depressed. If the toes spread apart in different directions like open eagle claws, a death in the family is imminent. A good sign is when the toes curl up nicely together.

Interpretations of chicken feet are aligned with certain circumstances and occasions. During a wedding, the feet of the ceremonial chickens may show signs of compatibility between the bride and the groom. During New Years, chicken feet are great indicators of how things will be in the coming year. During a soul-calling ritual (*hu plig*), the chickens' feet show whether or not the soul is happy and if it has been reunited with the host body. Chicken-feet interpretation is an integral part of our belief system.

What the chicken feet show may not be definitive. If the chicken feet provide mixed messages, the tongue and skull are taken out and inspected. The skull of a young chicken is easily popped off. As it is detached from the head, it will split into mirror-image halves. When the halves are held next to each other, the skull should be clear to almost transparent. In the middle where the two halves come together, dark black spots are indicative of troubles ahead. The left side of the skull pertains to the husband's side of the family and the right side pertains to the wife's side of the family. If a dark spot appears in the middle between the two halves, something bad will happen to a member of the immediate family.

The tongue is commonly read during soul-calling ceremonies. When the tongue is pulled out, two narrow and round cartilaginous extensions are drawn out. These extensions diverge from the tip of the tongue. There is a short pointy spike between them. When the tongue is held upside down, the extension will take the shape of a "V" and the spike will stand erect between them. If the spike stands straight up and the end of the extensions curl in in unison, the soul is said to have come back and united with the host body. On the other hand, when the extensions bend in different directions, the news is negative in nature.

The thigh bones of a chicken are rarely used, but they can be a strong indication of potential negative occurrences within the family. At the middle of every thigh bone, there are usually one or two black dots. If the two dots line up along the length of the bone then there is nothing to worry about. The two dots lining up perpendicularly to the length of the bone means an eventful future awaits. Sometimes, there is only one dot on each thigh bone, and it does not mean anything.

Though a person may not want to live with a constant indicator or reminder of things that can potentially happen, every now and then curiosity gets the best of us and we do look at chicken parts with piercing eyes and wonder if something good or bad is about to happen. That is what being Hmong is all about. Then again, some people have no idea what to look for in a chicken, and they may seek out professional psychics instead.

Psychics or fortune-tellers play a prominent role in the Hmong belief system. Rarely do Hmong people claim to have psychic power. Hmong fortune-telling or psychic analysis is commonly derived from three things: the 12 animals of the yearly cycle, the lunar months, and time. Interpretation of the alignment of these three variables varies slightly from one fortune-teller to the next, but all true fortune-tellers commonly give vague answers or predictions. When it comes to psychic reading pertaining to an illness associated with a certain evil spirit, the person seeking the reading will have to go home and offer a resolution to the spirit. When the illness goes away within a certain time frame, it is believed to be true and the resolution is followed through. Take the hypothetical situation of a man with a headache. He goes to see a psychic. The psychic reader aligns the time, date and month and comes to the conclusion that it has to do with a certain evil spirit that the man has come in contact with. The psychic may ask the man if he has been to the woods or a strange and unusual place. The man may have gone hunting at a swamp. In that case, the psychic reader will call out to the spirit of the swamp and offer a resolution offering a chicken and 100 bundles of spirit papers. So, in three days, if the headache goes away, the man slaughters a chicken and burns 100 bundles of papers offering them to the swamp spirit. If the man's headache is still pounding after three days perhaps he should consult a shaman, or better yet, take two Tylenols and forget about the evil swamp spirit. On the other hand, if his pain is gone and he does not follow through with the resolution the consequences can be severe.

Hmong readily seek help outside their comfort zone and reach out to fortune-tellers and psychic readers of other religions. In the world of Buddhism, monks are a very reliable source of spiritual guidance for Hmong people. We may not practice Buddhism, but the divine power and teaching of Buddha is well respected in the Hmong community. Palm reading is also highly regarded by Hmong people.

Another component of the Hmong belief system that is highly regarded is moral ethics. Hmong refer to our ethics as Heaven's rules. In a traditional setting, these values are reiterated so often that they become common sense. In today's world, however, we are bombarded with different cultural beliefs and ethical perspectives that can cloud our sense of right and wrong. The disparity between Hmong moral values and those of mainstream Americans is quite large because Hmong people come from a male-dominated society.

In the patriarchal world, moral ethics are in favor of the men. Married men may have extramarital affairs. They can even marry a second or third wife and it would be morally acceptable. Women, on the other hand, cannot do such a thing, because it is morally wrong for married women to be intimate with men other than their own husbands. To see how our moral ethics work, let us look at an incident that happened in a small village in Laos during the spring of 1974 when an elderly lady of the Xiong clan passed away. During burial, her body would not fit into the coffin. The problem was that her legs were curled up and out in a compromising position. Her sons had to literally crush her legs and thighs to straighten them out so she would fit into the coffin. The reason, as it was told, was that her husband was poor and not very bright. When the couple was young, she had openly committed adultery. The husband could not do anything about it, so he cursed her something like this:

"I am dumb. I may not be able to do anything about your cheating on me, but there is Heaven above. It sees everything. It may not matter now, but some day you will suffer for years in your dying bed, and for one year before you die, you will show the whole world how you cheated on me."

As it happened, the lady was bedridden for many years before she finally passed away. Was it a coincidence? Perhaps, but Hmong people believe that she was cursed (khaum).

Hmong have a firm belief in sins and curses. In the realms of both ying and yang, no crime goes unpunished. Sin is punishable in many ways. Redemption occurs when a settlement is reached and all parties involved are satisfied. The ultimate judgment for the most heinous crimes is a lightning strike. Heaven is the supreme judge and Thor (xob) is the enforcer. When a Hmong man feels powerless against a more powerful force, he kneels and calls out to Heaven to look down on him; he asks Heaven for justice. When conflicts between people cannot be resolved because somebody is not being truthful, Hmong people will call on Heaven to pass judgment. This usually takes one of two forms. The parties dip their hands in hot oil (raus roj) or drink holy water (haus dej dab). In the super-hot oil, the dishonest person's hands and arms will be burned to a crisp and either they will lose the hands or die as a result it. In the case of the holy water, the liar will die according to a specified cause of death within a certain time frame. In either case, the dishonest one and his descendants will be cursed for many generations. The one who is truthful will live a healthy and prosperous life. That is why Hmong people do not take the drinking of holy water or curses lightly.

Spiritual beings that abuse their power in their domination over human beings are said to be punished by Heaven. Hmong people believe that a person who drowns in any body of water is being taken by sea serpents or dragons. A dragon that takes a life every once in a long time is said to be morally acceptable. However, one that takes too many lives in too short a period of time commits a moral breach. In such a case, lightning will strike down the dragon and kill it. Heaven has final judgment on all beings.

Traditionally, Hmong did not know how to cast evil spells. When Hmong migrated into Southeast Asia, they learned such skills from the Khmer and Laotian natives. Evil spells come in many forms. The most common forms are woven cow models (*nyuj ciab nyuj ncau*), kua shee (*kua si*), cow hide and flint (*tawv nyuj zeb ntais*), death spirits (*dab phim pauv*), and kher kong (*khawv koob*). These are different forms of evil spells. Although there is no clear evidence that such spells work, there are people who claim to have acquired the ability to cast spells. There are also people who have claimed that they or their loved ones have fallen victim to evil spells. Any evildoing can be morally justified only when the evildoer has suffered at the hands of the victim to the point where the evildoer cries bloody tears. Otherwise, evildoers will have to endure the wrath of Heaven.

Slaughtering animals for religious purposes has always been a part of Hmong religious practice. Even today, Hmong people still slaughter chickens, pigs and cows on a regular basis. Some Hmong youth don't seem very eager to talk about how they "kill" chickens in their kitchen. It is, however, a practice that goes hand-in-hand with everything Hmong religion stands for. Acknowledging it and trying to understand its purpose should help young people deal with this part of our culture. Animal sacrifice, as it is often called, is misleading when it comes to Hmong religious practices. The use of domestic animals in Hmong traditions and religious rituals serves multiple purposes. The spirit of the animal helps to protect or uplift the souls of humans. The meat is used to provide for attending guests.

The slaughtering of animals in Hmong religious rituals is contrary to the Western concept of animal sacrifice, which carries a negative stigma reminiscent of sacrifices in ancient civilizations. The use of live animals in the Hmong world is not a horrendous act. On certain occasions, the slaughter of an animal serves no religious purposes. At a wedding celebration, for example, usually a sizeable pig is slaughtered just to have fresh meat for a feast. In all cases, the animals are treated as humanely as possible and are put to death swiftly just like at the slaughterhouse.

Offering food to the spirits in rituals such as laida can sound very primitive. So it is. But the significance of the practice goes way beyond what meets the eye. Today, we keep the memories of loved ones who have passed on alive with photographs on the wall in the living room. Traditionally, Hmong people did not have that luxury. We keep their memory alive by calling out their names one by one, inviting them to join us during festive occasions. There have never been ghostly figures seen hovering over the food that is being offered to a spirit. It is a belief and tradition that has been carried on religiously for centuries.

Hmong may have been outcasts throughout history, but the core of our faith has been enduring and has remained unchanged for generations. Our religious practices are unique and we can call them "our own." It may seem impractical and nearly impossible in the modern world, but Hmong people should do what we do best. We improvise and adapt to keep the name and the belief system alive.

8 THE ARTS

Don't go whistle on the hill, you will not have food to eat.
Don't go whistle at the creek, you will not have clothes to wear.

Txhob mus xuav yij xuav kauv tuaj nraum toj, tsam tsis muaj nrog luag noj.
Txhob mus xuav yij xuav kauv tuaj nraum hav, tsam tsis muaj nrog luag hnav.

—a verse from Hmong funeral chant

Different peoples have preserved their cultures through different forms of art. From the cave paintings in Africa to the cathedral ceilings in Europe, people have captured their daily lives through their art. Unfortunately for Hmong, our ancestors did not leave paintings for us to peek into our past. Pictures of Hmong people taken more than 100 years ago are available, but those snapshots were taken fairly recently. Hmong life prior to those photos was preserved in stories told orally from generation to generation. With heavy reliance on oral traditions, Hmong have an extensive collection of knowledge about their history, customs, traditions, religious rites, folksongs, and chants. These are the arts that tell us about the past.

If an elderly Hmong man should see Leonardo da Vinci's Mona Lisa, he would probably not know what to think. Take an elderly woman to see an opera and she would fall asleep in the middle of the show. It is not that Hmong are ignorant. Hmong just do not understand or see the practicality of the modern arts. For Hmong people, art needs to be more than just a form of entertainment.

In the traditional agrarian life, Hmong people have been so captive to their struggle to survive that there has been little time for entertainment.

For most people, entertainment was a luxury they could not afford. More importantly, entertainment had to serve a practical purpose. Because of this, the arts in the Hmong world took on a very different role from the arts in the Western world. Dancing, acting, and painting, for example, were impractical in the agrarian lifestyle, and so did not exist until recently.

Luxury was not a common concept for Hmong, so there was no money to be made in the arts. There were no nobles, kings, and queens thirsting for entertainment. Thus, an ingenious artist would have starved to death in the Hmong world. William Shakespeare would have been reduced to a beggar if he walked into the Hmong world during his time.

Although practicality characterized Hmong arts in the past, contemporary views of the arts is slowly gaining acceptance in the Hmong community. These days, the entertainment industry is growing and Hmong arts are evolving. Dancing, for example, was not part of Hmong culture. The Hmong language does not have a word for "dance" because dancing did not exist in the Hmong world either as a social activity or performing art. However, a few decades ago young people began to borrow dance moves from the Chinese, Laotian, Thai and Westerners and started calling them "Hmong traditional dances." Likewise, contemporary music and singing did not gain acceptance until the 1980s.

Playing a traditional musical instrument has been a part of Hmong culture as a skill that contributes to survival as well as a form of entertainment. Playing the flute (tshuab raj), for instance, was not a skill developed just to entertain others. It was a means to attract a preferable soulmate. It was also a skill that helped a man learn to play the kheng. Not everyone could put their musical skills into practical use, but there were real benefits, and financial gain was not one of them.

Visual arts were not meant to be hung on the wall to be admired. They were to be part of a clothing article, instrument or equipment to improve its look. Colorful embroidery artworks became a part of a shirt or sash to be worn by a girl to bring out her beauty. The ability to do the intricate needle work was an essential skill to make clothing. A girl who was able to produce gorgeous embroidery work would be able to sew beautiful clothes for herself and her future husband and children. A man who could weave flawless carrying rattan baskets would make a sturdy and long-lasting basket that his wife and children could carry with pride. Artistic skills were part of everyday life's practical skills. Art in Hmong tradition was never meant to be a profession to earn a living and surely not to bring fame and fortune. A person with artistic insight and creativity adds joy to life, and, more importantly, is better suited for success in the Hmong world.

A type of embroidery pattern called snail base (*qab qwj*) after the shape of a snail shell.

In today's world, the seemingly ancient arts of the Hmong people are antiquated and impractical. Keeping these arts alive in the modern world is a losing effort. That is because societal norms are vastly different from traditional Hmong society. Young people cannot understand the meaning of these aspects of Hmong culture. For the few who are willing to learn and are interested in their survival, Hmong arts can be fascinating and enriching.

A fascinating example of a performing art in the Hmong world is singing folk songs and chanting rites. To the untrained ear, they all sound the same. That is because every song and every chant is a poem. Let us take a look at a Hmong folk song translated into English to illustrate its poetic nature.

Intro. → Nia yai...

Male stranger, when it rains the rain falls on
the leaves of <u>grass</u>   *one stanza*

one set You say you will marry us, but your words have
no <u>class</u>
Male stranger, when it rains the rain falls on
the leaves of <u>rye</u>
You say you will marry us, but your words are
but a <u>lie</u>
It breaks the heart to end on the leaves of a
hemp <u>tree</u>   *conclusion*
This song is dedicated to the men who are not
<u>trustworthy</u>

Niam yai...
Txiv leej tub cas yuav los kob nag tshauv nag
ntxej ntxaum ntxaum ntxiav daim nplooj <u>nqeeb</u>,
txiv leej tub lub ncauj lam daj tias yuav los
twb hais tsis muaj ib lo lus <u>tseeb</u>.
Txiv leej tub cas yuav los kob nag tshauv nag

ntxej ntxaum ntxaum li ntxiav daim nplooj <u>yuaj</u>,
txiv leej tub lub ncauj lam daj tias yuav
los twb hais tsis muaj ib lo lus <u>ruaj</u>.
Chim laj xeeb xaus xi daim nplooj <u>mag</u> nrov
nreeg hmoob leej tub tus txawj <u>dag</u>.

Hmong folk songs have a beginning and an ending. The song above starts with "nia yai," which is standard for White Hmong. A song is made of many sets (*txwm*) and each set is made of two stanzas (*fab*). A stanza has two phrases that rhyme at the end. In the example above, in the first stanza the words "grass" and "class" rhyme. Both phrases are usually related but not necessarily. The first phrase is usually an analogy, anecdote, or a comparison. The second phrase or second half of the stanza bears the actual message in the stanza. The second stanza is a repeat of the first stanza with the rhyming words changed.

The conclusion marks the ending of the song and expresses the feeling of the singer. A Hmong folksong can be as short as two sets or as long as dozens of them. A good example of a very long chant is the wedding chant of the origin of Hmong wedding rituals (*txheej tshoob*), which has more than 50 sets and takes nearly an hour to perform. To be creditable, songs and chants have to come purely from memory. Singing or chanting by reading off of a script is unconventional — even unacceptable.

Hmong folksongs and ritual chants are full of repetitions, analogies, idioms, jargon, similes, and more. They follow a similar poetic pattern. Each has a beginning and ending. In the sample above, the first two words are the sounding off of a song. This differs regionally and by dialect. For example, Hmong from China will sound off their songs differently from those in Laos or Vietnam. Dialectically, Green Hmong will start their songs differently from White Hmong. Green Hmong usually start with "cha how." White Hmong commonly start with "nia yai," which means something like "oh dear." The starting words will sustain for a little bit and then the actual song follows.

The differences in songs and ritual chants are apparent if careful attention is paid to style, rhythm and content. There are three main categories of songs and chants. There are songs just for entertainment and courtship. There are also songs and chants for special occasions like weddings and New Year celebrations. Then there are the death songs and chants for funeral rituals. The songs and chants cannot be used interchangeably. In other words, courting songs (*kwv txhiaj*) are not to be used in funeral chants (*txiv xaiv*) and vice versa. The way these songs and chants are performed also varies drastically.

Here is the breakdown of Hmong songs for entertainment and courtship. The most common of folksongs is called kuexia (*kwv txhiaj*) in White Hmong or lootsung (*lug txaj*) in Green Hmong. Kuexia is usually sung during courtship. The other type of folk song is called lutao (*lus taum*). Lutao is a slightly different form of singing. It is geared toward philosophical expression. It is often sung by older singers to tell a story or express a philosophical thought. The defining characteristic of such songs is the expression uoachia (*ua ciav*), which means "all of a sudden." It is used often at the beginning and during transition between sets. An example of a lutao song can be one that tells the story of sibling love. It is a poetic narration of how the sister is separated from the brother due to marriage. Her married life away from her brother and family does not include her in family gatherings. Women who have gotten married and moved away from their families could become quite emotional when they listen to such a song. To Hmong people, songs are meant for communication, self-expression and story-telling and can be as vivid as motion pictures.

Songs and chants for special occasions include those for weddings. These are called wedding songs (*nkauj tshoob*) and wedding chants (*zaj tshoob*). There are also chants for social functions such as raising the pole to kick off New Years celebration (*nkauj nkaum toj*). In any case, a song describes the nature of the event while illustrating its importance and function.

Funeral and religious chants take a more serious tone, and the language carries deeper meaning. Mandarin words are added to make the chanting more mysterious and empowering. The voice is also more somber and eerie. These are not to be practiced or chanted inside the house if there is no funeral service being held there, because they may stir the house spirits. Funeral chants are discussed in greater detail in the chapter on funerals.

In the Hmong world, each successive generation loses some of the authenticity of the Hmong culture. Hmong people have not only lost the true art of singing and chanting, but we have made drastic changes to this part of our culture within the last half century. Take a close look at a modern folksong (*kwv txhiaj*) and you will see that the lyrics resemble those of American rap songs more than Hmong traditional songs. Let us compare two Hmong folksongs. Here is a stanza sung by my father, Kou Shue Cha, who was a reputable singer when he was young:

A bronze ring is not as worthy as a lead ring. This year, for Choua Yee Leng Cha, (young man with power of eight people) dating Mai Sia Moua Gao Da (Mai Sia with ghostly beauty) is not as satisfying as dating Pa Ther Vee Lee Choua Poua (Broken Flower the divorcee).

A bronze ring is not as worthy as a copper ring. This year, for Choua Yee Leng Cha, dating Mai Sia Moua Gao Da is not as satisfying as dating Pa Ther Vee Lee Choua Chia.

Ntiv tes tooj npab zoo tsis cuag ntiv tes tooj txhuas, xyoo no Cuav Yim Leej Cab daj dee Maiv Xia Muam Nkauj Dab twb yuav zoo tsis cuag li Paj Tawg Maiv Vwj Lis Cuab Puas.

Ntiv tes tooj npab yuav zoo tsis cuag ntiv tes tooj liab, xyoo no Cuav Yim Leej Cab daj dee Maiv Xia Muam Nkauj Dab twb zoo tsis cuag li Paj Tawg Maiv Vwj Lis Cuab Tshiab.

Compare the traditional song above to one that the new generation of singers would sing:

Your mother and father know how to eat and give birth, they eat banana (in Hmong) with banana (in English), so they give birth to you and you are very beautiful and your skin is smooth like a yellow foreign girl.

Your mother and father know how to eat and give birth, they eat banana (in English) with banana (in Hmong) so they give birth to you and you are very beautiful and your skin is smooth like a white foreign girl.

Koj leej niam leej txiv yuav txawj noj los txawj yug, cia koj leej niam leej txiv twb yuav noj txiv tsawb ntxuag npas nav nam es thiaj li yug tau koj tus me zoo zoo nkauj dawb dawb mos nyoos cuag li nkauj mab daj.

Koj leej niam leej txiv yuav txawj noj los txawj yug, cia koj leej niam leej txiv twb yuav noj npas nav nam ntxuag txiv tsawb es thiaj li yug tau koj tus me zoo zoo nkauj dawb dawb mos nyoos cuag li nkauj mab dawb.

If these two sets of folksongs are compared, we find major differences. The traditional song is indirect and the meaning is profound. The words were carefully chosen with poetic rhythm. The second song is very direct. The words are simple and used loosely to reflect modern day society.

Hmong traditional folksongs are like nursery rhymes. They were learned from master singers with style and carefully-chosen words to tell a story. These days, people make up their own songs, some of which don't even rhyme. It has become more like freestyle rap. That is where the authenticity of the art is being compromised.

Storytelling is another example of a native tradition that is a true art. It is an oral tradition that takes great skills that not everybody has. Story-telling requires more than simply reciting the words. A captivating story requires the teller to act, do monologues, sing, chant, and recite in heartwarming tones. It has been used to entertain young and old alike. It has been passed on from one generation to the next for hundreds of years.

Another Hmong art that has been passed down from generation to generation is needle work. Embroidery is deeply important and valued. In certain parts of Thailand, Laos, and China, Hmong women still have the patience and time to make clothes one stitch at a time — the way traditional Hmong embroidery has been done for generations. It is an art in the greatest sense of the word. There are methods of doing fine needlework. There is a name for every pattern. Talent in needle work is not only an ability to make fine stitches with needles, but the ability to envision and create new patterns that are pleasing to the eye. The colors are carefully combined as part of the beauty. Hmong women are legendary in the art of embroidery, but they don't master it without practice. From childhood, Hmong women have learned the art as apprentices. To become an artisan, Hmong girls spend hours learning the fine art of embroidery. Young girls spend every moment of their spare time practicing needlework, which has been the practice of embroidery for hundreds of years.

Prior to migration to the West, Hmong embroidery played an essential part in everyday life. Every piece of embroidery became a part of an article of clothing. Whether a girl made a lopsided work or a masterpiece, it would find its way into somebody's wardrobe. That was how Hmong people treated the art of needlework.

In the 1970s and 1980s, when Hmong migrated into the Western world, Hmong women started exploring the different ways they could market their skills. Hmong women sewed their artwork onto little cubes hanging from a chain of beads and marketed them as decorative ornaments to be hung on rearview mirrors and even Christmas trees. Some women sewed their embroidery masterpieces onto stuffed animals such as turtles. My mother sold a bunch of those turtles for $5 each. The time she put into making them generated no more than a few pennies per hour. One of the most familiar artworks is the story cloth. It is needlework that illustrates the stories of the Hmong people. A story cloth is an adaptation of Hmong embroidery that defies the tradition of utility, but it has gained acceptance and popularity among Hmong people and mainstream Americans.

Unlike embroidery, adaptation in Hmong traditional music has been a slow process. Traditional Hmong music is soothing and heartwarming as opposed to the rhythmic and fast-paced music of today. Each Hmong musical instrument is played separately without the accompaniment of other instruments. Traditional instruments do not lend themselves to today's loud and high-energy music fans. The Hmong harp, for example, cannot compete with the deafening volume of electronic instruments.

Hmong musical instruments are played spontaneously and by ear. There is no written music — no notes to read. The music itself is not merely to make sounds that are pleasing to the ear and soothing to the soul, but also to express conditions of the heart and express the thoughts and feelings of the musician. Each note represents a word. A song carries a message. Each instrument has a pattern of tonal phrases. Several tones run together to create a recognizable expression. Even those who cannot play an instrument learn to recognize the messages carried by the tones' variations and patterns. Thus, Hmong people can comprehend the meaning of the song. Oftentimes, tone patterns in the words of folksongs are echoed as if the words are sung through the instrument rather than accompanying them. To fully appreciate Hmong music, one must learn to decipher the message as well as hear the soothing sounds made by the instrument.

The music relays the message through the eight distinctive tones of the Hmong language. When a common phrase is spoken, the words in the phrase follow a tonal pattern. To make them even more standard meaning, Hmong give these phrases a theatrical twist to capture a heartfelt expression. Here's an example:

> Heaven [and] earth, oh you strangers ...
> *Ntuj teb yuas lawv e ...*

When the phrase is sung out, the first word (Ntuj) has a tone that is equivalent to a G note on a musical scale. The words "teb," "yuas," "lawv" and "e" have the tones E, C, E and D respectively. Whenever these tones are played sequentially, they are associated with this phrase, no matter what instrument is played. Most common musical phrases are easily recognized if there is enough exposure because Hmong is a tonal language. As such, the tones are recognized and the message understood. How is it possible? Growing up as a child in the Hmong world, hearing this music and song is an everyday occurrence. Over the course of time the sounds become second nature. An instrument can be mastered by learning to create the appropriate tonal patterns. The playing of an instrument and the daily involvement with music are extremely intrinsic parts of Hmong culture.

Hmong music has normally been played in the most intimate situations. It is not meant to entertain large audiences. Hmong musicians often play to entertain small groups of friends and family members. More frequently, however, musicians play to entice someone during the evening hours. Young men will play the flute to serenade a potential soulmate.

Music may also be played to signal one's presence so others are aware. For example, in a world where there are no telephones and young people cannot openly court each other, a young man would play a bamboo flute in the evening outside the home of his girlfriend so that she knows he is present. Then, after dinner and household chores are done she will find a way to meet him. Perhaps, in the middle of the night when the family is fast asleep and her suitor cannot just knock on the wall or the door for fear of awakening her parents, he will play a quiet musical instrument like a mouth harp just outside the wall of her bedroom. He hopes his music will awaken her without arousing others.

There are many traditional musical instruments in the Hmong world. A musical instrument that is uniquely Hmong is the kheng or reed pipe. Other instruments include the woodbine bamboo flute (*lev les*), the harmonic bamboo flute (*raj nplaim*), mouth harp (*ncas*), wind tunnel bamboo flute (*raj ntsia*) and Hmong violin or see sao (*xim xaus*). Most of these instruments closely resemble Chinese musical instruments. With the exception of the mouth harp, they may have been adopted from the Chinese. Whether or not an instrument is a Hmong creation, the music and the way it is played are unique. All these instruments reverberate to Hmong tunes and are aligned to the Hmong language of tones.

Hmong musical instruments are works of arts themselves. The kheng is a piece of artwork. Refining a piece of wood, strips of tree bark and six stocks of bamboo into a kheng takes great care and artistic skill. Moreover, the digits of the kheng require fine tuning. Thus the art of making musical instruments is an important part of the culture.

There are other Hmong crafts that are admirable in their own special ways. Rice winnowing baskets (*vab*), flour sifters (*vab tshaus*), carrying baskets (*kawm*) and storage bins (*mej loos*) are woven out of flat bamboo strips and split rattan stalks. This fine craftsmanship is passed on from generation to generation. A man is expected to be able to make these household items for his family's use. Some men can weave more beautiful and durable baskets than others. Basket weaving is revered not only as an art, but as a practical and traditional skill passed down over generations.

Another craft that is valued by Hmong is metal work. Who can dismiss the spear-shaped Hmong knives? No farming could be done without

Anna Vang (left) and Chia Vang wear traditional White Hmong costumes.

Leo Cha in traditional White Hmong costume, carrying a kheng (*qeej*).

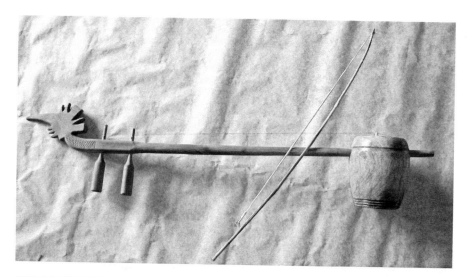

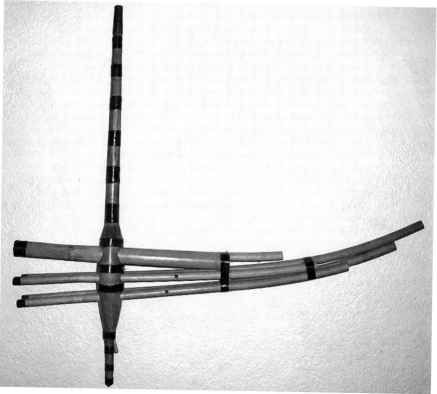

Top: This is called seesao (*xim xaus*), the Laotian name for the instrument. *Bottom:* Kheng (*qeej*) is a common musical instrument with many uses in the Hmong culture.

Hmong Chinese woman's outfit. Notice the colorful beads.

farming equipment such as hoes and rice cutters. Hmong blacksmiths can produce tools big and small. They can produce scores of metal tools by heating raw metal until glowing red and pounding them into shape one piece at a time. Since the 1800s and early 1900s, Hmong have forged steel into gun barrels and produced homemade muskets that were used as weapons of war.

Beautiful jewelry is another craft that Hmong have been producing for many generations. From necklaces to rings, Hmong produce delicate masterpieces out of sterling silver. Hmong in China wear homemade silver headwear that is brilliant. Hmong in Laos produce silver earrings that are finer than human fingers can pick up. Hmong jewelry is made almost exclusively from sterling silver. It is unique and beautiful in design and refinement and is not molded and engraved with sophisticated tools or machines. Hmong craftsmen make it by hand with antiquated tools going back many generations. Hmong people wear their jewelry proudly.

Hmong traditional arts and crafts withstand the test of time for their beauty and practicality. However, Hmong youth today do not seem to appreciate Hmong crafts for what they are. Furthermore, they cannot rival contemporary arts. More importantly, these ancient arts are not practical anymore.

Some artistic skills have stood the test of time, but some will disappear as Hmong people assimilate into mainstream society. These days, dances and contemporary music are being accepted as a part of Hmong culture, but they are newly adopted. The guitar has replaced the kheng as the musical instrument of choice. As we shift into a more contemporary culture, it is wise to not forget what is uniquely ours.

9 POLITICS AND LEADERSHIP

A grove of trees has one that is tallest, a family of brothers has a leader. (*Ib koog zoov muaj ib tug siab, ib cuab kwv tij muaj ib tug coj.*)

— a Hmong proverb

This chapter is written without malicious intent toward Hmong people or leaders. I draw information from years of studying Hmong history, my involvement in Hmong leadership, and living through decades of political turbulence. Extensive discussions with Hmong elders, leaders and youth have helped me formulate the pictures painted in this chapter. There may be experts who will disagree with certain things in this chapter. However, I believe that the information discussed will provide food for thought for future generations to come.

Hmong elders often say a leader has to be like an open-bottom carrying basket (*ua qab kawg tshau*). Such a basket does not retain objects that are thrown into it. That way, the objects will not be a burden to the carrier. A Hmong leader should not take everything to heart or take things personally to cloud his judgment and affect his ability to perform his duties. What goes in one ear has to be allowed to come out the other. In essence, a good leader needs to be patient and be able to tolerate others.

An enduring characteristic of an adorned leader is honesty. One who is not honest will be cursed, if not killed, by his constituents. Hmong people usually do not confront authorities directly, but they will curse unruly leaders to kingdom come behind their backs. Even leaders who are honest and impartial will still have disgruntled constituents, so it is extremely important for Hmong leaders to be honest. People do recognize good qualities in their leaders.

Hmong people are reluctant to support their leaders wholeheartedly. They want their leaders to be selfless public servants without benefits — not even monetary allowances for personal necessities. Of course, leaders have to receive some financial compensation so that they can be committed to their jobs without having to worry about where their next meal is going to come from. Without financial support, it would be impossible to have a totally committed leader and governing system. Hmong people are poor citizens who cannot financially support their leaders. We cannot afford to provide support for an organization to provide leadership for the people either. In the case of General Vang Pao, he was not elevated into his leadership role by Hmong people. He went up the ranks of the Lao Royal Army. Subsequently, his war efforts were funded by the United States Central Intelligence Agency. As a general, Vang was not financially supported by Hmong people directly. Even so, Vang Pao's determination to fight off the advances of communism in Laos during the Vietnam War was a popular idea among Hmong people, but they were reluctant to help. Most of Vang Pao's soldiers did not voluntarily enlist themselves — they were drafted into the war. If it wasn't for the financial backing of the United States government and the empowerment of the Lao government, Vang Pao would not have had the ability to draw Hmong people into the war. Even today, Hmong people are still reluctant to provide financial support to our community leaders. Individual leaders either receive funding from government entities or they help the community at their own expense.

At the clan level, a revered Hmong leader usually has an extensive knowledge of various aspects of Hmong culture. He also has to have strong leadership and communication skills. Such a leader is usually appointed by elders or elected into the position by his clansmen. He is commonly referred to as the one who leads to eat and to do (*tus coj noj coj ua*). Wherever there is a large concentration of Hmong with the same last name, a leader is usually selected or elected to keep the clan together. Rarely do Hmong people voluntarily accept a man as their leader when he asserts himself into that position. This is particularly true if he does not know much about the Hmong culture.

Traditionally, the elders will select a middle-aged leader to deal with the different aspects of society. The young and the very old are usually not the preferred leaders. A man between 30 and 50 is ideal. This is because

Hmong people believe that young leaders are not strong mentally as in the saying, "Taking a young man to be the leader is like taking a corn stalk to be a hoe handle" (*Muab tub hluas los ua hau, zoo puav tam li muab quav kws los ua ko hlau*). A corn stalk is not rigid enough to be a handle and when used on a hoe, it is not effective. As for using an elder as the leader, Hmong people say, "Old dogs do not guard the yard, old men do not resolve problems" (*Dev laus tsis zov loog, neeg laus tsis nquam plaub*). Elders are believed to be too rigid to resolve conflicts between people. Elders, however, are wise and well respected. As such, they serve as honing stones. They are the pillars of the community. In a world where knowledge and ideas cannot be found in print in the library, they are found in elders. That is why when a leader is selected by the elders, people respect him.

A true Hmong leader usually does not deal with every aspect of society. He would normally deal with social and political issues, but leave issues concerning religion to the spiritual leaders. In parts of the world where Hmong live homogeneously, this leader is recognized by the dominant culture. The spiritual leader is normally recognized by the clan. In the Western world, Hmong people do not have regional statesmen who govern just Hmong citizens. So, we have established an organization to oversee and resolve societal issues. This organization is called the "18 clans," representing all the clans. Spiritual leaders are still up to the individual clans. Although this structure has worked well in the past, it is losing its effectiveness, for Hmong have become less dependable on each other. More often than not, conflicts are being resolved by the police and the courts rather than through community leaders. No matter how Hmong people live, strong leadership is something people yearn for.

Although Hmong people are highly ethical, it is not uncommon to find Hmong to be unruly. Hmong see rules and laws as instruments of oppression against individual liberty when they are put in place by people. Rather than respecting the law, they fear and dread it. Moral ethics, on the other hand, are respected by Hmong. Hmong people generally do not commit crimes against other people or their property. We believe that criminals will never escape punishment whether or not they get caught. If they do not pay in life, they will in death. As such, Hmong usually have high moral and ethical standards, and so do we expect of our leaders. To get all Hmong to adhere to laws and civil codes, however, is a challenge.

Unity has been the weakest link for Hmong people throughout history. Hmong have always been divided physically, mentally, and politically.

Within the last century, there has not been a single Hmong leader who united all Hmong people in any region of the world. Even the most powerful Hmong leader in recent history, General Vang Pao, did not have the full support of all the Hmong people in Laos. Vang Pao's nemesis, Fai Da Lao, and his clansmen were firmly against Vang Pao to this day. This kind of division among Hmong people has made us an easy target for domination.

Sometimes, the division among Hmong people can be brought on by external forces. During the last ditch effort to gain independence from Chinese oppression by Zhang Xiu Mei (*Tsab Xyooj Mem*) in China, the Chinese were able to persuade the war weary and starving Hmong majority to surrender. In the end, Zhang was left with only his core supporters, and they were left to be slaughtered by the Chinese. The division of Hmong people influenced by the enemy continued in Laos when the French assigned Touby Lyfong to his father's post which was formerly Lao Kaitong's post. That left the Lao clan furious, creating a division between the Ly and Lao clans. That division escalated into the pro–Western and pro-communist factions within the Hmong population that boiled over to the Vietnam War era. During that time, most of the fighting and killing of the Hmong people in Laos was between the two factions. The Hmongs' gullible nature has proven detrimental time after time throughout history.

The inability to see eye to eye has been costly for Hmong people. A rising Hmong leader usually fights for the good of all Hmong. Ordinary people, however, have to consider their individual freedom and the well-being of their families. Often, individuals are at odds with their leaders, which causes people to defect, pitting Hmong people against each other. During the Vietnam War, for example, Hmong villagers had to either join Vang Pao by picking up arms to protect their villages from communist infiltration or join the communist revolution by rejecting American influence. More often than not, members of the same village would split and become enemies. The lack of vision for all Hmong people creates division between Hmong people, and it makes us very weak.

Hmong people recognize and embrace strong leadership in crises, but in times of peace leadership is highly contested and authorities are challenged. Furthermore, Hmong want peace and liberty, but we do not want to live under the authority of other human beings, let alone serving and financially supporting them with royalty. The crazy war of the Pa Chay

Vue rebellion is a perfect example. When Hmong people rallied behind Vue to keep the French off their backs, everyone was on board. Sure enough, the French were kept at bay. The French regrouped to strategize. Hmong people, on the other hand, went back to their daily routines of farming and taking care of their individual families. Vue went back to fending for himself and taking care of his family, which made him an easy target for assassination. One has to wonder if the Hmong people had recognized Vue's leadership abilities and raised an army to protect him, how the outcome of the rebellion would have turned out differently. Had Hmong been able to unite and make sacrifices in time of peace to support a government, life would have been very different for Hmong people.

One of the reasons why Hmong are so divided is because of the clan system. The clannish nature of Hmong people makes it impossible for the general public to throw their support behind a true leader. There is always tension and envy among the clans. To think highly of the success of each individual clan makes it difficult for individuals to see the fairness in a true leader who serves the general population. In other words, no matter how great a leader is, Hmong people will always think of clan pride and everyone else is an outsider who cannot be trusted. On the other hand, most leaders do put their clansmen before others. It is unfortunate, but clan loyalty causes great divisions among Hmong people.

Hmong people have a tendency to be competitive and non-cooperative. Hmong have a saying, "When you support others, they become better and they disrespect you" (*txhawb luag, luag zoo luag saib tsis taus yus*). Hmong people would not financially support just anybody to achieve greatness. They usually support their clan members. Support is reserved for the closest of kin to make the clan greater than other clans. This is one of the most destructive characteristics of Hmong people as a whole, and it is demoralizing for people with leadership potential.

Hmong people always strive to achieve individual liberty, but they are reluctant to pay for it. Liberty comes with a price. Financial and human resources have to be sacrificed to achieve liberty. Hmong would not willingly commit to either financial or personal sacrifices. During the Vietnam War, for example, Hmong people did not send their sons into battle voluntarily. They were forced to do so. To the Hmong people, paying to obtain liberty is not true liberty. Having to sacrifice the lives of loved ones to protect liberty is liberty not worth fighting for, at least not until it is absolutely necessary. This is the reason Hmong were not able to establish a strong government to unify and protect their own people from foreign aggression.

Hmong have always strived to be self-sufficient. We believe that working for another individual is disgraceful. A real man has to be able to fend for himself. That means living off the earth without having to depend on anybody else for survival. Essentially, food, clothes, security, and shelter must be achieved through individual success. In generations past, this mentality has made it very difficult for Hmong to live in large communities. When the population grew too large to be sustained by the land, Hmong had to spread out. As a result, it is nearly impossible to govern and protect the people as a whole. In today's world, people still prefer to fend for themselves without depending on others, but we have come to accept the fact that working for others is a viable means of making a living. Most Hmong people in developing countries and young people in part have learned to assimilate into mainstream society and become more successful. The pride of individual success overshadows the need for the Hmong people as a whole to thrive.

As immigrants in the Western world, Hmong people remain humble but proud. Rather than yielding to other Hmong or asking each other for help, they would rather submit to outsiders. Perhaps Hmong just do not trust each other. Then again, maybe Hmong people want to retain their dignity — what we call "to not lose face" (*tsis xav poob ntsej muag*). This lack of trust and support for each other makes it difficult for us to help and work with each other.

In parts of the world where Hmong are empowered to govern themselves regionally, the power hierarchy continues to exist as it has for generations. How does it work? Within a family unit, the most able adult male is the decision maker. Next up the chain of command is the clan leader. The clan leader answers to the village or town chief. The village chief answers to the regional government. If there is information that needs to be defused, it can easily be sent down the chain of command. Issues can also be resolved through the chain of command. For example, if a family member has a problem, the head of the household resolves it. If he cannot resolve it, he takes it to the clan leader. If the clan leader cannot resolve it, then it is taken to the town or village chief, and so on and so forth. What makes it so challenging for Hmong people is that when we live under the domination of another society, it is beneficial to settle issues on our own. When a problem gets to the top level of decision-making, the result is never in the best interest of either party. Hmong have a saying, "Chinese medicine Chinese boil, Hmong medicine Hmong boil" (*Suav tshuaj Suav rhaub, Hmong tshuaj Hmong rhaub*). It means we keep our problems to ourselves, and resolve them in our own way. Only when Hmong cannot solve our own problems should we trust others to solve them for us.

Traditionally, when problems are brought to the head of the village or town, a tribunal hearing is conducted. Both parties are given a chance to plead their cases. A panel of elders (*kev txwj laus*) is appointed by the village leader. These elders are the ones who will determine the outcome. The village leader is like the judge and the elders are like the jury. Without penal codes, Hmong people settle problems with logic. A panel of judges or elders, with consensus, will order the guilty party to pay restitution to the victim as they see fit. The restitution and judgment can be disputed. A clan with strong influence and unrivaled reputation can argue a strong case and the judgment can be strongly in favor of members of such a clan. Usually, when the guilty party does not have a strong support system, judgment is heavily against him or her. In some instances, an innocent person can be found guilty of a crime simply because he has no kin to stand up for him. This is where the true altruistic nature of the Hmong people is most evident.

Clan leaders usually have the best interest of their subordinate in mind when they seek true justice. Oftentimes, they will make a case for their clansmen in a dispute whether the people who are directly involved are satisfied with the resolution or not. The clan leaders can persuade people to accept their resolution. A decision is often made in the best interest of the individuals, but the reputation of the clan as a whole is taken into consideration. This usually creates rivalry between clan leaders and leads to problems in the community.

Where Hmong are allowed to govern themselves, due process is anything but fair, which causes people to not trust each other. When someone causes an infraction against another, the accuser has to initiate a formal complaint to the village chief. The village chief summons the accused for questioning. Sometimes, a perpetrator of a crime is caught red-handed. In such a case, the criminal can be physically restrained and taken to the chief. In restraining a person who has committed an infraction against others, a rope, chain or trap (*cuab*) can be used to restrain that person. In some cases, family members of the victim can taunt or assault the accused without repercussion. For example, if a man is caught committing adultery with another man's wife, the husband can tie up the hands of both the wife and the accomplice. As he does so, he can verbally and physically insult them both, and nobody can do anything about it — at least not until they reach the security of the village chief. However, if the perpetrator is from a clan with a strong leader, people usually think twice before taunting him.

In any case, to initiate a complaint, a man has to approach the village chief. A certain amount of money has to be given to the leader, and a formal complaint has to be properly verbalized in order for the chief to take him seriously (*cuab phaj nqes ntim*). The exact wording of the complaint varies depending on the nature of the complaint and regional norms.

During tribunal proceedings, it is customary to use philosophical and proverbial expressions (*paj lug*). The use of such expressions is primarily for posturing, but it sends a strong message of superiority in verbal articulation and intelligence. One's ability to argue his case determines his fate. Otherwise, a competent clan leader can be a savior. With strong leadership in the clan, clan members will not fear the wrath of others. Loners can be taken advantage of. That is why Hmong people value kinship and their fellow clansmen. In the Western world, where problems are not resolved by clan leaders, but by the judicial system, the clan system is devalued.

Leadership in the Hmong world touches every facet of life, but none is more important than spiritual leadership. Even with modern medicine and easily accessible medical treatments, Hmong still turn to spiritual healing. Strong spiritual leadership makes tragedy easier to cope with, and it keeps families together. The spiritual leader keeps the religious rituals and family traditions alive. That is why in every clan there has to be a spiritual leader.

In parts of the world where Hmong are integrated into a dominant culture, the traditional societal structure proves to be ineffective. In some cases, the traditional way of resolving conflicts can be destructive. Hmong leaders are bypassed and individuals deal directly with the leading authorities of the dominant culture. A man who has a conflict with his Hmong neighbor, for example, can have a choice between taking the neighbor to the clan leaders or to the court. In the Western world, such issues are likely to be resolved by the police or in court. Modern society has no room or patience for traditional practices, and Hmong leaders become powerless.

As Hmong people make educational and technological advances, a new class of leaders is starting to emerge. These are educated Hmong people. As is often the case, education comes at the expense of cultural knowledge and awareness. The educated leaders tend to be more liberal in their thinking. Usually, these leaders do not see eye-to-eye with the more traditional and conservative elders. This incongruence in philosophy between the new breed of leaders and traditional leaders is a polarizing force in Hmong communities throughout the Western world.

Traditionally, leadership has been the sole responsibility of the men, but the tide is changing in favor of women. In today's world, Hmong women are taking charge of leadership in the Hmong community. With their newfound rights, women have become promising prospective leaders. Senator Mee Moua of Minnesota, for example, has overcome all odds and become the highest-ranking Hmong government official in the United States. This power shift will change the politics and leadership in the Hmong world forever.

If Hmong are to retain our inherent identity and continue to exist as a people with our own culture, we need strong leadership. Whether they be men or women, tomorrow's leaders will have to work with an even more diverse Hmong population — politically, socially and economically. Hmong people are broadening our religious beliefs, so Hmong leaders have to take that into consideration as well. Today's potential leaders may have more resources and more training, but there is so much more to know and understand to become an effective leader.

There is an urgent call for Hmong leaders. As General Vang Pao rides into the sunset, he is making a plea to all Hmong people to elect the next leader and support him or her wholeheartedly. For the last several years, he has been calling out for unity in his public speeches. I believe that Hmong people hear him. Maybe it is just that no one has the "know how" and capability to answer his call. Then again, maybe the next Hmong leader is just waiting for the perfect storm to give him or her the energy and power to rise above the crowd like many other Hmong leaders have done in the past.

10 WHERE DO WE GO FROM HERE?

When you live in the world of others, imitate their skills. When you live in the land of others, imitate their kind. (*Nyob luag ntuj yoog luag txuj, nyob luag av yoog luag tsav.*)

— a Hmong proverb

On January 16, 1980, my family arrived at Portland International Airport after spending five years in a refugee camp in Thailand. Altogether, there were seven of us: my grandmother, my father, my mother, my three sisters and me. We were led from the terminal to the waiting area like a bunch of lost children. Next, we squeezed into cousin Tong Kao Cha's Toyota Corolla station wagon, and we were on our way to our new home.

As we pulled out of the airport parking lot, I kept thinking to myself, "This guy is Hmong and he drives a car." I was so amazed because until then I had never been in a car driven by a Hmong person.

Tong Kao gave us a quick run-down of the etiquette of our new country. "In this country," he said in a stern voice, "we cannot do the things we used to do in our country. People here don't walk outside. They step out of the house into the car and go to work. When they get home, they park their cars, go inside the house and stay there. The white-skin people don't sit around outside and talk. They don't even talk to the people who live in the house next to theirs."

As I listened to those words, I wondered how people could live in such a strange way.

After being in the United States for nearly 30 years, I went back to

188

Thailand to visit my relatives from my mother's side of the family. My early observation was: "Why do these men just sit around outside talking and laughing so loud for hours on end wasting precious time?" Then after just a week, I was chatting into the night with these same men, my cousins, with no concern for time. Oddly, I felt right at home. That was the world I came from.

The "norm" is a perception constantly tossed about and influenced by the society in which we live. Hmong people are alike in many ways. The fact that we live in different parts of the world causes us to have differences. Therefore, it is impossible to establish norms for all Hmong throughout the world, let alone create a uniform culture for all. Thus, we will have to continue to live with the phrase, "A different world, a different body of knowledge" (*ib rab teb ib tsa txuj*), but let us not forget who we are and where we come from.

As I work with Hmong teenagers every day, I see their struggle to understand their own lives and their split self-identity. Every time I bid farewell to a Hmong elder as he or she passes on, I see a piece of Hmong identity disappear. It is disheartening to see a beautiful culture slowly vanish before my eyes. In an attempt to help maintain and retain our culture and to keep the Hmong name alive, I provide some suggestions in this chapter on what we need to do to hold onto Hmong language, art, cultural traditions and religion while we continue to live as subordinates in other, more dominant, cultures.

The suggestions in this chapter are based on my life experiences, discussions with elders, debates with teenagers and training in bilingual-multicultural education. These are merely suggestions. How a person lives his or her life is a matter of personal choice. The decisions we make now will determine the fate of our descendants for generations to come. If many generations from now, our great-grandchildren no longer bear any characteristics of our cultural identity, it will be shameful. After all, the obstacles we face today are nothing compared to what our ancestors faced in past generations.

For thousands of years, Hmong fought against invaders and oppressors to keep Hmong culture alive and pure. Like glaciers, Hmong populations flowed onto the fertile lands of the valleys and low-lying areas of southwestern China when the tide of war swayed in their favor. When pushed to near extinction, Hmong retreated to the safety of the rugged mountaintops. Today, we need to learn to think in terms of society as a whole by expanding the way we think and treat other people who cross our paths, as well as learning to embrace a national identity. We must realize that we no longer live in clan-centered isolation.

Even as late as the industrial revolution, Hmong just stood by and watched others advance in education and technology. It has been less than a century since Hmong started associating with other ethnic groups in a positive way and entered the world of education. In recent years, Hmong have demonstrated a willingness to embrace modern technology and have learned to adapt to the modern world. Even so, we are still reluctant to let go of the things that define us culturally, which places us in a dual-life. This dual-life means we remain traditional at home but become assimilated into mainstream society.

The struggle to remain pure and hold onto our cultural identity is getting more and more challenging with each successive generation. Our biggest challenge nowadays is our inability to show our children what it means to be Hmong. We are again fighting a battle to keep Hmong culture alive, but this time the battle is among the Hmong people themselves.

To survive culturally, we have to be active by educating our children about their culture, history and language. One of the most important ways to teach them who we are as a people is to look into our past. Before we can prepare ourselves to face the challenges of tomorrow, we need to study the past and learn from our own challenges and mistakes.

In my own efforts toward discovering the past and studying the present, I have come to believe that one of our greatest drawbacks is the self-focused ideology of our people. We place our immediate family members before our extended family. The more closely-related family members take precedence over the clan, and the clan comes before Hmong people in general. Whereas the people of a proud nation would likely put what is good for the common people over their own lives and the safety of their loved ones, Hmong people tend to think otherwise. There is a lack of commitment to the phrase, "Even if there is no me, as long as there is the nation," which is echoed by many Hmong leaders, including General Vang Pao. Perhaps the reason Hmong do not have a country of our own is because of our failure to make personal sacrifices for the good of the people. Making personal sacrifices might be something future leaders should contemplate.

Historically, Hmong leaders were believed to possess great strength and extraordinary powers. Leaders of this nature have a tendency to be strong-willed and ruthless. They also have a tendency to attract both followers and rivals because they want supreme power. Rather than striving to make a name for ourselves and become the only leader, we might want to think about the people as a whole. Instead of expecting the people to serve a leader, we might want to start thinking about leaders serving the people. This way, we can become a true democratic society.

One of the most polarizing issues involving Hmong leadership today is the separation between traditional leaders and book-smart leaders. There seems to be a great disparity between the two. I think we need to recognize a true leader for who he is and not judge him either by his cultural fluency or academic achievement. A person who knows everything there is to know about Hmong culture and tradition may not have leadership skills no matter how much he wants to assert himself as a leader. On the other hand, a highly educated individual may not have the ability to be an effective leader. Cultural fluency and academic achievement are bodies of knowledge, not character traits. Individual knowledge and skills are best used to complement each other for coming together to be part of the society in which we live.

Attributes like cultural fluency and academic achievement need not become the defining characteristics of leaders or grounds for defining adversaries. A person who is knowledgeable in the Hmong culture, academically inclined, trustworthy and blessed with an innate ability to lead would probably gain the trust of Hmong people. However, a person of this nature would likely not want to lead Hmong people if the majority continue to demonstrate an inability to think, work and act as civilized people.

In any society, it is crucial to have true leadership with common goals without the tendency to betray each other. It is also crucial to have devoted followers without the temptation to sabotage their leaders. Throughout history, we have learned that many Hmong leaders have fallen to the hands of our adversaries because of traitors among us. There were those who were willing to sell our leaders and the Hmong people for personal gain and security. A good example of this is when the self-proclaimed Hmong King, Wu Pa Yia (*Vwj Paj Yias*), was betrayed by his own cousin in the 1700s. Betrayal in itself is defeating and leads to despair and mistrust among the people.

Hmong people are reluctant to help other Hmong if they are not closely related. A good example of that is the 2005 desecration of Hmong graves at Wat Thamkrabot, Thailand, where Hmong refugees from Laos had settled. When Thai laborers started digging up Hmong graves, Hmong people just stood by and watched. There were well over a quarter-million Hmong living throughout Thailand at the time and not a single Hmong made an effort to stop an act that struck at the core of Hmong religious conviction — respect for our ancestors. The reason was simply that they feared for their own lives and safety. The graves being dug up were those whose relatives had left for the United States. Hmong people showed very little unity in developing a resistance plan until Hmong living in the U.S. became involved. We have to learn to love and help our neighbors even if they are not related to us.

We cannot correct the mistakes of the past, but we can prevent the same mistakes from recurring. As a minority, we may put ourselves at risk when we stand up for others, but sometimes the potential gain in social justice justifies the risk.

Another example of short-sightedness among Hmong people is the lack of understanding that there is power in numbers. Hmong often do not cooperate with each other. We tend to be greedy. We compete with one another. This makes us vulnerable and puts us at a great disadvantage. As individuals, it is impossible to hold cultural functions and perform religious rituals. We cannot compete with corporations as individuals and become financially successful.

As an example of how Hmong lack cooperation, we can just look at the markets that litter the large Hmong communities throughout the United States. In Fresno, California, there are seven Hmong markets in the south area. They all sell the same products, thus competing for the same customers. I have to wonder what the result would be if the owners of these markets were to form a cooperative where they could work at developing a supermarket with all-around services. I will bet that they would be able to serve customers better and offer greater potential for economic gain. The same would work in other facets of our lives if we could learn to work together in larger numbers.

In recent years, Hmong community leaders have begun to realize the strength in numbers. A good example is the action Hmong people took when General Vang Pao was accused of trying to buy arms to overthrow the communist regime of Laos in 2007. In an effort to sway the outcome of the court proceedings, Hmong leaders throughout the United States organized rallies in support of the general and his alleged accomplices. Whether the rallies had any influence on the federal judge in Sacramento,

California, or not, no one really knows. What is known is that the voices of thousands of Hmong people protesting spurred massive media coverage. In the end, the charges against the general were dropped. So rather than trying single-handedly to accomplish things, we should make every effort to cooperate and support each other. There is strength in numbers.

As a people, Hmong blame our shortcomings on the lack of having a nation of our own. The elders have always said, "We do not have a country and that is why other people do not respect us." It is true that Hmong do not have a country, but we can still earn others' respect by being respectful toward each other. Other people will not respect us if we do not value ourselves. We need to respect the elders, men, women and children. We need to recognize the importance of all Hmong people throughout the world. Quite often, I see Hmong people in Thailand turn their back on the Hmong people in Laos. Hmong people in the United States exploit their Hmong neighbors. Hmong street gangs try to annihilate one another. Hmong leaders despise each other because of differences in opinion. Business people try to compromise each other rather than provide support and work together. Cultural leaders criticize and accuse each other of evil-doing as opposed to working toward achieving a common goal and uniting people. The list goes on. These are matters that do not earn Hmong people respect from others. Such conditions make young people dislike being Hmong. As a people, we have to learn to respect one another more.

Hmong people lack unity. In order for us to survive as a people, we must stand united. In every major conflict in recent memory, Hmong were not only divided, but we were our own adversaries. During the Cold War in Laos, for example, half of the Hmong people were on the side of Pathet Lao (communist revolutionaries) and the other half fought for the United States. It pitted brother against brother. A lot of Hmong people were killed by their own kind. In the end, Hmong were the biggest losers. The ones fighting for democracy became refugees. The ones fighting for the Pathet Lao came under strict Communist rule. In their division, Hmong further destroyed their unity.

Hmong people have to make adjustments to our way of life so that we can co-exist with people of other ethnicities, especially with those of the dominant culture. Having lived both the traditional Hmong life in the mountains of Laos and in 21st-century-America, I have seen a lot of social, economic and cultural changes in Hmong people. I believe Hmong people in the United States have retained and maintained the Hmong culture better than those who live in other parts of the world, perhaps because of the great number of different people living here and the level of acceptance by the dominant culture. Despite the many challenges we have to overcome, we can retain our culture and thrive in a strange land, co-existing with people who are vastly different from us. We have to keep our customs and traditions alive while at the same time being sensitive and accepting of other people.

In today's world, we can create a global community of Hmong people having common beliefs and interests, standing on common grounds, and pursuing common goals without the need to have a country of our own. We have to learn to adapt to an ever-changing world and live in harmony with the people around us and be grateful.

The migration of Hmong people from the isolated agrarian life to urban communities has placed Hmong people in a peculiar situation in regards to health. When Hmong lived in isolation without modern medicine, communicable diseases were kept in check naturally. In urban America, large families living in cramped apartments bring people very close together, and germs are easily spread. The flu virus, for example, is more difficult to contain in crowded conditions.

As Hmong people congregated into large populations and came into direct contact with urban dwellers, they were not immune to communicable diseases, nor were they informed about the healthy lifestyle of urban dwellers. Hmong became highly susceptible to chronic diseases such as diabetes, hypertension, the common flu, venereal diseases and more. Through education, younger generations are now better informed about healthy lifestyles. The older generation, who had little or no formal education, still lives in the same way our ancestors lived for thousands of years.

Sometimes we must make changes to our lives even if such changes go against tradition. A good example is the traditional way of dining. Whether it be a family dinner or a large family gathering, it is customary to set the table with community dishes where every dish is within easy reach of everybody at the dining table. Diners stick the spoons or forks with which they are eating into the community dishes and put the food directly into their mouths, bypassing the plate they hold in their hands. As the spoons or forks go from mouth to food and back, germs can spread like wildfire. Therefore, we are at a higher risk of spreading communicable diseases. Adapting to simple steps practiced by urban dwellers can reduce health risks.

This is not to say that we should abandon our traditions. It is merely a suggestion that we need to re-evaluate a practice that conflicts with safe health practices, especially in urban environments. We have to make changes to promote healthful living in the modern world.

Food is part of culture, and in part, it makes us who we are. To Hmong people, a meal is just not a meal without rice. It is rice with some kind of meat for breakfast, lunch and dinner. Hmong usually do not eat very much variety when it comes to food. At issue are the nutrient-depleted steamed rice, the oily foods, fatty pork and the high-sugar-content drinks that Hmong people love dearly. When cooking rice, Hmong usually wash the rice once or twice with water before cooking. This washes away important nutrients. Cooking also commonly involves meat with a high fat content and dishes prepared with a lot of oil. Thus, our diets lack nutrients and are full of unhealthy things. These unhealthy food choices, along with lack of exercise, have taken a heavy toll on Hmong people in the Western world. We are seeing more and more obese children and sick elders. Making healthier choices, preparing meals in a healthier way and leading more active lives must become part of our culture in the modern world.

Part of what defines the Hmong culture is its arts. Hmong arts are admirable in their own way, but they have become less popular among younger generations, perhaps partly, because they have lost much of their practical application. The culture itself has moved a step away from them and adopted contemporary pop culture. Arts such as needlework are becoming obsolete. These needle skills are no longer practical in today's world because they are not marketable job skills. There must be ways to preserve this art through creative marketing and adaptations. One ingenious contemporary use of Hmong needlework is the story cloth. Story cloth is not a traditional Hmong craft, though today it has gained popularity as an important Hmong work of art. The story cloth is one of many adaptations that came about during the 1980s. Other adaptations include ornaments, decorated stuffed animals, Western-style accessories lined with embroidery artwork and more.

Perhaps another means to keep Hmong art alive is to view it in a different light. Rather than Hmong themselves looking at traditional practical application, we might need to focus on the beauty and uniqueness of our ancient traditional art and determine that it is of great value and must be preserved and collected. Hmong art should be admired for its aesthetic nature as well. It is worthy to preserve and collect the pieces they are.

Music is probably the most difficult of the arts to maintain. Young people who are interested in music turn to guitars and electronic synthesizers rather than traditional instruments such as the bamboo flute or kheng. The most likely traditional instrument to survive is the kheng, because it is an essential component of funeral rituals. It does not have to compete with modern music where it would be required to play in harmony with other instruments.

Hmong craftsmen are hard to find these days. Hmong craft is time-consuming, and it is not practical in a world where time is money. A man would rather spend a few dollars on a cheap-looking knife than spend hours hammering one out for himself. Hmong arts and crafts are becoming a thing of the past because we do not have people learning the trades as professions. In past generations, nearly every man was a craftsman — it was a necessity. In the Western world, it is often possible to earn the money to buy a ready-made item. Hmong craft, however, is more likely to survive in remote parts of the world where Hmong still do subsistence farming. These people may be an important resource for urbanized Hmong. Yet even there, tradition is under attack.

One might think that all the Hmong arts and crafts survive in remote parts of China or Laos. That is not entirely true. Pop culture has swept through the entire Hmong world. The spare hours Hmong women and girls traditionally spent practicing needlework and learning to play musical instruments in remote villages are now spent talking on cell phones and watching videos made in America. Where technology is accessible, young people would rather spend their spare time on the internet than learn the antiquated arts of generations past. In the evening, instead of serenading each other with traditional musical instruments, young people share contemporary music and songs on CD players and iPods. In remote parts of Thailand where Hmong still lead very traditional lives, young boys would still rather learn how to play the guitar than the bamboo flute. Other art forms are hit just as hard and for many of the same reasons. Unless we take an active approach to preserving the arts, we are going to lose them.

In addition to art there are other things that are more at the heart of Hmong cultural identity. We have looked at some rituals, but there is none more reflective of defining who we are as the wedding ritual. There are issues concerning Hmong traditional weddings that are worth considering for changes as we move toward assimilation with the Western world. Wedding traditions are deeply rooted and practices pit family against family and clan against clan. Hmong people are reluctant to make the changes necessary to make weddings more pleasant and equitable.

Traditional Hmong wedding celebrations focus too much on the bride's family and not enough on making the occasion the happiest day of the bride and groom's life together. The couple getting married is a reason to celebrate, but the bride does not usually take part in the celebration. The bride and groom could be included in the decision-making and the festivities. After all, it is their "big day." When the feast begins, the bride and groom should be given the opportunity to give a speech and be at the head of the drinking procession. The bride should be allowed to share her thoughts and feelings with everyone. Rather than the bride and groom trying to make the parents happy, it should be the families making the bride and groom happy on their wedding day. At least, the bride and groom should be given the opportunity to shine at some point during the ceremony.

As to what we call the "bride price," this is nothing more than parents selling a daughter to her husband. In the Western world, I don't think Hmong parents really want to convey the notion that they sell their daughters. Young men generally do not want to have to pay for their wives. Most female Hmong students I have taught do not want to be bartered like a commodity. Furthermore, a woman is just as capable as a man when it comes to taking care of aging parents. In today's world, a marriage is viewed as two people becoming one, not the bride becoming the property of the groom. So a groom should not have to pay for his bride.

Hmong people in the Western world hesitate to re-structure an ancient system because we cannot get everybody to agree to the changes. Once we have everyone agreed on not collecting money for their daughters, the abolition of the bride price is as easy as, as we say, peeling an egg (*tev qe*). The most practical way to do this, I believe, is for those parents who are financially well-off to not collect the bride price for their daughters. After all, a few thousand dollars is of little consequence for some parents — getting the bride and groom started on a positive financial footing is more rewarding. As more parents are abolishing the bride price, it is likely that we will eliminate it altogether. This antiquated custom has no place in our community as we know it today.

Something else that has to be let go of is the use of tobacco in Hmong rituals. Whether it is at a wedding or a funeral, Hmong people use tobacco as a means to calm unsettled nerves. This is a tradition that can be traced back to the ancient world of Hmong people in China where every Hmong man, young and old, smoked. A pinch of tobacco (*ib kab luam yeeb*) for the bong, pipe, as a gesture of goodwill to set the stage for a rational formal conversation between men is the expectation for Hmong people. Today, particularly in the West, we have learned that tobacco smoking is unhealthy. Knowing what we know about the danger of tobacco, the use of tobacco or cigarettes during cultural rituals should be limited, if not eliminated. It is an unnecessary burden that has lost its perceived value in our society.

Another substance that has been a part of Hmong cultural traditions and rituals for a long time is alcohol (*dej caw*). Rice wine, which is hard liquor, has been used extensively during weddings and funerals. In remote parts of China and Southeast Asia, rice wine is still the preferred alcoholic beverage at community and family gatherings. In other parts of the world, especially in the West, beer and soda have slowly replaced rice wine. In any case, the use of alcohol by responsible adults is not the big issue. The issue here is the use of alcohol in ceremonies and rituals where young people are involved. Allowing, and sometimes requiring, teenagers to drink alcohol at weddings and funerals sets an unhealthy precedent. Besides, developed nations like the United States have laws that prohibit people from drinking alcohol before a certain age.

Hmong people value a big funeral. A big funeral is one where lots of people are in attendance, food and drinks are in abundance and many head of cattle are slaughtered. Such a funeral can cost up to $50,000 in the United States. Therefore, some people have to make financial sacrifices throughout their lives to save up for their own final expenses. If they don't save up, their final expenses will incur a large debt for their survivors. A proper funeral is crucial in the Hmong culture, but too much emphasis on it places an unnecessary burden on people. I see people deprive themselves of a comfortable life to save up for final expenses. When they die, the money they saved is used to buy food and drink for people who attend their funeral. Many heads of cattle and pigs are slaughtered in their honor. To Hmong people, that is reverence for a life.

Hmong people need to keep funerals short and simple to reduce their cost. After all, a funeral is a set of rituals to conclude a life, not a celebration of death. We need to channel our finances to maintain a decent life and not so much toward the after-death rituals. Once a person's life is over, the burden on their survivors should be minimal.

Hmong use funeral rituals to convey a message of love and caring. Therefore, we have a tendency to pour our hearts out in the form of wailing and chanting to the deceased as though he or she can still hear. This is our way of telling the deceased of our love and regrets. It is part of Hmong culture. I believe that Hmong people use such occasions to express feelings and thoughts we don't share adequately with our loved ones while they are alive. Perhaps we might spend time talking to and doing things with the people we love. We should not be embarrassed to show our loved ones that we care about them when they are still alive — just as we normally do when they have passed on.

Hmong parents are rather conservative when it comes to teaching culture to their children. In fact, certain things are not meant to be discussed under normal circumstances. How to select a burial site, for example, is something Hmong people do not talk about casually. Only at the time of death do the elders talk about such a thing. Hmong people believe that once a potential grave site is pointed out, and there is no one to be buried, somebody will die to fill the site. Another superstition is that if a son learns a trade from his father, he will inherit all the father's problems as well. Whether it is just an uncomfortable feeling or a taboo, teaching does not take place on a regular basis between parents and children. As primary teachers, parents should take advantage of every teachable moment. We need to pause and take the time to teach and re-teach our children without reservations if we are going to retain and maintain our culture and traditions. A particular trade is really not the reason to teach — it is the cultural knowledge that hangs in the balance.

In regards to teaching and learning, language is crucial. Language is the cornerstone of every culture. It is the only way we can preserve and tell "the story." The problem is that the Hmong language is extremely difficult to maintain. The reason for this is that Hmong have been living in small isolated groups for thousands of years and the language has diverged into many dialects. Therefore many of the dialects are unintelligible to one another. Oppression also played a role in our ancestors' inability to maintain a uniform language and writing system. In recent years, Hmong have integrated with dominant cultures and the Hmong language has become less functional. The dominant language becomes the preferred mode of communication, if not the key to survival.

In China, some of the more widely spoken Hmong dialects include flower, green, white, black, and light. In the United States, Hmong speak only two dialects: green and white. These two dialects are quite intelligible with only minor differences. It may not be possible to consolidate the regional variations in our culture and language; however, we should be able to maintain it and prevent it from further disparity.

I believe that literature is the key to the maintenance of our language, culture and customs. Literature records what we still have, and so every effort should be made to unify Hmong people linguistically. There are people who use the subtle differences in our language and customs to create division between Hmong subgroups. The Hmong name is barely known to the world, and we need to work together to bring awareness to our plight. I believe all Hmong people share the same roots, have a similar struggle, and share a common goal. We are the same people no matter what dialect we speak or what costume we wear. Hmong have been divided and conquered enough; it is time to unite and stand together.

In parts of the world where Hmong are in a constant struggle to survive and opportunities are limited, they keep hopes and dreams alive with religious faith. Our customs, beliefs, and rituals give us hope for a brighter future. We seem to accept the fact that we are poor because it is fate. To alter this demoralizing fate, we turn to the divine powers of suka, tsee xai, dathong and other religious rituals. This idea seems antiquated, but there are those who still believe in it. In a world where opportunities are readily available, as in the United States, we should learn to control our own fate with the power of knowledge, hard work and perseverance. In other words, instead of waiting for divine intervention and luck, we should rely on hard work and education to direct the future.

The hope for better luck in the next life plays a major role in our everyday decisions. Hmong people believe that if things do not go the way they want, they can count on the next life to improve their fate. If two lovers cannot be together in this life, they can just die together and be reborn into the next life so that they will be with each other. If someone lives in misery, there is no way out but to live with it, because the next life will be better. This philosophy has given many people the strength to live under hopeless conditions. It has also led to human tragedy. People who have given up on life would use such a rationale to sit idly and wait for this life to end. When people have some hope of a better next life, they have reasons not to try harder to bring about changes for themselves in this life.

Whether there is a next life or not, the current life is what is real.

This is not to deny that the soul lives on, but I have not encountered an individual who passes on and comes back through reincarnation to pick up life where he or she left off. Even if there is a next life, I strongly believe that one should make the most of this life and do one's best to make it good. Life is too precious to leave it to chance. We have to make every effort to make the current life worth living. No one should allow the quality of life to be wasted away.

Speaking of quality of life, Hmong have traditionally lived in a male-dominated society. Hmong people have been severe in regards to gender inequality. Hmong wedding rituals are a perfect example. In working with Hmong teenagers, I often see males relating to female classmates as though they were of lower status. A big fear among girls is that the man they marry will marry a second wife. This is not unusual; we see it every day. As Hmong men, we have to realize that we are no longer living in a patriarchal world. Men do not dominate women anymore. Hmong women do not need Hmong men to survive anymore. In fact, today's women do not want to just survive, they are seeking education and assuming responsibilities for their own well-being. They want to have a good life. Whether it is a girlfriend or a wife, if a Hmong man does not want to give her hope for a better tomorrow, she will seek a greener pasture.

In China, young Hmong men are afraid to court beautiful Hmong women, because fair ladies are often swept away by rich Chinese bachelors. Oftentimes, I see Hmong women in the United States marry men of other ethnicities because they lose faith in Hmong men or they do not want to have to deal with the Hmong culture. But, it is important that Hmong men and women stick with each other to maintain our identity. It takes both men and women to bring positive changes to our society. Social justice can be achieved only when people fight for it, not when they run away from the problems. For the sake of the people, everyone needs to do their part in helping to bring equality to our community. It is easy to jump ship, but what if there comes a day when you have a yearning to get back on board? What then?

As Hmong, we are part of a very small indigenous population. For peaceful co-existence we need to adapt to a life that reflects the laws and habits of the dominant society. We must learn to improve our socio-economic status, participate in civil service, and pursue higher education. All the while, we must always remember that in our struggle to keep our identity, language and culture alive in the modern world, we need to include all Hmong people throughout the world and not just our family members. It is unity, and not division, that is the key to survival. We need to focus on how we are similar and not on how we are different. That way, Hmong will stand a better chance of enduring over centuries and enriching the global human family with the uniqueness we have to offer.

REFERENCES

Nieto, Sonia. "Critical Multicultural Education and Students' Perspectives." In *Critical Multiculturalism: Rethinking Multicultural and Antiracist Education*, edited by Stephen May, 209–235. Philadelphia: Falmer Press, 1999.

Vang, Thomas S. *A History of the Hmong*. USA: Lulu.com, 2008.

Withers, Andrea C. "Hmong Language and Cultural Maintenance in Merced, California." *Bilingual Research Journal* 28 (2004): 299–318.

Wu, Rong Zhen. *Haiv Hmoob Liv Xwm*. Quezon City, Philippines: Association Patrimoine Culturel Hmong, 1997.

Xiong, Yuepheng. "Chinese Odyssey." *INK: Hmong Magazine*, Vol. 1 (spring 1997).

Yang, Va Thai. *Kab Ke Pam Tuag: Cov Zaj*. Guyane, France: Association Communauté Hmong, 1985.

_____. *Kab Ke Pam Tuag: Txheej Txheem*. Guyane, France: Association Communauté Hmong, 1985.

_____. *Kab Tshoob Kev Kos*. Guyane, France: Association Communauté Hmong, 1989.

INDEX

Numbers in **bold italics** indicate pages with photographs.

St. Louis Community College
at Meramec
LIBRARY